T0391115

Risk Management in East Asia

Yijia Jing · Jung-Sun Han · Keiichi Ogawa
Editors

Risk Management in East Asia

Systems and Frontier Issues

Editors
Yijia Jing
Institution for Global Public Policy
and School of International Relations
and Public Affairs
Fudan University
Shanghai, China

Jung-Sun Han
Division of International Studies
Korea University
Seoul, Republic of Korea

Keiichi Ogawa
Graduate School of International
Cooperation Studies
Kobe University
Kobe, Japan

ISBN 978-981-33-4585-0   ISBN 978-981-33-4586-7 (eBook)
https://doi.org/10.1007/978-981-33-4586-7

© The Editor(s) (if applicable) and The Author(s), under exclusive license to Springer Nature Singapore Pte Ltd. 2021
This work is subject to copyright. All rights are solely and exclusively licensed by the Publisher, whether the whole or part of the material is concerned, specifically the rights of translation, reprinting, reuse of illustrations, recitation, broadcasting, reproduction on microfilms or in any other physical way, and transmission or information storage and retrieval, electronic adaptation, computer software, or by similar or dissimilar methodology now known or hereafter developed.
The use of general descriptive names, registered names, trademarks, service marks, etc. in this publication does not imply, even in the absence of a specific statement, that such names are exempt from the relevant protective laws and regulations and therefore free for general use.
The publisher, the authors and the editors are safe to assume that the advice and information in this book are believed to be true and accurate at the date of publication. Neither the publisher nor the authors or the editors give a warranty, expressed or implied, with respect to the material contained herein or for any errors or omissions that may have been made. The publisher remains neutral with regard to jurisdictional claims in published maps and institutional affiliations.

This Palgrave Macmillan imprint is published by the registered company Springer Nature Singapore Pte Ltd.
The registered company address is: 152 Beach Road, #21-01/04 Gateway East, Singapore 189721, Singapore

CONTENTS

1   **Risk Management in East Asia: An Introduction**   1
Yijia Jing, Jung-Sun Han, and Keiichi Ogawa

Part I   National Risk Management Systems in the Region

2   **Understanding China's National Emergency Management System**   15
Xiaoli Lu, Lei Sun, Shuaize Fu, Yue Sun, and Kaiyu Shao

3   **Disaster Risk Management in Japan with Special Reference to "Sendai Framework"**   37
Toshihisa Toyoda

4   **Patterns of Risk Management Policies and Systems in South Korea: Special Reference to Water-Related Disaster Management**   61
Seungho Lee

Part II   Participatory Risk Management

5   **The Deliberative Option: The Theoretical Evolution of Citizen Participation in Risk Management and Possibilities for East Asia**   93
Cuz Potter

vi CONTENTS

6   Participation Willingness and Interactive Strategy
in Collaborative Risk Governance   119
Chun-yuan Wang and Yanyi Chang

Part III   Risk Management in a New Era

7   Postmodern Risks: The Fourth Industrial Revolution
in East Asia   141
Daniel Connolly

8   School Safety Management: International Framework
and Japanese Practice   167
Aiko Sakurai

Part IV   International Cooperation in Risk Management

9   Aid Policies in Disaster Risk Reduction: Japan
and the Development Assistance to Disaster-Prone
Developing Countries   199
Hazuki Matsuda and Keiichi Ogawa

10 Transboundary Fine Dust and "PM 2.5 Diplomacy"
in Northeast Asia: Cooperation and Future Challenges   223
Muhui Zhang

Index   247

NOTES ON CONTRIBUTORS

Yanyi Chang is an Associate Professor and Chair of the Department of Public Administration of Chung Hua University. His main research interests are China climate change governance, local government and public policy, mixed methods research, public management, and qualitative research software. His research has been published in journals such as *International Journal of China Studies, International Journal of Organizational Innovation, Journal of Environmental Protection and Ecology, Journal of Social and Administrative Sciences*, and *Universal Journal of Management*.

Daniel Connolly is Assistant Professor at the Division of International Studies, Hankuk University of Foreign Studies. His research and teaching interests integrate the history of international relations with science and technology studies. His recent research includes "New Rules for New Tools? Exploitative and Productive Lawfare in the Case of Unpiloted Aircraft" in Alternatives and "New Frontiers of Profit and Risk: The Fourth Industrial Revolution's Impact on Business and Human Rights" in New Political Economy.

Shuaize Fu is a Ph.D. candidate at School of Public Policy and Management, Tsinghua University. His research interests include cross-agency collaboration, collaborative sensemaking in crisis, and professions in government. His recent research focuses on labor process and self-identity of emergency call takers.

viii   NOTES ON CONTRIBUTORS

Jung-Sun Han is Professor at the Division of International Studies, Korea University. Majoring in modern and contemporary Japanese history and culture, Han has worked on the interwar and wartime Japanese political thoughts and the Japan-Korea relations via visual culture of modern Japan. Han's books include, *An Imperial Path to Modernity (Harvard University Press, 2013)* and *Drawing an Empire* (co-authored, Seoul, 2006). The latter book, *Drawing an Empire*, has won the best academic book prize in Korea and has been translated into Japanese (漫画に描かれた日本帝国, 2010). Currently, Han's research focuses on the contemporary Japanese civic activities on conserving war-related sites and the recent works on the topic are *"Relics of Empire Underground" (Asian Studies Review, 2016)* and *"The Heritage of Resentment and Shame in Postwar Japan" (Japan Focus, 2017)*.

Yijia Jing is a Chang Jiang Scholar, Dean of the Institute for Global Public Policy, and Professor of the School of International Relations and Public Affairs, Fudan University. He conducts research on privatization, governance, and collaborative service delivery. He is editor-in-chief of Fudan Public Administration Review and co-editor of *International Public Management Journal*. He is the founding co-editor of the Palgrave book series, *Governing China in the 21 Century*, and the founding editor of the journal *Global Public Policy and Governance*.

Seungho Lee is Professor at the Graduate School of International Studies, Korea University. His research interests are institutional change in water policy, water-related disaster management, transboundary water management, and public private partnership projects in water supply and sanitation services with reference to China, Korea, Southeast Asia, and Europe. Recent publications include *"Security and Development in Transboundary Water Management Between North Korea and China in the Yalu River Basin (2020),"* and *"Regional Cooperation Through the Greater Mekong Subregion (2020)."* Professor Lee often consults with various ministries of the Korean government, K-water, UNESCO, GGGI, and UNESCAP.

Xiaoli Lu is Associate Professor at Tsinghua University's School of Public Policy and Management, Associate Director at Tsinghua's Center for Crisis Management Research, and Executive Director of the Behavior and Data Science Lab. Lu has published widely on topics of crisis and disaster management, and organizational issues. His recent book is *Managing Uncertainty in Crisis: Exploring the Impact of Institutionalization on Organizational Sense Making*. His research has been funded by the National Science Foundation of China, Ministry of Education, Ministry of Science and Technology, Ministry of Emergency Management and China Earthquake Administration.

Hazuki Matsuda is an Assistant Professor at the Graduate School of International Cooperation Studies, Kobe University, Japan since 2018. Prior to joining Kobe University, she was an academic researcher at the University of Tokyo and Lecturer at the Yokohama National University. She holds a Ph.D. in Human Security Studies from the University of Tokyo. Her research interests include natural resource management in Latin American countries, human security studies, and Japan's development cooperation studies. She currently teaches the courses Japan's ODA Experiences and Risk Management at Kobe University, and Global Governance at the School of International Studies, Kwansei Gakuin University, Japan.

Keiichi Ogawa is a Professor/Department Chair in the Graduate School of International Cooperation Studies at Kobe University in Japan. He has served in various graduate schools, including as Visiting Professor at Columbia University and international organizations such as UNESCO and World Bank. His research interest lies in economics of education and education finance. He has worked on development assistance activities in over 30 countries and has authored or co-edited seven books and over 90 journal articles/book chapters. Many of them are issues related to educational development and cooperation in international settings. He holds his Ph.D. in Comparative International Education and Economics of Education from Columbia.

Cuz Potter is associate professor of international development and cooperation at Korea University's Division of International Studies. His teaching and research examines the relationship between urbanization, economic transformation, and social change. His current research problematizes the relationship between rapid economic growth and social justice through an exploration of large-scale residential projects, displacement, and gentrification in Southeast Asia. Past research has examined logistics, Nairobi's slums, US urban revitalization, urban entrepreneurialism, and industrial districts. He is a co-editor of and contributor to

Searching for the Just City, an interrogation of Susan Fainstein's concept of the Just City.

Aiko Sakurai is Professor, Toyo Eiwa University and International Research Institute of Disaster Science (IRIDeS), Tohoku University. She got her Ph.D. in 2007 from Graduate School of International Cooperation Studies (GSICS), Kobe University. Her recent research focuses on comprehensive and sustainable school disaster safety in Japan and the Asian Countries, including Indonesia, Philippines, Nepal, Vietnam, and Myanmar. She is a co-editor of a book, *Disaster Resilience of Education Systems: Experiences from Japan*. She is also a board member of SEEDS Asia, a Japan-based NGO focusing on DRR education.

Kaiyu Shao is a lecture at the Business School of China University of Political Sciences and Law. She received her Ph.D. from Faculty of Economics and Business, KU Leuven, Belgium. Her research interests include multimodal analysis, business-society interface, and politicized organizations. Her research paper has recently been awarded the "Best Critical Business Ethics Paper" by the Critical Management Studies Division of Academy of Management.

Yue Sun is Ph.D. student at Center for Crisis Management, School of Public Policy and Management, Tsinghua University. Her research interests focus on organizational behavior in crisis and the recent research discusses uncertainty in crisis and government response.

Lei Sun is Postdoc Research Fellow at Center for Crisis Management, School of Public Policy and Management, Tsinghua University. His research interests include public disaster awareness and response, disaster subculture, and disaster management. His recent research concentrates on the mechanisms and theoretical explanations that underlie public perception of earthquake risk and response behaviors in China, as well as the role of cultural factors in them.

Toshihisa Toyoda in Economics at Carnegie Mellon University, is Professor Emeritus at Kobe University and at Hiroshima Shudo University, Japan. He was the former president of the Japan Society for International Development Studies. His research interests include development economics and economics of disasters. He has published numerous papers in international journals of economics. He is also the co-editor of

Economic and Policy Lessons from Japan to Developing Countries (Palgrave Macmillan, 2012) and *Asian Law in Disasters* (Routledge, 2016).

Chun-yuan Wang is Professor at Department of Police Administration and Director of General Education Center, Central Police University. His research interests are crisis management, strategic management, and policy analysis. Dr. Wang has published more than 30 English and Chinese articles in leading journals, such as *Public Administration Review, Public Management Review, Administration and Society, Review of Public Personnel Administration, and Chinese Public Administration Review.* He received 2009 Best Ph.D. Dissertation Award and 2015 Best Journal Article Award which both awarded by Taiwan Association for Schools of Public Administration and Affairs (TASPAA).

Muhui Zhang is an Assistant Professor at the Graduate School of International Studies, Pusan National University. His research focuses on international relations and political economy in East Asia. Prior to the current position, he served as assistant professor at the School of International Relations and Public Affairs, Fudan University, and political affairs officer at the Trilateral Cooperation Secretariat among China, Japan, and South Korea. His current research project examines regional free trade agreements and environmental issues in East Asia.

LIST OF FIGURES

Fig. 2.1 Annual death tolls caused by work safety accidents from 2001 to 2018 (*Sources* The Statistical Communique of the People's Republic of China on National Economic and Social Development and China's Work Safety Yearbook) — 16

Fig. 2.2 Annual death toll caused by natural disasters from 2001 to 2018 (*Note* The number of deaths for the years 2008, 2010, and 2011 include missing victims. *Source* Ministry of Civil Affairs) — 17

Fig. 2.3 Milestones in the development of the NEMS in China since 2003 (*Source* The Authors) — 18

Fig. 2.4 Distribution of the founding years of county/district-level EMOs (*Source* Lu and Han [2019]) — 19

Fig. 2.5 Distribution of the stakeholders from whom prefectural EMO leaders can quickly access the listed equipment and supplies in X Province (*Source* Lu and Han [2019]) — 29

Fig. 2.6 Distribution of the stakeholders from whom county/district EMO leaders can quickly access the listed equipment and supplies in X Province (*Source* Lu and Han [2019]) — 30

Fig. 3.1 Historical Development of Major Disaster Laws in Japan (*Source* Author) — 45

Fig. 3.2 Sendai Framework for Disaster Risk Reduction (*Source* Created by the author based on the Sendai Framework [2015]) — 47

xiv LIST OF FIGURES

Fig. 4.1   Disaster risk management and response organizations
           in South Korea (*Source* Modified based on Kim and Sohn
           2018, 56; Korean Society of Hazard Mitigation 2012, 21)   70
Fig. 4.2   Annual precipitation history of South Korea
           between 1986 and 2015 (Unit: mm) (*Source* Kim et al.
           2018, 2)   73
Fig. 4.3   Economic losses caused by natural disasters of South
           Korea in recent 10 years (Unit: KRW Million) (*Remarks*
           *others primarily indicate heat waves and relevant costs.
           Source Ministry of the Interior and Safety 2019, 12)   74
Fig. 4.4   Flood warning dissemination system in South Korea
           (*Source* Modified based on Ministry of Environment
           2019, 257)   86
Fig. 8.1   Comprehensive school safety (*Source* Created
           by the author based on GADRRRES 2017)   169
Fig. 8.2   Roles and responsibilities for school safety
           in the educational structure (*Source* Created by the author
           based on MEXT 2019)   178
Fig. 8.3   School safety system in the Japanese education sector
           (*Source* Created by the author based on MEXT 2019)   179
Fig. 8.4   A photo of the remaining building of OES (taken
           by the author in July 2019)   183
Fig. 8.5   A photo of the Kitakami River Bridge (left) and OES
           (right) (taken by the author in July 2019)   183
Fig. 9.1   Components of disaster management (*Source* Created
           by the authors based on UNDRR 2020; UNGA 2016)   201
Fig. 9.2   Japan's ODA and the evolution of DRR framework
           (*Source* Created by the Authors)   215
Fig. 10.1 Annual PM 2.5 concentration in Major Chinese Cities
           (2013–2018) (*Source* Clear Air Asia (2019), compiled
           by the author)   234

LIST OF TABLES

Table 2.1	National Coordination Commands	22
Table 2.2	Distribution of the missions of county-level emergency management offices in X Province, China	23
Table 3.1	The Great Hanshin Earthquake project cost (100 million yen)	54
Table 3.2	The Great East Japan Earthquake project cost for 2011–2015 (100 million yen)	55
Table 4.1	Disaster management supervision agency in South Korea by disaster or accident type	66
Table 4.2	Economic losses caused by natural disasters of South Korea in recent 10 years (Unit: KRW Million)	75
Table 4.3	Summary of damage from top 10 typhoons in South Korea from 1925 to 2006, ranked by loss of lives and by property damage	77
Table 4.4	The most devastating typhoons in South Korea from the 1950s to the 2000s	78
Table 4.5	Flood-related ministries, laws, and plans in South Korea	82
Table 4.6	Specifications of dams in South Korea	83
Table 4.7	Specifications of multi-purpose dams in South Korea	84
Table 5.1	Typology of risk analysis approaches	96
Table 5.2	Characteristics of risk analysis approaches	103
Table 5.3	Percent change for and against resuming construction by survey	113
Table 6.1	List of in-depth interviews	128
Table 8.1	Details of the three pillars of comprehensive school safety	170

xvi LIST OF TABLES

Table 8.2	Details of the overlap between pillars	170
Table 8.3	Linking the Sendai Seven Targets to the education sector	173
Table 8.4	Status of school collaboration with households and communities in 2015 (N = 48,497 Schools)	182
Table 8.5	Summary of recommendations by the investigation committee of OES incident	185
Table 8.6	Allegations and judgment in the OES incident case	189
Table 10.1	Multilateral frameworks on transnational fine dust	231

CHAPTER 1

Risk Management in East Asia: An Introduction

Yijia Jing, Jung-Sun Han, and Keiichi Ogawa

Referring to the identification, analysis, calculation, and control of probable dangers and threats to people, property, and process, risk management is an issue of global relevance and salience. The recent outbreak of the Covid-19 pandemic, unsurprisingly, has put risk management at the central stage of public governance and civil resilience. The ongoing Covid-19 and past disasters remind citizens of different countries that there is a recurring need to prepare for and respond to calamitous

---

Y. Jing (✉)
Institute for Global Public Policy, School of International Relations and Public Affairs, Fudan University, Shanghai, China
e-mail: jingyj@fudan.edu.cn

J.-S. Han
Division of International Studies, Korea University, Seoul, Republic of Korea
e-mail: jsnhan@korea.ac.kr

K. Ogawa
Graduate School of International Cooperation Studies, Kobe University, Kobe, Japan
e-mail: ogawa35@kobe-u.ac.jp

© The Author(s), under exclusive license to Springer Nature
Singapore Pte Ltd. 2021
Y. Jing et al. (eds.), *Risk Management in East Asia*,
https://doi.org/10.1007/978-981-33-4586-7_1

disruptions and disturbances that are often unpredictable. Historically the concept of "risk management" was applied to the calculation of industrial risks in the private sector. More recently, the range and type of risks have expanded to cover the public sector as well (Beck 1992; Hopkin 2002, Drenan and McConnell 2007). Along with the conceptual evolution, risk management has been made difficult across the world. Perhaps it is inherently difficult to control such risks created by natural forces, sociopolitical failures, or scientific and technological progresses, since they are "not made to man's measure," to paraphrase Camus (Camus 1948, 35). As the belated and ineffective response to the Covid-19 pandemic in many developed and developing countries reveals, the globalized world poses compounded uncertainties in nature and transborder emergencies in scale (Beck 1999). Still, governments and societies have strived to reduce risks and mitigate disasters. The challenges are daunting since risk management is far beyond simply an instrumental solution to pragmatic queries. It engages political calculation of costs and benefits, governmental capacity of power reshuffling, institutional designing of social resilience, and reformulation of cultural traits and values.

East Asia, as a disaster-prone region with thousand years of civilizations, has a traditional emphasis on building preparedness and resilience for natural disasters and human-induced hazards and emergencies. Past disasters, like the 2008 Great Sichuan Earthquake in China and the 2011 Great East Japan Earthquake, saw good efforts of East Asian countries in helping each other, by means like dispatching rescue teams to each other and providing assistance in cash and goods. Such a trend has been further strengthened in these countries' recent cooperation and mutual support in their fight against the Covid-19 pandemic, in which both governments and civil societies donated cash and medical supplies to each other. While China, Japan, and South Korea are geographically and culturally contiguous and hence share some characteristics in their risk management principles and practices, there are also many significant differences due to their different socioeconomic and political systems. The commonalities and variances in East Asia risk management systems are also reflected by their recent responses to the Covid-19 challenges. In light of the continuing global pestilential risks, this book highlights a first systematic exploration of the three national systems of risk management and a couple of frontier issues.

RISK MANAGEMENT: A MULTIDIMENSIONAL GOVERNANCE CHALLENGE

Modern economy and technologies have created better conditions for human-led and human-controlled life and orders. Nonetheless, communities, societies, and nations are still suffering severe natural disasters, as well as the risks created by human achievements. Earthquake, tsunami, nuclear leakage, locust plague, dam break, epidemic, major security accidents, sanctions, and wars may overwhelm capacities of human societies in the short term or local areas and result in serious, mutually enforcing, and persistent damages. Covid-19, the most severe public health crisis since World War II, has caused the loss of lives of over half a million by June 29, 2020 and may lead to negative economic growth of the world for the first time since 2009.[1] Modern governments, as legitimate providers of public goods and services, are expected to organize effective all-phase responses by establishing appropriate legal and institutional systems. Beyond that, risk management has been a way of life in the modern risk society, shaping every aspect of life and business.

The cumulated knowledge and capacities of risk management have been increasing. Right now, risk management has some established rules and principles practiced around the world with varying success. A process view emphasizes the transparent dissemination of knowledge and active promotion of risk awareness, physical and institutional preparedness, emergency response, and post-disaster recovery and reconstruction. An institutional view emphasizes the establishment of legal and policy systems that mandate and support public and non-public institutions to engaging themselves in all these processes of risk management, the climax of which may be the establishment of a specialized government agency of risk management. Nonetheless, every disaster is different. Human preparedness seems often dwarfed by the disasters, with Covid-19 as a recent case.

There are several fundamental causes of risk management as a "wicked" governance issue. A first cause is that risk management is an issue based on probability and aims at the future. While the probability and damages of risks are hard to predict, both individuals and societies may tend to discount the future and feel reluctant to invest for the future. Consequently, there may not be a strong political motivation and will. A second cause is that existing governance systems are usually based on normal conditions and growth-driven expectations. The coalition of growth

4   Y. JING ET AL.

and development may not be able to invest enough for risk management. Third, the unbalance between costs and benefits in time, space, and human groups may lead to moral hazards like free-riding behavior. Fourth, risk management as a regular human institution is often made ineffective by the irregular risks. Finally, there is often difficult to reconcile different values, making risk management an issue of political debates. Hence the design and operation of risk management systems in any country may well reflect how these issues are perceived and handled.

East Asian Risk Management: Systems and Frontiers

The experiences of China, Japan, and South Korea in seeking appropriate and robust risk management may shed light on global risk management knowledge and practices. For one thing, East Asia has been an axis of global economic development and modernization. Risk management has been emphasized in all three countries in their public governance and international cooperation. Systematic studies are needed to disclose the existent and evolving patterns of risk management in the region that may be useful for countries of developed and developing status. A second concern is that China, Japan, and South Korea share the Confucian norms and the developmental practices that may create important consistency in their risk management system. Marked by the interventionist state in defining risks at the national level and molding the voluntary responses and preparedness at the social level, is there any chance to develop a distinctive East Asia model of risk management? This book may provide some preliminary exploration in this aspect. A third concern is that China, Japan, and South Korea are in the front of the radical technological development, so-called the Fourth Industrial Revolution, and are facing new opportunities and challenges of risk management. While the use of emerging technologies in risk management has created new capacities, the societal and technological transition also calls for new types of risk management. The frontier practices in East Asia may offer useful insights for all countries in this new era of the Fourth Industrial Revolution.

In recent decades, all three countries have struggled to strengthen their national risk management system. In the case of China, formal emergency management systems emerged relatively late and were mainly responses to major disasters, including the 2003 SARS and 2008 Sichuan Earthquake.[2] Overall, the establishment and development of risk management in China have been treated as a representative component of the modern state governance system and capacities promoted by the government since 2013. China's effective responses to the Covid-19 pandemic in 2020 have been a fundamental touchstone of its decade-long efforts to modernize its emergency management capacities.

Until late 2019, China announced to have established an emergency management system with Chinese characteristics. Such a system includes more than 70 laws and policies like the 2007 *Law on Responses to Emergencies*, the 2002 *Law on Safe Production*, and the 2013 *Regulations on the Emergency Response Plans* issued by the State Council. Subsequently, more than 5.5 million emergency response plans were made. The working system of emergency management in response to major disasters is composed of one general response manual, 15 manuals of specific disasters, and seven safeguard mechanisms. In 2018, the Ministry of Emergency Management was erected, which has established joint response mechanisms with more than 32 government and state agencies.

Such a system has some essential components. First is the centralized and firm leadership arrangement. According to the level and nature of emergencies, the party, the government, and its vertical hierarchy, and the professional agencies will decide the division of labor and the coordinating mechanisms. For example, responses to Covid-19 were directly coordinated by the Central Party Committee. Political and social mobilization may be exercised to varying extent. Second is the all-phase and prevention-oriented operational mechanisms. Emergency management covers all phases of disasters and emphasizes avoidance of and preparedness for emergencies. Third is the systematic and scientific rule system, including laws, bylaws, and policies. A sound institutional system is emphasized. A fourth component is a sufficient reserve of capacities and resources, including the application of high-tech.

Japan has experienced severe national disasters over the years, including earthquakes, tsunami, and typhoons. One of the worst natural disasters in history was the Great Hanshin earthquake (Kobe earthquake), which occurred on January 17, 1995, and up to 6434 people lost their lives; about 4600 of them were from Kobe, Hyogo Prefecture. More recently, the 2011 Great East Japan Earthquake was a magnitude 9.0 (Mw) undersea megathrust earthquake off the coast of Japan that occurred March 11, 2011. It was the most powerful earthquake ever recorded in Japan, and the fourth most powerful earthquake in the world since modern record-keeping began in 1900.

From the lessons learned from significant natural disasters, the government of Japan has been aware of the importance of reducing natural disaster risks before a disaster occurs. Knowledge and technology concerning disaster prevention, mitigation, and preparedness have been developed and transferred to vulnerable developing nations to minimize physical damage and human casualties by disasters. Therefore, not only within Japan but also internationally and as a donor country, Japan has played a crucial role in investing in Disaster Risk Reduction (DRR) policy and programs, becoming the world's single biggest direct donor in the context of DRR. The World Conferences on DRR has been hosted since 1994 in Japan to show Japan's efforts to tackle disaster risks on a global level, in which international frameworks on DRR have been adopted including the Yokohama Strategy and Plan of Action for a Safer World, the Hyogo Framework for Action (HFA) and Sendai Framework for Disaster Risk Reduction.

Probing into the South Korean developments of risk management policies and practices, the continuities and changes in the public approaches to the three types of risks are articulated. The first is the time-honored, traditional risk to human civilization, i.e., the water-related natural disasters. The second is the modern risks manufactured by the very scientific, industrial, and technological progresses, such as the nuclear risk. The third is the newly emerging postmodern risks caused by the development of intelligence technologies. Blurring the boundaries of real, virtual, and biological, the intelligence technologies are generating new risks of manipulating human decision making. In part due to the rapid industrialization and modernization, what characterizes the contemporary South Korean society is the coexistence of the three types of risks. In dealing with these risks simultaneously, it is discernible that a subtle shift in risk management policies and practices is taking place to incorporate local and site-specific measures into what has so far been a highly centralized and hierarchical risk management system.

In managing the traditional hazards to people and property, the Ministry of the Interior and Safety is at the center of administrating risk management by taking full responsibility for operating the Central Disaster and Safety Countermeasure Head Quarters. To enhance the efficiency in coordinating various disaster management agencies in coping with multifaceted hazardous conditions, including the Covid-19 outbreak in South Korea, the Prime Minister may undertake the task of coordinating relevant agencies' responses. In other words, the administrative structure of disaster risk management takes a strong top-down feature with an emphasis on the role of experts and bureaucracy. At the same time, there is a growing need and call to promote decentralized, citizen-participatory risk assessment and decision making in managing complex risks manufactured by industrial and technological developments. It is well-known that the compounded risk in modern society is not only generated exogenously but also embedded in conflicting interests and values among experts as well as experts and citizens. To manage the modern and, to some extent, postmodern risks, one can find the tendency to incorporate citizen viewpoints and voices based on local and tacit knowledge in South Korea.

RISK MANAGEMENT COOPERATION IN EAST ASIA

In order to better prevent and respond to disasters, there is an increasing need for coordination and cooperation among China, Japan, and South Korea in risk management. The recognition of the importance of trilateral cooperation was reflected by the biennial Trilateral Ministerial Meeting on Disaster Management, first held in Kobe City of Japan on October 31, 2009. The three parties signed the Trilateral Joint Statement on Disaster Management Cooperation, which specified various areas of trilateral cooperation. Till now, the three countries have taken a turn to host the Trilateral Ministerial Meeting on Disaster Management for six times. Heads of disaster management departments conduct in-depth discussions on cooperation forms, contents, and effectiveness to further strengthen trilateral and bilateral cooperation among the three countries.

The trilateral cooperation focuses on three aspects. The first is the sharing of information and technology. The three countries agree to share information on major domestic natural disasters, relevant domestic laws, regulations, systems, and policy regarding disaster management, research outcomes of catastrophes, and relevant technologies. Enhancing compatibility of information has been an important issue in the practice of information and technology sharing among the three countries. They also exchange communication technology, sponsor joint R&D projects, and host international and regional conferences on disaster management. The three countries emphasize sharing their disaster management technologies and experiences with developing countries.

The second is to establish a mechanism of mutual visits and exchanges. In addition to visits and exchanges among disaster management government officials, researchers and academia, the three countries have also established a joint visit mechanism to organize visits to disaster-prone areas or severe disaster-hit areas to share important experiences and lessons in disaster management, recovery, and reconstruction.

The third is cooperation on capacity building of disaster mitigation and relief. China, Japan, and South Korea have effectively improved their disaster mitigation and relief capabilities by carrying out trainings for disaster management personnel, drawing on the international experience and practices of on-site rescue and relief and strengthening satellite disaster monitoring. Since the adoption of Sendai Framework for Disaster Risk Reduction 2015–2030 (SFDRR) in 2015, the three countries have also been promoting the implementation of this framework in cooperation.

THE BOOK AND ITS ROAD MAP

In 2011, the three countries of the region, China, Japan, and South Korea decided to encourage trilateral intergovernmental high-education cooperation programs called CAMPUS Asia (Collective Action for Mobility Program of University Students in Asia). For that, Fudan University (China), Kobe University (Japan), and Korea University (South Korea) organized a CAMPUS Asia program "Risk Management Experts in East Asia" and launched regular double degree student exchanges and joint research projects in areas of risk management. The "Risk Management" program has received lots of attention and praise from the three Ministries of Education due to its excellent operation and outcomes.

This book is a joint endeavor of the three partner universities to develop a book with in-depth and state-of-the-art analysis for the academic community of East Asia and the world. Currently, there is still the absence of a book that can further our comparative knowledge of the three systems and encourage both policy transfer and cross-country cooperation in risk management in this region. Hence this book has been designed in a way to well compare the three systems and to grasp some frontier practices with theoretical and pragmatic importance.

The three beginning chapters focus on the evolution of risk management policies and systems in each country, paving a general framework to understand the commonalities and differences of the three national systems. In the first chapter, Xiaoli Lu et al. discuss the modernization of China's National Emergency Management System (NEMS) since 2003, which has successfully coped with a series of major emergencies and significantly reduced casualties and damage. They analyze the historical development, guiding principles, and contemporary constitution of NEMS and the government-society interaction under NEMS, arguing that China's NEMS has been moving toward an all-hazard, all-phase, and all-stakeholder model. In the second chapter, Toshihisa Toyoda examines the characteristics and challenges of the Japanese system of reconstruction from natural disasters with particular reference to the Sendai Framework. He also reviews the evolutionary development of the disaster management system in Japan. He discusses the central notion of "Build Back Better" (BBB) with particular reference to the Sendai Framework, showing the importance of integrated approach of disaster management cycles, particularly the integration of reconstruction and Disaster Risk Reduction. He also discusses Japan's initiatives of BBB, and their background from the viewpoints of history, law, and economics. In the third chapter, Seungho Lee traces the evolution of the South Korean disaster risk management system from the 1960s with a focus on the water-related hazard control policies and practices. Given the salience of water-related disasters in creating the most detrimental social and economic effects in South Korea, it is relevant to examine how the risk management system has been developed to mitigate damages caused by typhoons, floods, and drought. In introducing the risk management system in South Korea, Lee presents a highly centralized, top-down feature of risk management system. Yet, he also points out the subtle change in the system to explore the decentralized bottom-up approaches in the early 2000s as the nature of water-related risks has become more complexed due to the climate changes.

This brings to the next two chapters' topic—the role of citizen participation in risk management. Cuz Potter discusses the case of citizen deliberation on nuclear power in South Korea. The chapter introduces the theoretical shift from the empiricist and technocrats centered to the post-empiricist and deliberative decision-making processes in environmental risk management. The latter process is marked by the growing citizens' role in risk assessment and management. It then presents the recent South Korean case of assessing and managing nuclear risks as an Asian example for the theoretical shift. Likewise, in Chapter 5 Chun-yuan Wang et al. explores citizen participation in risk management by looking at participation willingness and interactive strategies between citizens and governments. Using in-depth interviews, they find that effective risk information communication and translational leadership will contribute to risk awareness and trust, and consequently improve citizen participation and network-based risk governance.

The following two chapters dwell on two important frontier issues of risk management. Daniel Connolly discusses postmodern risks engendered by the technological disruption also known as the Fourth Industrial Revolution in East Asia. Marked by the phenomenal development in intelligence technologies associated with datafication and predictive analytics, a categorically different hazard is being manufactured. By analyzing the dissemination of fake news and the increased digital addiction in South Korea, Connolly argues that they are the precursor of an entirely new type of risks threatening the human autonomy in decision making and the individual identity formation. Aiko Sakurai provides a case of disaster in the postmodern Japan, developing her analysis of risk management in school systems. She examines to draw lessons learned from experiences to make schools safer by using a case from the 2011 Great East Japan Earthquake. She also provides suggestions for future collaboration to enhance school resilience through risk management at school to protect children under school supervision, and the need to exchange experiences and regional cooperation in Asia.

The last part of the book extends to discussions on international cooperation in risk management. In their chapter. Hazuki Matsuda and Keiichi Ogawa discusses the conceptual framework of the Disaster Risk Reduction (DRR) in the context of aid, and assess the Yokohama Strategy, as well as the Hyogo Framework for Action (HFA) and Sendai Framework, underscoring that Japan played an influencing role in determining some of its policies. They also outline the historical evolution of Japan's development cooperation from the DRR perspective, examining some cases of DRR programs implemented in disaster-prone developing nations. They conclude that Japan's development cooperation policies transformed along with changes in the international environment, and these shifts also affected, to some extent, the national DRR framework, adjusting to new global circumstances. In the last chapter, Muhui Zhang discusses another kind of international cooperation driven by negative externalities—the joint efforts between China, Japan, and South Korea in curbing regional air pollution. The study finds that transnational cooperative networks, data sharing, and joint scientific research have increased in recent years, indicating a preliminary "air governance" regime in Northeast Asia. However, regional cooperation on transboundary air pollution in Northeast Asia is never a purely environmental issue, but has been heavily shaped by mixed concerns of domestic politics and diplomatic interests.

Overall, the chapters included in this book demonstrate dynamic developments of risk management in multiple fronts in East Asia. The patterns and inspirations of these developments may be further explored in the future.

Notes

1. The death toll of the world due to Covid-19 is from: https://voice. baidu.com/act/newpneumonia/newpneumonia/?from=osari_pc_1 Accessed on June 29, 2020.
2. In China, the term "emergency management" has been used to denote government-led risk management functions aiming basically at preventing and handling all kinds of disasters and emergency situations.

REFERENCES

Beck, U. 1992. *Risk Society: Toward a New Modernity*. London: Sage Publications.

Beck, U. 1999. *World Risk Society*. Cambridge: Polity Press.

Camus, A. 1948. *The Plague*. New York: Modern Library.

Drenan, T., and McConnel, A. (2007). *Risk and Crisis Management in the Public Sector*. London: Routledge.

Hopkin, P. 2002. *Holistic Risk Management in Practice*. London: Witherby.

PART I

National Risk Management Systems in the Region

CHAPTER 2

Understanding China's National Emergency Management System

Xiaoli Lu, Lei Sun, Shuaize Fu, Yue Sun, and Kaiyu Shao

INTRODUCTION

China is prone to frequent, diverse natural disasters as well as industrial accidents due to the rapid urbanisation and industrialisation of the nation.

X. Lu · L. Sun (✉) · S. Fu · Y. Sun
Center for Crisis Management Research, School of
Public Policy and Management, Tsinghua University, Beijing, China
e-mail: sunleiyanshan_2008@126.com

X. Lu
e-mail: luxiaoli@mail.tsinghua.edu.cn

S. Fu
e-mail: fushuaize@foxmail.com

Y. Sun
e-mail: mango950506@163.com

K. Shao
Business School, China University of Political
Science and Law, Beijing, China
e-mail: shaokaiyu2020@163.com

© The Author(s), under exclusive license to Springer Nature
Singapore Pte Ltd. 2021
Y. Jing et al. (eds.), *Risk Management in East Asia*,
https://doi.org/10.1007/978-981-33-4586-7_2

It also faces serious public health emergencies and social unrest. In the last two decades, devastating accidents and disasters, such as the Severe Acute Respiratory Syndrome (SARS) crisis in 2003, the Wenchuan Earthquake in 2008, Tianjin Port Explosion in 2015, and the ongoing COVID-19 epidemic, have seriously impacted Chinese society. Lessons learned from the government's responses to these major disasters have triggered policy changes, which have helped modernise the National Emergency Management System (NEMS).

The Chinese NEMS has withstood the formidable tests of the above mentioned major emergencies. Statistically, the number of deaths caused by industrial accidents has decreased steadily and the annual mortality rate due to natural disasters has dropped below 2000 in recent decades (Figs. 2.1 and 2.2). Moreover, the current NEMS has shown its strength in responding to the COVID-19 epidemic. It has featured a decisive lockdown, the rapid mobilisation of critical resource production and logistics, a newly equipped contact-tracing system, the promotion of strong national solidarity, and the construction of the innovative Fangcang shelter hospitals to isolate patients with mild or moderate symptoms to mitigate peak demand in hospitals (Chen et al. 2020). However,

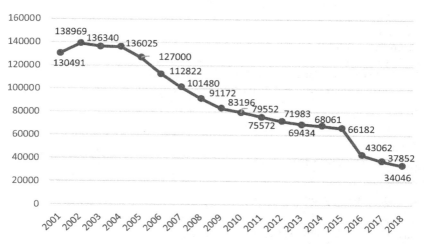

Fig. 2.1 Annual death tolls caused by work safety accidents from 2001 to 2018 (*Sources* The Statistical Communique of the People's Republic of China on National Economic and Social Development and China's Work Safety Yearbook)

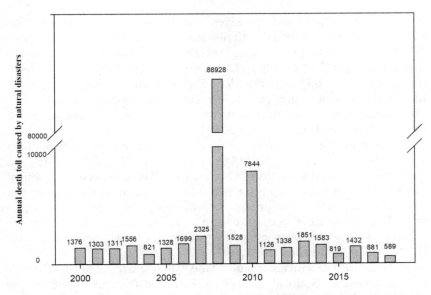

Fig. 2.2 Annual death toll caused by natural disasters from 2001 to 2018 (*Note* The number of deaths for the years 2008, 2010, and 2011 include missing victims. *Source* Ministry of Civil Affairs)

challenges remain for the NEMS, such as the lack of collaborative sense-making of unknown unknown type crises (Lu and Xue 2016).

The first half of the chapter provides an overview of the Chinese NEMS, including its historical evolution, recent trends, and interactions with society at large. The second half presents the challenges that remain for the NEMS. The conclusion offers suggestions for future directions of the Chinese NEMS.

THE HISTORY OF THE NEMS IN CHINA

The Establishment of the Modern NEMS

Before the 2003 SARS crisis, the Chinese NEMS was scattered across various response systems based on specific disaster agent (Lu and Han 2019). They were managed by vertical administrative-sector lines (Xue and Zhong 2009, Lu and Han 2019). The 2003 SARS crisis resulted in hundreds of deaths and had severe social and economic impacts; the national response to it revealed significant flaws in the traditional Chinese NEMS (Xue 2010). In a national working conference on SARS prevention and control (28 July 2003), China's central leadership acknowledged deficiencies in the response. President Hu Jintao and Premier Wen Jiabao identified problems, such as a failing emergency response mechanism, insufficient crisis management capacities, and a lack of local preparedness (*China Daily* 2003; Lu and Xue 2016).

Drawing on the lessons learned from the response to the SARS crisis, China began rebuilding its NEMS in 2003 (Lu and Xue 2016). The new system is based on the roadmap 'One Plan and Three Subsystems', which involves (1) creating contingency plans, (2) restructuring the institution, (3) clarifying the mechanisms in the emergency management process, and (4) drafting emergency management-related laws and regulations. Figure 2.3 shows an overview of the milestones in the development of the NEMS in China since 2003.

In terms of the emergency plan, the China State Council officially promulgated the 'National Emergency Response Plan for Public Emergencies' on 8 January 2006. The plan classifies public emergencies into four major types, including natural disasters, industrial accidents, public health emergencies, and social unrest. It also categorises emergencies based on the severity, including: I (highly significant), II (significant), III (major), and IV (routine). The plan specifies the organisational mechanisms of emergency response and provides general guidance on the prevention and management of public emergencies (Gao 2013). Based on these national-level plans, ministries responsible for specific types of disasters and governments across the hierarchies created their contingency plans subsequently. According to the Ministry of Emergency Management

Fig. 2.3 Milestones in the development of the NEMS in China since 2003 (*Source* The Authors)

(MEM) (2019), the Chinese government had formulated more than 5.5 million contingency plans by September 2019.

The Chinese government also upgraded the institutional structure of the NEMS, streamlining several of its key response mechanisms. In 2006, the National Emergency Management Office (NEMO) was established, followed by the creation of Emergency Management Offices (EMOs) at different levels of the hierarchy and in various policy sectors. The number of newly founded district/county-level EMOs peaked in 2008 (Fig. 2.4). On 5 March 2008, Premier Wen Jiabao announced the preliminary establishment of the modern NEMS. In 2016, the central government triggered another round of reform, which started with the release of two important documents called 'Guidance on Reforming the Disaster Risk Reduction System and Mechanism (2016–2020)' and the 'Guideline on Promoting the Reform and Development of Work Safety'. The two documents served as guiding principles for the development of natural-disaster and industrial-accident management, respectively. In 2018, the establishment of the MEM further integrated the responsibilities of nine permanent organisations and four national-level interagency coordination committees.

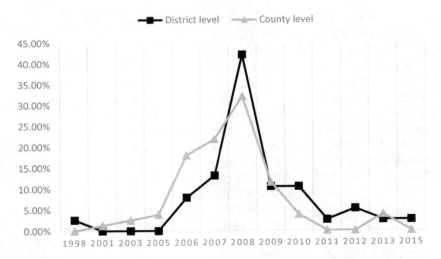

Fig. 2.4 Distribution of the founding years of county/district-level EMOs (*Source* Lu and Han [2019])

The organisations include:

1. State Administration of Work Safety (including the State Administration of Coal Mine Safety).
2. Fire Department of the Ministry of Public Security.
3. Emergency Management Office of the State Council.
4. China Earthquake Administration.
5. Departments relevant to geo-hazard management in the Ministry of Land and Resources.
6. Departments relevant to disaster relief in the Ministry of Civil Affairs.
7. Departments relevant to forest fire management in the State Forest Administration.
8. Departments relevant to drought and flood control in the Ministry of Water Resources.
9. Departments relevant to prairie fire control in the Ministry of Agriculture.

The four national-level interagency coordination committees include:

1. Headquarters of State Flood Control and Drought Relief.
2. National Committee for Disaster Relief.
3. State Council's Commission on Work Safety.
4. National Headquarters of Forest Fire Prevention.

In terms of legislation, the Chinese government released the 'Regulation on Preparedness for and Responses to Emergent Public Health Hazards' on 9 May 2003 as part of its response to the SARS crisis. It was followed by the Emergency Response Law of the People's Republic of China, which was promulgated on 30 August 2007. The Emergency Response Law prescribes the responsibilities of government and other stakeholders in different phases of emergency management. The enactment of this law initiated a comprehensive legislative process towards a general legal system of public emergency management in China.[1] By 2019, China had issued and implemented more than 70 laws and regulations related to emergency management. The current response to the ongoing COVID-19 epidemic has revealed several deficiencies of the Emergency Response Law and the Law of the People's Republic of China on the Prevention and Control of Infectious Diseases. In July 2020, the National People's Congress triggered the revision of both laws.[2]

Trends in the Development of the NEMS in China: Towards All-Hazard, All-Phase, and All-Stakeholder Management

The modern Chinese NEMS, in line with global trends, is moving towards comprehensive emergency management. It aims to adopt an all-hazard, all-phase, and all-stakeholder emergency management model with distinct Chinese characteristics.

All-Hazard Management

The establishment of the MEM synthesised the scattered emergency-management responsibilities of different vertical administrative lines. The MEM is responsible for preparing and responding to two major types of emergencies, natural disasters and industrial accidents. Before the establishment of the MEM, the emergency response relied on two major institutional arrangements. The first involved the above-listed interagency coordinating headquarters based in specific ministries for managing each type of disaster (Table 2.1). The second involved the State Council Emergency Management Office, which was responsible for collecting and synthesising emergency information for national leaders and helping with coordination.

The coordinating headquarters vary in terms of power structure. Some headquarters are ranked as national-level commands, while others are ministry-level commands. For instance, the Headquarters of State Flood and Control and Drought Relief operates at the national level and is led by a vice premier and assisted by a standing working office affiliated with the MEM (formerly the Ministry of Water Resources). Several temporary coordinating commands have evolved into regular standing committees as certain crises have become more salient. For example, the food safety emergency plan specifies that the coordinating headquarters will be activated when a food crisis unfolds. After the nation increasingly faced food safety issues, the State Council's Commission on Food Safety was founded in 2010. It consists of an executing vice premier, two vice premiers, and leaders from other supporting agencies (Lu and Han 2019). To cope with some transboundary crises, such as the 2008 Snow Storm Catastrophe, an ad hoc, temporary emergency command centre for disaster relief and coal, power, oil, and transportation assurance was established in the National

22   X. LU ET AL.

Table 2.1   National Coordination Commands

Type of coordination command	Responsibilities	Examples
Political Bureau of the Communist Party of China Central Committee/State Council	Transboundary crises, catastrophes	Leading group of the CPC Central Committee for Novel Coronavirus Prevention and Control
Ad hoc State Council Command	Single- or multi-type emergency; activated under the State Council to coordinate transboundary crises and catastrophes; the response is based in one specific ministry and supported by other ministries	Emergency Command Center for Disaster Relief and Coal, Power, Oil, and Transportation Assurance
Standing National Coordinating Commission	Single- or multi-type emergency	Headquarters of State Flood Control and Drought Relief; National Committee for Disaster Relief
Standing State Council's Commission	A single type of emergency	State Council's Commission on Work Safety; State Council's Commission on Food Safety
Standing Ministry Coordinating Commission	A single type of emergency	Leading Group of National Communication Assurance; The National Headquarters of Forest Fire Prevention

Source revised based on Lu and Han (2019)

Development and Reform Commission. This command led the response to the unexpected ice storm and the subsequent breakdown of the electric grid and transportation infrastructure in southern China (Lu and Xue 2016).

At the national level, the NEMO scrutinises, organises, and assesses the information reported from local EMOs and functional departments and reports it to State Council leaders. In some provinces, such as Beijing, the local district/county-level EMOs also serve as the daily operating offices of the local emergency management committees. In general, most

EMOs across hierarchies maintain several key functions (Table 2.2). Lu and Han (2019) surveyed EMOs in X Province and found that they all maintained emergency on-shift duty and information-reporting functions; however, only 48% of the EMOs engaged in risk assessment and evaluation. According to Lu and Han's (2019) survey results, we can summarise the core practical functions of EMOs in China. First, each EMO provides an information hub in the governmental system; the local departments or agencies report to it when they detect an emergency. After receiving and assessing this information, the EMO then decides whether to report it to the appropriate government leaders or a related agency. Second, each EMO assists local government leaders as they deal with an emergency by providing relevant information, such as the distribution of reserved emergency resources and the division of functions among different government agencies. Third, each EMO is responsible for coordinating agencies in preparation for all kinds of emergencies. Last, each EMO oversees all of the emergency plans; besides designing the general emergency plan, it checks and keeps on file the specific emergency plans of all the agencies.

Due to their limited capacities, the NEMO, MEM, and National Health Commission have not been able to serve as a single all-hazard

Table 2.2 Distribution of the missions of county-level emergency management offices in X Province, China

Mission	Percentage
Emergency on-duty shift and information reporting	100.0
Coordination	98.4
Law enforcement	92.8
Assisting executives on emergency response	89.6
Training and drilling	86.3
Educating the public	84.0
Contingency planning	77.6
Releasing information	76.8
Systems/platforms for information and communications technology	70.4
Monitoring and early warning	60.8
Recovery management	49.6
Risk assessment and evaluation	48.0

Source Lu and Han (2019)
Note The numbers represent the proportion of surveyed EMOs taking part in the corresponding mission

agency for the management of so-called transboundary crises[3] (Lu and Han 2019). In most major transboundary crises, temporary national-level commands have been set up under the State Council or the Standing Committee of the Political Bureau of the Communist Party of China (CPC) Central Committee to coordinate large-scale responses and recovery efforts. The Emergency Command Center for Disaster Relief and Coal, Power, Oil, and Transportation Assurance is a case in point. Another example is the recent response to the COVID-19 epidemic. The Standing Committee of the Political Bureau of the CPC Central Committee set up a Leading Group of the CPC Central Committee for COVID-19 Prevention and Control on 25 January 2020.

All-Phase Management

The all-phase principle aims to connect activities before, during, and after an emergency, particularly the mitigation phase, which is often ignored. In China, the mitigation efforts mentioned in the current national emergency plan refer to improving public awareness of hazards and increasing participation in hazard-mitigation practices through social education campaigns, risk identification and analysis, and early warning (Lu and Han 2019).[4] Beyond the development of traditional engineering measures for pre-disaster mitigation, there have been few initiatives undertaken in the last decade. In early 2010, the tentative Geo-Hazard Migrant programme was initiated in some provinces, such as Shandong and Shaanxi. Since then, under this programme, Shaanxi Province planned to relocate roughly 2.4 million residents of communities deemed vulnerable to flash floods, landslides, and mudslides in ten years (Meng 2010, Shaanxi Daily 2010). Shaanxi Province has already achieved its stated goals by the end of 2020 (Li 2015, Liu 2020). In June 2020, the State Council decided to conduct a general survey of composite natural disaster risks, the first ever in China. The State Council expects to complete this comprehensive evaluation by 2022.[5]

Compared with its handling of the mitigation and preparedness phases, the Chinese government's mobilisation of emergency response and short-term reconstruction after catastrophic disasters has proved faster and more comprehensive. As the COVID-19 epidemic began unfolding in January 2020, numerous protection resources and medical professionals were sent to Wuhan, the epicentre of the outbreak. According to a white paper released by China's State Council Information Office (2020), the National Health Commission mobilised around 42,600 medical workers and more than 900 public health professionals to assist with the response in Hubei Province to cope with the surges in medical demand. The military dispatched more than 4000 medical workers to Hubei. The Wenchuan Earthquake offers another example of national mobilisation in the post-catastrophe reconstruction phase. After the Wenchuan Earthquake, the State Council launched the Paired Assistance to Disaster-Affected Areas Programme (PADDA), in which economically developed provinces were assigned to assist the reconstruction of the earthquake-affected counties and districts. The provinces became responsible for providing necessary resources to the assigned counties or districts with which they were paired to assist with their post-earthquake reconstruction. Although sometimes suffering from drawbacks, such as sustainability issues or mismatches between supply and demands, the PADDA programme accelerated the reconstruction process (Xu et al. 2014; Zhong and Lu 2018).

This type of mobilisation does not work for all types of emergencies. After a major industrial accident, the State Administration of Work Safety often launches a nationwide campaign to suspend production in the affected industry. This type of mobilisation generates only limited positive effects in some industries, such as that of Chlor-alkali, and fails in most cases. Consequently, the private sectors often criticise this strategy.

All-Stakeholder Management
While the government plays a dominant role in the Chinese NEMS, other actors, including military forces, private sectors, and nongovernmental organisations (NGOs), also contribute to emergency management. The military sector has a long history of participating in emergency responses to major disasters, such as the Tangshan Earthquake in 1976, and the Yangtze River Flood in 1998. In 2005, the Central Military Commission issued a regulation regarding the military's participation in disaster rescue, institutionalising its role in emergency response. Military leaders have long maintained formal positions in long-standing coordination committees and temporary incident commands. The deputy chief of staff of the People's Liberation Army of China served as a member of the National Headquarters of Flood Control and Drought Relief and the vice commander of the Headquarters for Earthquake Relief. In response to the 2013 Lushan Earthquake, a joint CPC committee between the military and the local government was established to coordinate relief efforts (Lu and Xue 2016; Lu and Han 2019).

In 2014, the State Council released an industry development policy to grow the emergency management industry, which would specialise in supplying professional products and services for emergency prevention, preparedness, monitoring, early warning, disposal, and rescue (Lu and Han 2019). The aim to develop such an industry appears to be unique to China. Under this policy, some cities began to build industrial parks to host various enterprises producing emergency response products. Thus far, this new industry has made limited observable impact, and its research and development capacity continues to be not satisfied.

Since the 2008 Wenchuan Earthquake, NGOs have increased their participation in emergency management (Zhang et al. 2015), which has resulted in two significant trends in recent years. First, although the capacity of most NGOs has remained weak, some have become major players in emergency response, partnering with local governments; a key example is the Blue Sky Rescue Team. Second, Chinese NGOs have become involved in the global response to major international disasters, such as the earthquakes in Nepal and Haiti. Several NGOs have gone beyond short-term responses by working with local partners to provide long-term recovery assistance, such as in the establishment of the Nepal Office of the China Foundation for Poverty Alleviation.[6]

Interactions Between the Government and Society

Emergency Communication

Central-level emergency communication channels continue to take a scattered approach to the releasing of emergency information. Apart from the common practice of holding press conferences, other channels include the National Emergency Broadcasting System,[7] the newly created 'China Emergency Information' website,[8] and the National Emergency Incident Early Warning Release System.[9]

Based on the lessons learned from the SARS crisis, the Chinese government established a news spokesperson system to communicate with the public and the media. During the spread of H1N1, the government held news conferences to inform the public about case details. With the help of epidemiologists, these timely communications reduced public panic (Xue and Zeng 2019). During the COVID-19 epidemic, the central and local governments, such as that of Hubei Province, have organised regular press conferences to inform the public about the disease, its spread, and advice on its prevention.

Following the Wenchuan Earthquake, the China Media Group initiated a National Emergency Broadcasting System, which has since served as an important channel of emergency communication. This system became functional as part of the response to the Lushan Earthquake in 2013. It has become a multichannel communication platform, involving a website, social media, and mobile applications, to meet various needs during emergencies and normal times.

The newly founded MEM also plays an active role in emergency communication. In 2019, MEM worked with Xinhua News Agency to build the 'China Emergency Information' website, which synthesises all disaster information for the public. In normal times, the website shares and updates disaster-related knowledge and rescue skills. Before an emergency, it releases early warnings and forecast information. During a disaster, it releases disaster damage and relief information. The disaster information is supplied by over 700,000 registered disaster-information officers nationwide, who collect and monitor disaster information promptly. The MEM releases updates after synthesising and confirming the collected information.

In 2015, the National Early Warning Center, affiliated with the China Meteorological Administration, was established to release warnings to the public. The centre maintains the National Emergency Incident Early Warning Release System.

Disaster Education

In 1989, China established the China National Commission for the International Decade on Natural Disaster Reduction in response to a United Nations initiative.[10] The commission was responsible for guiding China's efforts towards natural-disaster reduction, including disaster education. In 1996, the State Education Commission designated the last Monday in March as National Safety Education Day to promote comprehensive safety education among students in primary and secondary schools (Deng 2012). After the Wenchuan Earthquake, natural-disaster education gained more attention. The State Council set 12 May (the date of the 2008 Wenchuan Earthquake) as National Disaster Prevention and Reduction Day. The State Council also began including disaster and safety education in the national education system (Zhu and Zhang 2017). Now schools begin each semester with courses on disaster education.

Remaining Challenges for the NEMS in China

The modern Chinese NEMS has distinctive characteristics that are rooted in its history and the current sociopolitical context. Although it has accomplished significant achievements, the ongoing reform of the NEMS must overcome the following challenges.

Limited Social Participation in Disaster Mitigation and Emergency Preparedness

The government plays a dominant role in emergency management, which leads to the insufficient participation of other stakeholders in mitigating and preparing for emergencies. Similar to most countries in the mitigation phase, public participation has been limited in identifying and assessing risks, and few measures have been taken to reduce potential losses. Lu and Han's (2019) survey showed that in the emergency preparedness phase, emergency office directors at the prefectural- and county-levels did not maintain close relationships with other stakeholders, which are necessary for acquiring response resources. EMO leaders tend to access resources and gather supplies from other agencies or departments in horizontal coordination within the same prefecture or county government (Figs. 2.5 and 2.6, respectively).

Failure of Initiative and Over-Response

The modern Chinese NEMS has demonstrated effectiveness and efficiency in several routine emergencies or expected crises. However, its response has been inadequate in addressing irregular and unexpected emergencies. Faced with 'new' situations for which the NEMS has not established a response routine, the system shows a high level of inertia. It takes longer for the system to be activated, however, once it was activated, the NEMS tends to invest an overwhelming amount of resources and efforts into political mobilisation.

The reasons for the failure of initiative in the face of unknown unknown crises partly lie in the bureaucratic rigidity of the NEMS routines, which tend to be formed based on previous disasters. Most emergency plans that guide emergency response are not the result of deliberation over bureaucratic realities and local hazard situations. Instead, most are based on templates. Generally, the plans are drafted for

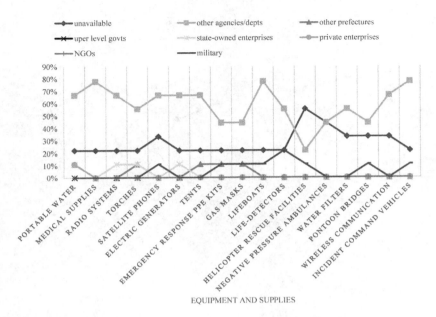

Fig. 2.5 Distribution of the stakeholders from whom prefectural EMO leaders can quickly access the listed equipment and supplies in X Province (*Source* Lu and Han [2019])

routine crises rather than to address situations that have not been experienced (Lu and Xue 2016). There are only some exceptions in regions that have experienced major emergencies, such as Sichuan Province. The earthquake contingency plan of Sichuan Province addressed local situations and response system. Another significant problem is that emergency plans tend to be out of date. The national emergency plan has not been updated since 2005 when the first version was released, and the same is true of the National Contingency Plan for Public Health Emergencies.

Typical Coordination Problems

Coordination is notoriously difficult in administrative contexts (Kettl 2003, Boin and Bynander 2015), and China is no exception. Coordination in vertical dimensions works relatively well, whereas horizontal coordination across organisations remains underdeveloped (Lu and Xue

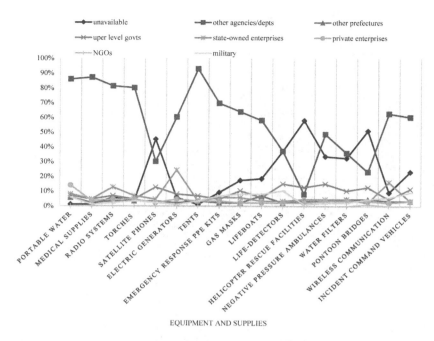

Fig. 2.6 Distribution of the stakeholders from whom county/district EMO leaders can quickly access the listed equipment and supplies in X Province (*Source* Lu and Han [2019])

2016). There have been significant data barriers in sharing information, which often hinder the early detection of risky anomalies. In the 2008 Sanlu Milk Scandal, the then Ministry of Public Health received information from the Gansu Provincial Department of Health through vertical administrative communication channels and immediately triggered a response within its vertical jurisdiction. However, it failed to share crucial information with other horizontal departments, such as the then State Administration for Industry and Commerce.

The situation is even worse in another common transboundary context: the coordination between state-owned enterprises and local governments. The former typically is overseen by the State-Owned Assets Supervision and Administration Commission of the State Council. Those in the latter group are empowered to handle crises in their jurisdictions according to the 'territorial management' principle specified in the Emergency Response Law. In the 2013 Qingdao Pipeline Explosion, the state-owned company, Sinopec, did not inform the Qingdao municipal government about the exact type and volume of the spilled oil, which severely hindered the disaster response. In the early stages of the leak, the Sinopec fire rescue team tried to keep the emergency under control and refused to accept the assistance offered by the local fire station operated by the municipal government.

Too Much Accountability and Too Little Learning

The Chinese government puts too much stake in the accountability system for individual leaders. It ignores opportunities to investigate the in-depth causes of disasters and does not engage in sufficient trial-and-error learning after catastrophic events (Wildavsky 2017). In 2009, the Communist Party of China Central Committee and the State Council issued 'Interim Provisions on the Implementation of the Accountability System for the Leaders of the Party and Government' to specify occasions when individual leaders are accountable, thereby seeking to pressure local leaders to report time-sensitive information to the central government (Lu and Han 2019). The accountability system gives too much responsibility to individual leaders and fails to help them organise relevant stakeholders to improve hazard detection institutionally. It has resulted in the resignation of many leaders while neglecting to ensure the careful investigation of the causes of disasters (Gao and Gao 2011).

CONCLUSION

Since the SARS outbreak in 2003, China has continually modernised its NEMS. Based on the blueprint 'One Plan and Three subsystems', China has drafted millions of contingency plans, established new institutions, streamlined response mechanisms, and improved the legal system. The current NEMS is moving in the direction of adopting an all-hazard, all-phase, and all-stakeholder model. In the past two decades, the NEMS has successfully dealt with a series of major emergencies and significantly reduced casualties and damages. However, reforming the Chinese NEMS is an ongoing process, and it faces several significant challenges.

The development of a future-oriented NEMS calls for a paradigm shift. To better implement the 'prioritizing prevention' principle and complete the 'shift from relief to prevention', the NEMS must integrate a bottom-up risk assessment mechanism into its traditional top-down approach. The bottom-up approach should incorporate frontline risk perceptions and mine the big data that have already been collected by local governments for years. Most municipals in China have maintained hotline systems for emergencies (110 in China), public services (12,345), and consumer complaints (12,315). These systems have archives of rich, unbiased data about the feedback loop with citizens. Many risk cues are embedded in the data, and the government has not paid sufficient attention to mining risk information from these data sources. Likewise, frontline workers and street-level bureaucrats can form judgements of potential risks through their daily interactions with stakeholders. The data from a system designed to collect the individual risk perceptions of people on the frontline could be analysed to help detect potential risks.

Acknowledgements This chapter is supported by the National Key R&D Program of China (2018YFC0809801) and National Natural Science Foundation of China (72042012 and 71774098).

Notes

1. Before the Emergency Response Law, emergency management laws scattered in various policy fields such as the Law of the People's Republic of China on Protecting Against and Mitigating Earthquake Disasters and the Law of the People's Republic of China on Flood Control, both released in 1997, and the Fire Prevention Law of the People's Republic of China, released in 1998.
2. See: http://www.gov.cn/zhengce/content/2020-07/08/content_5525 117.htm (last accessed on 12 July 2020).
3. According to Ansell et al. (2010), a transboundary crisis refers to a situation in which the functioning of multiple, life-sustaining systems or critical infrastructures is acutely threatened, and the causes of failure remain unclear.
4. In practice, there is no clear division between the mitigation and preparedness phases in China. Most mitigation efforts concern engineering measures, such as building dams and reinforcing rural residential buildings.
5. See 'China to carry out general survey on natural disaster risks' at http://english.www.gov.cn/policies/latestreleases/202006/08/

content_WS5ede4132c6d066592a4491cd.html (last accessed on 13 July 2020).

6. See: http://www.cfpa.org.cn/news/news_detail.aspx?articleid=824 (last accessed on 13 July 2020).
7. See: http://www.cneb.gov.cn/ (last accessed on 13 July 2020).
8. See: http://www.emerinfo.cn/ (last accessed on13 July 2020).
9. See: http://www.12379.cn/ (last accessed on 13 July 2020).
10. The China National Commission for the International Decade on Natural Disaster Reduction was renamed the 'China National Commission for International Disaster Reduction' in 2000, and then renamed again as the 'China National Commission for Disaster Reduction' (NCDR China) until today.

REFERENCES

Ansell, Chris, Arjen Boin, and Ann Keller. 2010. Managing Transboundary Crises: Identifying the Building Blocks of an Effective Response System: Managing Transboundary Crises. *Journal of Contingencies and Crisis Management*, 18 (4): 195–207.

Boin, Arjen, and Fredrik Bynander. 2015. Explaining Success and Failure in Crisis Coordination. *Geografiska Annaler: Series A, Physical Geography* 97 (1): 123–135.

Chen, Simiao, Zongjiu Zhang, Juntao Yang, Jian Wang, Xiaohui Zhai, Till Bärnighausen, and Chen Wang. 2020. Fangcang Shelter Hospitals: A Novel Concept for Responding to Public Health Emergencies. *The Lancet* 395 (10232): 1305–1314.

China Daily Reporter. 2003. President declares victory against SARS [Online]. Beijing, China: Chinadaily. Available at: http://www.chinadaily.com.cn/en/doc/2003-07/29/content_250040.htm (accessed 26 May 2014).

China's State Council Information Office. 2020. Kangji Yiqing Zhongguo Zai Xingdong. [Fighting COVID-19: China in Action]. Xinhua News Agency, June 7. http://www.gov.cn/xinwen/2020-06/07/content_5517737.htm.

Deng, Meide. 2012. Lun Zhongguo Zaihai Jiaoyu [Disaster Education in China]. *Chengshi yu Jianzai* 5: 1–4.

Gao, Mingyong, and Chong Gao. 2011. Xue Lan: Shigu Duofaqi Youxiao Jianguan Shi Zuibiyao de Gonggongpin [Effective Regulation is the Most Necessary Public Goods in the Era of High Incident Frequency: An Exclusive Interview with Professor Xue Lan]. *Xinjingbao*, August 6. http://www.bjnews.com.cn/finance/2011/08/06/141993.html.

Gao, Yue. 2013. SARS hou de "Yian Sanzhi" [One Plan Three Systems After SARS]. *Zhongguo Yiyuan Yuanzhang* 5 (5): 56–58.

Kettl, Donald F. 2003. Contingent Coordination: Practical and Theoretical Puzzles for Homeland Security. *The American Review of Public Administration* 33 (3): 253–277.

Li, Yongping. 2015. Shanxi Sheng Shannan Yimin Banqian Xiangguan Qingkuang Fabuhui [Press conference on the relocation of Southern Shaanxi immigrants]. December 24. State Council Information Office. http://www.scio.gov.cn/xwfbh/gssxwfbh/xwfbh/shan_xi/Document/1461027/1461027.htm.

Liu, Yingjun. 2020. Shanxi Wunian Wancheng Yidi Fupin Banqian 24.93 Wanhu 84.36 Wanren. [Shaanxi Province completed the relocation of ex-situ pro-poor of 249,300 households and 843,600 people in five years]. Peopleweekly. http://www.peopleweekly.cn/html/2020/wenchuandianxun_1020/44545.html.

Lu, Xiaoli, and Ziqiang Han. 2019. Emergency Management in China: Towards a Comprehensive Model? *Journal of Risk Research* 22 (11): 1425–1442.

Lu, Xiaoli, and Lan Xue. 2016. Managing the Unexpected: Sense-Making in the Chinese Emergency Management System. *Public Administration* 94 (2): 414–429.

Meng, Dengke. 2010. 240 Wan Dizhi Yimin, Shinian Banqian, Haozi Qianyi, zhi wei Anquan Jusuo—1.5 ge Sanxia, Ruhe Ban de Dong? [2.4 Million Geo-Hazard Migrants, in a Decade, Cost a Hundred Billion, for a Safe Community—1.5 The Three Gorges, how?]. *Nanfang Zhoumo*, December 23. http://www.infzm.com/content/53854?dooc.

Ministry of Emergency Management. 2019. Yingji Guanli Bu: Woguo Leiji Zhiding 550 Yu Wan Jian Yingji Yuan [Ministry of Emergency Management: China has formulated more than 5.5 million emergency plans]. Renmin Wang, September 18. http://www.mem.gov.cn/xw/bndt/201909/t20190918_336740.shtml.

Shaanxi Daily. 2010. Yuanli Dizhi Zaihai: Shinian Erbaiwan Yimin Dabanqian [Isolated from the Geo-Hazards: 2 Million Migrants in a Decade in the Process]. *Shaanxi Ribao*, August 25. http://www.ankang.gov.cn/Content-32489.html.

Wildavsky, Aaron. 2017. Searching for Safety. Routledge. 1st edition (May 4, 2017).

Xue, Lan. 2010. Zhongguo Yingji Guanli Xitong de Yanbian [Evolution of Emergency Management System in China]. *Xingzheng Guanli Gaige* 8: 22–24.

Xue, Lan, and Kaibin Zhong. 2009. Turning Danger to Opportunities: Reconstructing China's National System for Emergency Management after 2003. In *Learning from Catastrophes: Strategies for Reaction and Response*, ed. Howard Kunreuther and Michael Useem, 190–210. Upper Saddle River, NJ: Wharton School Publishing.

Xue, Lan, and Guang Zeng. 2019. A Comprehensive Evaluation on Emergency Response in China: The Case of Pandemic Influenza (H1N1) 2009. Springer: Singapore.

Xu, Ping, Xiaoli Lu, Kelvin Zuo, and Huan Zhang. 2014. "Post-Wenchuan Earthquake Reconstruction and Development in China." Disaster & Development: Examining Global Issues and Cases. ed. by N. Kapucu, and K. T. Liou, 427–446. New York, NY: Springer.

Zhang, Qiang, Lu Qibin, Hu Yameng, and Jocelyn Lau. 2015. What Constrained Disaster Management Capacity in the Township Level of China? Case Studies of Wenchuan and Lushan earthquakes. *Natural Hazards* 77 (3): 1915–1938.

Zhong, Kaibin, and Xiaoli Lu. 2018. Exploring the Administrative Mechanism of China's Paired Assistance to Disaster Affected Areas Programme. *Disasters* 42 (3): 590–612.

Zhu, Tian Tian, and Yue Jun Zhang. 2017. An Investigation of Disaster Education in Elementary and Secondary Schools: Evidence from China. *Natural Hazards* 89: 1009–1029.

CHAPTER 3

Disaster Risk Management in Japan with Special Reference to "Sendai Framework"

Toshihisa Toyoda

INTRODUCTION

In March 2015, the Sendai Framework for Disaster Risk Reduction 2015–2030 (UNDRR 2015) was adopted at the third UN World Conference on Disaster Risk Reduction held in Sendai, Japan. This has become the basis for the current international disaster response framework through 2030. The first World Conference was held in Yokohama in May 1994 and the second in Kobe in January 2005. These World Conferences on Disaster Risk Reduction have become important venues for deciding the initiatives of individual countries and how international cooperation should function in disaster risk management.

The United Nations designated 1990–1999 as the "International Decade for Natural Disaster Reduction." During this period, it launched global initiatives on disaster response, with the Yokohama conference serving as an interim meeting. Initially, the main purpose was the

---

T. Toyoda (✉)
Graduate School of International Cooperation Studies, Kobe University, Hyogo Prefecture, Japan
e-mail: ttoyoda@port.kobe-u.ac.jp

© The Author(s), under exclusive license to Springer Nature Singapore Pte Ltd. 2021
Y. Jing et al. (eds.), *Risk Management in East Asia*,
https://doi.org/10.1007/978-981-33-4586-7_3

"prevention" of natural disasters, as advocated mainly by seismologists and other natural scientists. The Great Hanshin-Awaji Earthquake of 1995 struck about 6 months after the Yokohama conference. In the wake of this disaster, many pointed out there had been overconfidence in scientific technology for preventing disasters. Reflecting on this, the field underwent a paradigm shift from "disaster prevention" to "disaster risk reduction." The Kobe conference emphasized integrating disaster risk reduction measures at all stages of development to reduce human, physical, economic, and environmental damage. These ideas were summarized in comprehensive guidelines called the Hyogo Framework for Action (HFA). The UN International Strategy for Disaster Reduction (UNISDR) was charged with promoting the HFA. The UNISDR promoted "mainstreaming disaster risk reduction" by emphasizing the importance of reducing risks beforehand rather than focusing on responses following a disaster. This mainstreaming trend was rapidly adopted by the international community in part because of the agreed promotion of the HFA.

The Sendai Framework adopted at the Sendai conference stipulated more specific guidelines due to the fact that little progress had been made worldwide on reducing disaster damage, despite the promotion of the HFA. In addition to further promoting the mainstreaming of disaster risk reduction, which requires advance investment, the idea of "Build Back Better" (hereafter abbreviated as "BBB") gained prominence as one of the core guidelines. This was led by UNISDR, which was renamed the UN Office for Disaster Risk Reduction (UNDRR) in 2019.

This chapter examines the characteristics and challenges of the Japanese system of reconstruction from natural disasters with special reference to the Sendai Framework. First, in the next section, the evolutionary development of disaster management system in Japan will be reviewed. In Sect. "Examining BBB", the central notion of BBB will be discussed with special reference to the Sendai Framework, showing the importance of integrated approach of disaster management cycles, particularly the integration of reconstruction and disaster risk reduction. In Sect. "Japan's BBB Initiatives and their Historical and Institutional Backgrounds", the Japan's initiatives of BBB and their background will be discussed from the viewpoints of history, law, and economics. The concluding remarks will be given in Sect. "Conclusion".

Overview of the Disaster Management System in Japan

Evolutionary Development of the System

Due to its national conditions, Japan is very prone to a variety of natural disasters since its ancient era. Before the Edo era (1600–1867), there are several historical records of such responses to spontaneous disaster events as a river control, developing new rice-fields, etc. In the Edo period, many disaster including earthquakes, fires, floods, and eruptions occurred (Tsukui 2012, 2–4). Under the feudal system, Bakufu (the central government) and Han (the local governments) were not only involved in reconstruction projects but also relief measures were taken for the victims. Emergency measures such as food and sheltering huts were provided, and systematic provision of rice and money to help people rebuild their lives for the time being was seen. Particular attention is paid to the "seven-three reserve system." The landowners and other influential people in the region were required to contribute 70% of the funds, and the central government subsidized about 30% of the reserve funds for disaster relief. Measured at present value, it was a huge sum of more than 100 billion yen. However, the Meiji government, which was established in 1867, used up the all reserves to pay for the construction of government buildings and other modernizing state policies.

In the beginning, the Meiji government adopted a policy of stockpiling by each prefecture, instead of the national government. However, as the government promoted modernization, wealth and military strength, and established a centralized system of power, the localized disaster management system was replaced by a central government system. The Relief Act was enacted in 1880, and the fund was set up by the government to provide subsidies for temporary huts, farm equipment, and other expenses in addition to provision of food. However, due to the damage caused by subsequent earthquakes and a tsunami, the fund was run out. Then, with the implementation of Act on Victims' Relief enacted in 1899, the funds were again provided on a prefecture-by-prefecture basis, entrusting the funding and payment criteria to the regions. Thus, whether the entity responsible for disaster management should be central or local was repeatedly raised. This question remains more or less even now.

The 1923 Great Kanto Earthquake was one of the most devastating disasters in Japan's history, with an earthquake, a tsunami, and a massive fire hitting the capital and six prefectures. It was a disaster of the worst kind. Some 99,000 people died, 43,000 were missing, and more than 700,000 buildings were destroyed. This was the first and only time martial law was declared for natural disasters in Japan's history. The person who was active in the reconstruction of this catastrophe was Shinpei Goto, the Minister of Home Affairs. He influenced on establishing the Japanese way of reconstruction by implementing policies such as land readjustment, city planning, and earthquake resistance of buildings. The related discussions will be given in detail in Sect. "Japan's BBB Initiatives and their Historical and Institutional Backgrounds".

Period 1945–1994

During World War II, not only was there significant damage to land and human life, but over 1000 deaths by frequent natural disasters each year. This trend continued after the war, and disaster legislation was repeatedly enacted and revised after major disasters.

The law that is the basis of the current disaster management system is Disaster Counter Measures Basic Act enacted in 1961 (hereinafter abbreviated as the Basic Act). It was legislated after the devastating damage caused by Typhoon Ise Bay in September 1959 and became a turning point in postwar disaster prevention measures. Besides, since more than 100 special laws for disasters had been enacted in the ten years after the war, it was necessary to consolidate disaster countermeasures into one. In Japan's disaster legislation, the Basic Act is a general law, while many other disaster-related laws are special laws (Tsukui 2012, 23).

The Basic Act covers natural disasters such as storms, tornadoes, heavy rains, floods, mudslides, earthquakes, tsunamis, large-scale fire, explosion, or other similar disaster that causes extensive damage.[1]

The Basic Act stipulates the following:

1. Definitions of the responsibilities of the state, prefectures and municipalities in responding to disasters. In particular, the primary responsibility for response must be assumed by municipalities, while they are supported by prefectures which are also supported by the state.
2. Establishment of Disaster Management Councils at the national and local levels.

3. Establishment of a national emergency (or urgent) response head-quarter and a local government disaster response headquarter.
4. Development of a disaster management plan.
5. Authority regulations for disaster countermeasures (e.g., evacuation instructions, establishment of warning zones, etc.).
6. Fiscal and Financial Measures. In particular, disaster response costs are to be borne by the entity responsible for the disaster. In the case of a great tragedy, it opens the way for municipalities to receive financial support from prefectures and the state. However, the expenditure items are defined except in exceptional cases, and hence the weight of expenditure on the recovery of damaged physical public facilities becomes higher. This point will be described in detail in Sect. "Japan's BBB Initiatives and their Historical and Institutional Backgrounds".
7. Disaster Emergency Declaration.

In principle, the disaster management system may be called a bottom-up type, as shown in (1). Still, it is not so simple because many guidelines and regulations and various financial subsidies come down from the central government. The more substantial disaster damage reveals, the larger this top-down relation becomes explicit. The item (7) is the ultimate form of top-down system, but in Japan, a disaster emergency has yet to be declared so far.

Among the many special disaster-related laws, the one that plays a vital role in emergency response immediately after a disaster is the Disaster Relief Act enacted in 1947. This act was enacted responding to the Showa Nankai Earthquake that occurred in 1946, which caused extensive damage in western Japan. Article 1 of this law states that "In the event of a disaster, the State shall cooperate with local governments, the Japanese Red Cross Society and other public organizations and the people to provide emergency relief to the victims, protect them and maintain social order." The entity providing the rescue under the Disaster Relief Act is prefectures. They will pay for the costs using a rescue fund, which is characterized by an obligation to accumulate. Depending on the financial status of a prefecture, the government bears part of the prefecture cost. Since both the government and the prefectures bear the costs, the municipalities are considered to be in a position to provide disaster relief activities. The Act lays down its "general standards" concerning the type, extent, method, and duration of rescue (Yamasaki 2016, 166). The types of rescue include everything from the provision of shelter and emergency temporary housing, the provision of food, and drinking water to the search for dead bodies, in a total of 11 items. If setting forth the general standards makes it difficult to carry out a rescue properly, the prefectures are admitted to relaxing the contents of a standard with the national government's consent. Such relaxed standards are called "special standards" (Yamasaki 2016, 166). The clear institutionalization and flexible application of this response is something of which the country can be proud. However, the principle of material donations has been stubbornly kept, and no cash transfers will be made to victims.[2] Besides, the fiscal and financial measures in the Basic Act, which is a general law, are focused on the rehabilitation of physical and social facilities. The system's principle is not to provide compensation for damage to private tangible property, except agriculture and fisheries, where it includes compensation for damage to private property. Special measures will be taken for small- and medium-sized enterprises, but the main focus will be on loans and interest subsidies. Loans and interest subsidies are also provided to individuals who have suffered severe damage within the Basic Act framework. It is a distinctive feature of the Japanese tradition that the government does not offer cash payments, although there are times when it does.

During this period, typhoons and floods were frequent. Accordingly, Flood Control Act and Soil Conservation and Flood Control Urgent Measures Act were established in 1949 and 1960, respectively. Also, some related laws were enacted. The government promoted public investment in flood and erosion control projects intensively from when the country was the least developing country after the war. As the country's economic growth progressed, the amount of public investment in these projects increased. As a result, a downward trend in wind and flood fatalities and damage to physical stocks was achieved (Cabinet Office 2015, 2–3; 2019, Appendix 54; Ishiwatari 2019).

The Period 1995–2010

Until 1995, large earth-physical disasters had not occurred for the previous three decades in Japan. The Hanshin-Awaji Earthquake suddenly hit the Kobe City area in January 1995. The affected area was one of the densest in terms of both population and industries; therefore, the enormous amounts of human lives and physical assets were lost.

Sixteen pieces of emergency legislation were enacted in the two months following the Hanshin-Awaji Earthquake. However, many of the measures were to implement special rules within the framework of the Basic Act. The disaster caused about 250,000 total and half-destroyed buildings in urban areas. About 80% of the casualties were crushed to death by collapsed buildings. Many citizens also suddenly lost their homes and other assets, and many lost their jobs. However, while the government has taken financial measures to restore the public facilities, it has not compensated any of the individual's assets (houses). The local prefectural and Kobe city governments jointly set up their reconstruction fund to support victims and implement various niche policies. These miserable conditions in the affected areas motivated politicians to take action, and three years after the disaster, Act on Support for Livelihood Recovery of Disaster Victims was enacted in 1998. The law was not applied to the Hanshin-Awaji Earthquake's victims, but it was very significant that a benefit for individual victims was institutionalized first time in Japan. Initially, a maximum of 1 million yen was available with an income limit. But, now up to 3 million yen is available to households whose houses have been totally destroyed without any income limit. It has helped the victims of earthquakes, tsunamis, floods, and typhoons over the past 20 years to rebuild on their own. However, if the Basic Act is strictly interpreted, it is a special law that lies outside the system's framework.

After the Hanshin-Awaji Earthquake, there was a new trend of increased civil society participation in disaster recovery. Although Japan had a tradition of mutual aid from neighboring communities in the wake of previous disasters, many volunteers came from far away to the affected areas to provide free services. This trend led to the establishment of the Act on Non-Profit Organization in 1998. Also, various voluntary disaster management organizations, which are the main actors in community-based recovery, were established.

In 1999, the criticality accident at a nuclear industry named JCO occurred, and the Act on Special Measures for Nuclear Disasters was enacted in 1999.

After 2011

In March 2011, the Great East Japan Earthquake left 21,839 people dead or missing, and the number of houses entirely or half-destroyed, or swept away, was amounted to more than 404,000: the most significant postwar catastrophe. The tsunami drowned most of the dead. Add to this the radioactive leak from the nuclear power plant at Tokyo Electric Power Company (TEPCO) made the situation immensely worse.

Since the situation was beyond the scope of the existing legislation, legislative activities such as revision of laws and regulations were actively carried out. In particular, the amendment of the Basic Act was enacted twice. The First Amendment of 2012 included such contents as Wide-area response for Large-scale Disasters, Improvement of Disaster Management Education, etc. In the Second Amendment of 2013, the Improvement of Support for Affected People was enacted, but there were no major concrete measures in particular.[3] Other essential pieces of legislation include the Act on Promotion of Tsunami Countermeasures enacted in 2011, Act on Reconstruction from Large-Scale Disasters enacted in 2013, Act for Establishment of Nuclear Regulation Authority enacted in 2012, etc.

Direct sock losses were estimated to be 16.9 trillion yen. The budget for a 10-year project of recovery was massive, exceeding 30 trillion yen. Special features include the construction of large-scale seawalls, large-scale rezoning and raising tsunami-affected lands, and group relocation. In addition to the hard budgetary measures, a reconstruction fund was set up in each municipality at government expense. Public works projects in Miyagi and Iwate Prefectures are in the final stages of reconstruction, but the rebuilding of visible and invisible assets in Fukushima Prefecture has been delayed. Livelihood reconstruction of the severely affected households in the trend of declining population, especially in an aging society, is not smooth, even if the public physical facilities are restored. In the region, it cannot be said that the recovery of households and individuals has made any progress in stabilizing their lives.

The Great East Japan Earthquake caused several municipalities to lose their administrative functions. In addition to the traditional state-prefecture-municipality vertical support system, there is also a need for other local governments that have not been affected by the disaster to assist. The importance of horizontal support from other local governments was well recognized. The counterpart support system was also observed, but in Japan's case, it is more common for local government officials (human resources) to be dispatched from the unaffected municipality to the affected one. In addition to the request from the central government, the National Governors' Association sent quite a few staff to the three affected prefectures. The government is also actively promoting public-private partnerships; the legal system in the Second Amendment of the Basic Act enacted in 2013 describes the importance for the administration of setting a goal of working in collaboration with volunteers.

Summary of Disaster Laws in Japan

Figure 3.1 shows major disaster management laws in the historical perspective and main amendments. Under the Basic Act as the general law, there exist about 200 disaster special laws. If a significant disaster event occurs and the existing rules are not well applied to it, either amendment of the existing laws or a new enactment of special measures is made quite frequently. For example, 16 new laws were enacted after the Great Hanshin-Awaji Earthquake, while about 60 laws were enacted after the Great East Japan Earthquake.

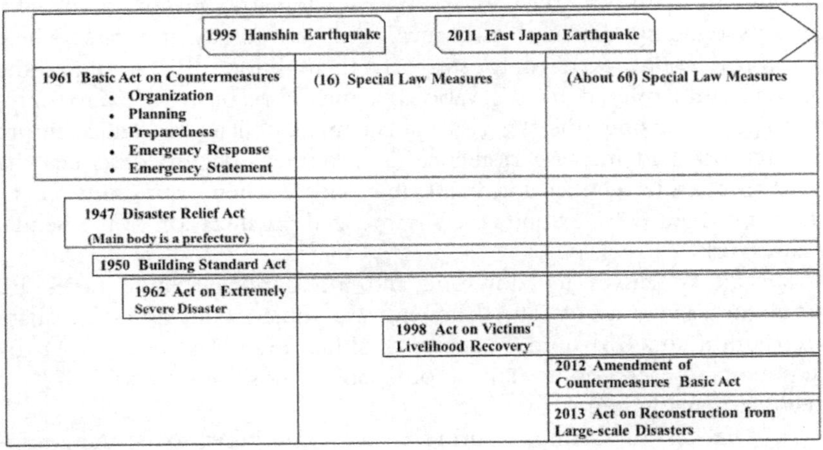

1995 Hanshin Earthquake	2011 East Japan Earthquake	
1961 Basic Act on Countermeasures • Organization • Planning • Preparedness • Emergency Response • Emergency Statement	(16) Special Law Measures	(About 60) Special Law Measures
1947 Disaster Relief Act (Main body is a prefecture)		
1950 Building Standard Act		
1962 Act on Extremely Severe Disaster		
	1998 Act on Victims' Livelihood Recovery	
		2012 Amendment of Countermeasures Basic Act
		2013 Act on Reconstruction from Large-scale Disasters

Fig. 3.1 Historical Development of Major Disaster Laws in Japan (*Source* Author)

Examining BBB

Sendai Framework

"The Sendai Framework for Disaster Risk Reduction for 2015–2030" (UNDRR 2015) provides four specific guidelines called "priorities for action." Priority 1 is "Understanding disaster risk," and priority 2 is "Disaster risk governance," which are fundamentally based on HFA. Priority 3, "Investing in disaster risk reduction for resilience," and priority 4, "Enhancing preparedness for an effective response and to 'Build Back Better,'" have seen increasing emphasis in the trends of international cooperation in disaster management over the past decade or so and are items that were newly added to this framework. Priority 3 explicitly addresses the economic debate discussed under mainstreaming disaster risk management. Priority 4 is difficult to understand at a glance because the short description includes the words "preparedness" and "Build Back Better." The text states that for nations to achieve BBB, especially developing countries, they must improve domestic resources through capacity-building, financial assistance, and technology transfers, which developed countries need to support. In addition, BBB signifies the opportunities offered by the various stages of reconstruction for integrating (mobilizing) disaster risk management policies to reduce future disaster risk and increase resilience. The framework also describes the need to consider gender and vulnerable people when promoting reconstruction. Figure 3.2 exhibits the summarized organization of the Sendai Framework.

Specific initiatives for domestic and international communities are listed for each priority. The following are some examples of adequate preparation and BBB under priority 4. While examples were chosen by summarizing each country's positions, Japan's positions are said to have been particularly important in (b):

(a) Disaster forecasting, securing evacuation centers, food, and equipment, evacuation drills, business continuity

(b) Disaster prevention, including creating standards for the recovery and reconstruction stages, and improving land-use planning.

What Does BBB Mean?

Ever since the BBB concept had been used abstractly as a development philosophy and was used explicitly in the Sendai Framework, BBB has

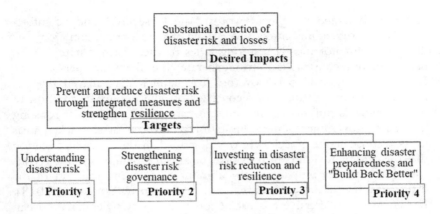

Fig. 3.2 Sendai Framework for Disaster Risk Reduction (*Source* Created by the author based on the Sendai Framework [2015])

been discussed in Japan and around the world as an essential post-disaster objective. However, its meaning is not necessarily fixed. Even experts on disaster risk management from various countries use the term with slightly different nuances.

The term BBB was first used in the memorial speech by the former US President William Clinton (2006) at Ache, Indonesia, which was hit hardest by the 2004 Indian Ocean tsunami. Afterward, it is said that the term became popular among United Nations, World Bank, and others in the international community during the reconstruction of Aceh. In terms of timing, the rebuilding of Aceh was an opportunity to promote the priorities of the HFA and the mainstreaming of disaster preparedness. Thus the term was formulated in this context.

The term "creative reconstruction," which can be considered the origin of BBB, also needs to be mentioned. Hyogo Prefecture officially used the term six months after the Great Hanshin-Awaji Earthquake. That is, the Hanshin Earthquake Reconstruction Policy Formulation Commission released a document in June, 1995, titled "Toward creative reconstruction from the Great Hanshin-Awaji Earthquake—a Hanshin-Awaji earthquake reconstruction plan," which was based on the discussions of an informal council on urban rehabilitation strategy that was established in February, 1995. The underlying philosophy was creating a "symbiotic society" in which people, communities, and nature are in harmony. It aimed for the keywords "safe," "secure," and "comfortable" when rebuilding cities, and argued that reconstruction from the disaster meant not merely restoring cities to their former state, but to use "creative reconstruction" to regenerate cities from new perspectives. It is said that then Hyogo Governor Toshitami Kaihara played a significant role in formulating this reconstruction philosophy. In addition to being Kaihara's philosophy, it seems to have been a means of resisting the central government's harsh limitation of aid to disaster-stricken areas in its reconstruction policies. It was described in the preceding section that the central government provided the affected region with the reconstruction expenses only up to the amount of restoring the cost of the damaged public facilities. In interviews conducted by Yamanaka (2018), Kaihara said that creative reconstruction "was a way to eliminate urban vulnerability through multi-networked cities," "was an attempt to rebuild using aspects of soft power such as the environment, medical care, welfare, and disaster management," "required a paradigm shift to transform ideas about national and regional revitalization," and "needed prescient policies not bound by the current system." The creative reconstruction promoted by Kaihara emerged from the region where the Great Hanshin-Awaji Earthquake occurred, and Japan's historical background. The background of the term involved the governors' position at a time of strict national regulations before decentralization, the characteristics of the times, and the geopolitical background of the urban Hanshin area that needed reconstruction. The term creative reconstruction has universality but was not immediately adopted by the world as a reconstruction philosophy. This is evident in the 10-year gap before the term BBB was widely adopted by the international community aiding the reconstruction of Aceh. However, their universal meanings have many similarities. A World Bank Group survey of Kobe's recovery from the earthquake reported in 2018 that in the creative reconstruction projects, there were areas where BBB succeeded and failed. The title of this report used the term "Creative Reconstruction" (World Bank 2018).

The definition of BBB originally given by UNISDR was "The use of the recovery, rehabilitation and reconstruction phases after a disaster to increase the resilience of nations and communities through integrating disaster risk reduction measures and means of development" (UNISDR 2015). In 2016 the definition was revised to, "The use of the recovery, rehabilitation and reconstruction phases after a disaster to increase the resilience of nations and communities through integrating disaster risk reduction measures into the restoration of physical infrastructure and societal systems, and into the revitalization of livelihoods, economies and the environment." Therefore, the term BBB used by the international community means using hard and soft disaster management policies to improve "livelihoods, economies and the environment" to "increase the resilience of nations and communities." When implementing BBB represented by this international concept, the widely varying conditions in different countries, especially in terms of hazard environments, reconstruction systems, and feasible human and financial inputs, will result in varying degrees of achievement. In particular, there are differences between developed and developing countries in the feasibility of policies emphasizing physical infrastructure (e.g., Toyoda 2016). This is why priority 4 requires preparations in areas such as funding, technology, and disaster management education. In either case, disaster management policies, reconstruction policies, and resilience should consider both hard and soft factors. Also, the ultimate goal of BBB is not only resilience in terms of physical safety, but a comprehensive policy system that emphasizes rebuilding livelihoods and improving economic and environmental aspects.

As described above, the Sendai Framework does not provide a straightforward definition of BBB, and the examples offered vary widely. Accordingly, when looking at reports from specialist conferences and on the status of initiatives in different countries, common phrases such as "reducing disaster risk," "reducing vulnerability," and "increasing resilience" are almost always used, but the specific initiatives vary. Therefore, while remaining organizations of UNISDR (now UNDRR) definition, this chapter will focus on "what can be made better" in 3 areas: (1) physical facilities, (2) rebuilding lives, and (3) the local society, economy, and environment.

Japan's BBB Initiatives and Their Historical and Institutional Backgrounds

Are Japan's Initiatives Right?

BBB has been accepted in Japan to the extent that this concept can be considered the main characteristic of the Sendai Framework. BBB has also been included as a guideline for national disaster management efforts (e.g., Cabinet Office 2018, 23–24). The most explicit indication of this is in "Disaster Management in Japan" (Cabinet Office 2019). The final page of this document states, "A concept of 'Build Back Better' is an approach to build up a more resilient community during the reconstruction phase after the disaster has struck. In order to reduce the potential risk of disaster damages, it is necessary to construct houses in the area of lower disaster risk, and to build the urban structure resilient to such disaster. The reconstruction phase from the disaster is an opportunity to take a fundamental approach including the land-use plan and building of disaster-resilient structures, with lessons learned from the disaster experience..." (Cabinet Office 2019, 49).

This document makes no clear reference to improving lives, the economy, or the environment as specified in the Sendai Framework. Even if "build up more resilient community" is synonymous with "making communities resilient," the subsequent examples are typically Japanese. The BBB examples given are the typical initiatives Japan has traditionally engaged in, i.e., policies aimed at the recovery and reconstruction of damaged physical facilities as has been overviewed in Sect. "Overview of the Disaster Management System in Japan". This process is centered around hard measures for making things (physical assets) better, such as making structures earthquake-resistant, creating safe spaces through land reallocation, raising seawalls, and group relocations to higher ground, these measures being adopted in the reconstruction from the Great East Japan Earthquake. It cannot be denied that criteria such as these for reducing the risk of future disasters are essential. The question is whether this process gives humans (disaster victims) sufficient consideration and communities in the devastated area. A variety of issues with this approach have been pointed out, such as whether sufficient compensation is given for restrictions on private land and other rights, whether hard initiatives incorporate the autonomous views of disaster victims, whether the local community can cover the future costs of maintaining physical facilities, and whether the rebuilding of people's lives is taken into account in hard projects.

Given that Japan's geographical environment necessitates dealing with a wide variety of natural disasters, there is an undeniable need to emphasize hard aspects and advance investments to reduce the risk of future disasters. As has been observed in Sect. "Overview of the Disaster Management System in Japan", national land conservation and measures to control the floods that are continuously occurring are part of increasing resilience. They should be funded every year as long as the budget allows, even if no disaster happens. However, in terms of BBB initiatives after a disaster, Japan's efforts are heavily biased toward the hard aspects as described above. This means only some parts of the Sendai Framework agreed to by the international community are being emphasized. Specifically, the reconstruction of people's daily lives—such as their livelihoods and the economy—is being neglected. The international community's understanding is that both hard and soft measures should be included in the process of reconstruction, with the goal of creating better conditions for both things and humans. Japan probably has one of the world's best policy menus for the reconstruction of hard facilities, but that does not necessarily mean it is such a disaster management superpower as being supposed to be in the world (Toyoda 2012).

Japan's disaster management system was overviewed in Sect. "Overview of the Disaster Management System in Japan" without pointing out any specific deficiencies. For example, the long-standing Disaster Relief Act (1947) includes almost all necessary measures at the response stage. However, the quality of the contents of some measures is poor compared with some developed countries. These inadequacies include poor living conditions in evacuation centers, an old-fashioned adherence to in-kind aid, no assistance for home evacuees, multi-year stays in temporary housing, disaster-related deaths, and inadequate housing reconstruction support (e.g., Yamanaka 2018).

Background of the Characteristics of Japan's Initiatives

It is pointed out that at least three characteristics exist behind the centrality of hard aspects in BBB in Japan.

Historical Aspect
The first is that the recovery from the Great Kanto Earthquake of 1923 became the norm for how recoveries from subsequent major disasters would proceed. As discussed in Sect. "Overview of the Disaster Management System in Japan", Shinpei Goto played a leading role in this development. Appointed Home Minister immediately after the earthquake, Goto drew up the "Fundamental measures for rebuilding the capital." This comprised 4 stipulations: (1) the capital should not be relocated, (2) reconstruction will require 3 billion yen, (3) a new city suitable for Japan should be built by adopting the latest urban planning methods from the West, and (4) a decisive attitude should be taken

with landowners when carrying out a new urban plan. Four days after the earthquake, "Deliberations on Rebuilding the Capital" (Goto 1923) based on this framework was submitted to the Cabinet. Although the proposal faced resistance and its budget was drastically reduced, Goto became director of the Capital Reconstruction Institute and tenaciously pursued not only recovery but the realization of his metropolitan plan. When added to Japan's experience rebuilding after World War II, a reconstruction system focused on hard measures based on urban planning and civil and architectural engineering took root. Technical staff is assigned not only at the national and the prefectural levels but throughout the basic municipal level. In light of these historical developments, the pre- and post-recovery planning at each level, from the national government to basic municipalities, has been structured around the restoration of physical facilities and "machizdukuri" (town planning). This is the most salient aspect of disaster management from the past to the present in Japan (e.g., Cabinet Office 2015, 12, 49).

Economic Aspect

During the reconstruction from the Great Hanshin-Awaji Earthquake, the central government only provided budgetary measures for restoring physical infrastructure. However, as mentioned in the previous section, the governor of Hyogo Prefecture launched a "creative reconstruction plan" designated not merely for recovery, but to rebuild better. This plan can be considered a successor to the spirit of Shinpei Goto, but it contained not only hard measures but a number of soft ones as well. While there were many setbacks due to the lack of central government support, the "medical industry city concept" can be considered a typical example of BBB. Without support of the central government, Kobe City and Hyogo Prefecture pursued and made many efforts to assemble research institutes and private firms related to the medical/health industry, and at last, successfully realized the medical industry city zone after about ten years from the disaster. In the aftermath of the Great East Japan Earthquake, differing from the case of the Great Hanshin-Awaji Earthquake, the central government prominently promoted BBB. The system of special reconstruction zones was implemented in 227 devastated municipalities from Aomori to Ibaragi Prefectures. According to the Reconstruction Agency (2020), the measures of the special reconstruction zones include (1) tax reduction, (2) interest subsidy, and (3) several deregulations such as land-use deregulation. For the period between 2012 and 2019, about 5000 small/medium enterprises invested about 3.3 trillion yen and created about 40,000 employments. Although some projects are concerned with primary industries like agriculture and fishery, manufacturing, and tourism, quite a few projects are related to the ongoing reconstruction projects. Even being acknowledged that the special reconstruction zones have played to sustain the affected local economies to some degree, but it would be doubtful how many enterprises will survive and contribute to the sustainability of the local economies. A special exception would be the case of the Fukushima Innovation Coast Concept, which is a national project that aims to build a new industrial base in order to recover industries in the Hamadori area that were lost in the Great East Japan Earthquake and nuclear disaster. It is a long-run project and has just started but seeks new industrial development in such areas of robotics and renewal energy, which fit the concept of BBB.

Although some typical BBB measures aiming at creating a better local economy and environment, in the long run, can be observed as mentioned above, there was little change in budgetary allocations, which were biased toward hard measures. Table 3.1 shows the accounting summary of the recovery/reconstruction projects of the Great Hanshin-Awaji Earthquake during the initial five years, in which almost all main projects were terminated. The central government invested about 6 or 7 trillion yen among the total project cost of 16.3 trillion yen, and it is seen that about 70% of total expenditures were spent on hard projects (Note that private housing construction is not included in these public projects) (Toyoda 2015). Table 3.2 shows the budget for the first five years' period of the recovery projects in the case of the Great East Japan Earthquake. The total budget during this period was 25 trillion yen, and it is seen that about 60% of expenditures were directed to hard projects (Note that some portion of private housing was supported by this budget). As a typical soft measure, about 300 billion yen was spent to help disaster victims rebuild their lives (based on the Act on Support for Reconstructing Livelihoods of Disaster Victims). This is less than 1% of the total budget of 32 trillion yen for total ten years' period of reconstruction.

The characteristics of Japan's reconstruction policies, which means heavy focuses on recovery of physical structures and urban renewal, are evident when budgets are examined.

It is admittedly said that some change from hard to soft measures can be observed compared to the case of Great Hanshin-Awaji Earthquake,

Table 3.1 The Great Hanshin Earthquake project cost (100 million yen)

Implementing body Project	Central Government	Prefecture	Municipality	Special reconstruction fund	Public external organization	Total	%
Public housing	9400	4410	3240	2710	8590	28,350	17.4
Welfare, culture, and education	1350	1090	960	190	110	3700	2.3
Industry, employment	9940	6040	3690	540	10,290	29,500	18.1
Disaster prevention facilities	1200	710	1170	30	40	3150	1.9
Urban maintenance, urban infrastructure	39,090	10,710	20,990	30	27,480	98,300	**60.3**
Total	60,980	22,960	29,050	3510	46,510	**163,000**	100
%	**37.4**	14.1	17.8	2.1	**28.5**	100	

Source Hyogo Prefecture

Table 3.2 The Great East Japan Earthquake project cost for 2011–2015 (100 million yen)

Classification	Five years total	(%)
Emergency response	9610	3.9
Disposal of disaster wastes	11,075	4.5
Public works	39,960	16.4
East Japan EQ subsidy	28,722	11.8
East Japan EQ special subsidy	43,415	17.8
Subsidies for domestic location	7772	3.2
Disaster-related public financing programs	18,300	7.5
Support of the victims' livelihood recovery fund	2564	1.1
Medical care insurance, long-term care and welfare for the disabled	3632	1.5
Education affairs	850	0.4
Employment affairs	5411	2.2
Agriculture, fisheries, and forestry	5351	2.2
Support of small and medium enterprises	3684	1.5
Resources and energy	5107	2.1
Atomic energy revival affairs	31,334	12.9
Disaster reduction measures in Japan	15,686	6.4
Total	244,041	100

Source Ministry of Finance

but the typical characteristics in reconstruction fund allocation in Japan remain stubbornly biased toward hard measures.

Legal Aspect

As has been observed in Sect. "Overview of the Disaster Management System in Japan", the fundamental law for Japan's disaster law system is the Basic Act (1961), which created the legal system that regulates Japan's disaster management policy. The Basic Act has sections on disaster prevention, emergency response, and recovery as part of the "disaster management cycle," but none on reconstruction. It mainly stipulates that

1. the lowest-level municipalities will be the primary agents of disaster management initiatives,
2. the basic governance structure will involve the central government providing aid via the prefectures, and

3. the emergency response will be carried out primarily by the prefectures based on the Disaster Relief Act (1947).

Budgetary measures are the primary concern of the municipalities responsible for actual recovery projects. These are stipulated in Article 7, "Fiscal and monetary measures," as (1) exceptional cases when the national government must pay for disaster recovery initiatives specified by other laws and regulations; (2) how to reduce the burden on municipalities that were severely damaged as determined by other laws and regulations; and (3) exceptional cases for issuing bonds for disaster recovery and other expenses. A typical example of the other requirements is the National Government Defrayment Act for Reconstruction of Disaster-stricken Public Facilities, that was enacted in 1951. It stipulates the targets of disaster management policies and designates that only physical infrastructure is subject to disaster recovery/reconstruction.[4] The responses of the relevant ministries are based on this law, and municipalities also carry out reconstruction projects based on it, which means they are centered on hard measures. After the Great Hanshin-Awaji Earthquake, there was a citizens' campaign over the tragic lack of support for disaster victims compared to the funding for hard initiatives, which pushed the Diet to act. Ultimately a Diet members' proposal was passed as the Act on Support for Reconstructing Livelihoods of Disaster Victims, which legally allowed cash benefits to individuals whose housing was severely damaged. Nevertheless, the government posture of only targeting hard disaster management policies based on the Basic Act has remained unchanged. The above Livelihood Reconstruction Act enacted in 1998 is a prefectural, not a central government policy (with the central government paying for half) funded from a separate account from the national treasury. Japan's disaster management policies remain institutionally designed to be biased toward hard measures, and this is reflected in the characteristics of Japan's BBB initiatives.

There are two approaches to modify the current bias toward hard measures existing in Japan's disaster management system. First, the Basic Act should be reorganized to designate recent advancements in the disaster recovery/reconstruction stages (Matsui 2019, 212–218). Namely, it should refer to the updated philosophy of all management cycles, including reconstruction and measures of restoration of human livelihood as well as physical facilities. Second, as a more reasonable settlement of the issues than the amendment mentioned above of the Basic

Act itself, laws for assisting disaster victims need to be brought together. Currently, soft measures are scattered among several laws like the Disaster Relief Act, the Livelihood Recovery Act, and the Reconstruction Fund Special Measures Act, and so on. If they are consolidated into a comprehensive law, victims and municipality officers can understand the contents more easily.

CONCLUSION

As discussed above, there is a subtle difference between how BBB is understood by the international community and the actual responses of Japanese policymakers. This chapter has pointed out historical and institutional roots in Japan that account for these differences. These are deeply rooted in the idea that disaster management is a hard problem, evident in areas from the departments' configuration at the relevant ministries and agencies to work performed by municipalities. Reconstruction policies for the emergency response have made rapid progress in preparing for anticipated significant disasters such as a Nankai Trough Earthquake or Tokyo Metropolitan Earthquake. However, the problem is that the system needs to shift to one that promotes recovery for humans (human reconstruction) in areas such as the rebuilding of people's lives and local economies (and the environment in the long run).

Japan has hosted all of the UN World Conferences on Disaster Reduction and has played a significant role in compiling the reports from these meetings. At present, a significant target of the Sendai Framework—which is mainly based on BBB. Countries around the world are executing it is to improve social resilience, along with rebuilding physical stock. In other words, Japan should also become a world leader in soft measures for rebuilding livelihoods, society, the economy, and the environment. To that end, soft aspects that have been overlooked, such as inadequate shelters, disaster victims living in temporary housing for more than five years, and economic stagnation in disaster-affected areas, need to be rectified via a thorough policy transformation. Besides, the world is paying attention to removing the hazards of a human disaster, i.e., the decommissioning of nuclear reactors that were damaged in the Great East Japan Earthquake. Unfortunately, this chapter was unable to address the longstanding challenge of incorporating BBB when rebuilding from a complex disaster involving both an earthquake and a nuclear blast.

Japan learned many lessons from the experience of significant natural (and unnatural) disasters. If she fails to apply these lessons and make radical reforms of legal and economic aspects in the disaster management system that this disaster-prone country requires as described in this chapter, Japanese people will face future tragedy again and repeatedly. There are many lessons other countries could learn from the deficiencies or failures caused by biasedness and inefficiency due to the Japanese system of disaster management (Toyoda 2012, 2016).

Of course, Japan's disaster risk reduction system has many salient features, particularly in such areas as science/engineering aspects and people's cooperative behaviors for disaster response, which significantly contribute to the system. Each country has some strong and weak elements in the disaster risk reduction system and should learn each other.

NOTES

1. Infectious diseases are not covered by the Basic Law. Therefore, the government's measures against COVID-19 in 2020 could not apply the Basic Law and separate special laws on infectious diseases were applied. Therefore, no mandatory lockdowns or instructions for action could be given, but rather gradual requests to the public and businesses were implemented.
2. Under the Disaster Condolence Act enacted in 1973, a certain fixed amount of condolence money is paid the dead (their families) and the seriously injured.
3. Six basic principles of disaster countermeasures were defined for the first time in Article 2, paragraph 2. The fifth of these concerns with the appropriate assistance to the victims based on age, sex, disability, and other circumstances. It is noted that "victims are to be appropriately assisted," but no mention is made of benefits.
4. There are also other laws which stipulate special measures for the agriculture, forestry, and fisheries industries as well as small- and medium-sized enterprises.

REFERENCES

Cabinet Office. 2015. *Disaster Management in Japan.* Tokyo: Cabinet Office, GOJ.

Cabinet Office. 2019. *Build Back Better Case Studies from the Great East Japan Earthquake, Great Hanshin-Awaji Earthquake.* http://www.bousai.go.jp/kyo iku/fukko/index.html. (In Japanese).

Clinton, W. 2006. *Lessons Learned from Tsunami recovery: Key Propositions for Building Back Better*. New York, NY: Office of the UN Secretary-General's Special Envoy for Tsunami Recovery. https://reliefweb.int/report/thailand/lessons-learned-tsunami-recovery-key-propositions-building-back-better.

Goto, S. 1923. *Deliberations on Rebuilding the Capital*.Tokyo: Tokyo Institute for Municipal Research, Municipal Reference Library Collection. https://www.timr.or.jp/library/docs/kuranonaka/lib001.pdf. (In Japanese).

The Great Hanshin-Awaji Earthquake Memorial Research Institute. 1999. *Great Hanshin-Awaji Earthquake Reconstruction Journal*, 3. Kobe: The Earthquake Memorial Research Institute. (In Japanese).

Ishiwatari, T. 2019. *Investing in Disaster Risk Reduction: Scale and Effect of Investment in Flood Protection in Asia*. Global Assessment Report on DRR. Geneva: UNDRR. https://www.researchgate.net/publication/333995670.

Matsui, S. 2019. *Law and Disaster*. Abington: Routledge.

Reconstruction Agency. 2020. *Report*. Reconstruction Agency, Tokyo: GOJ. https://www.reconstruction.go.jp/english/index.html.

Toyoda, T. 2012. Disaster Management and Policy. In *Economic and Policy Lessons from Japan to Developing Countries*, ed. T. Toyoda et al., 236–252. Basingstoke: Palgrave Macmillan.

Toyoda, T. 2015. The Reality of Economic Reconstruction. In *Earthquake Recovery Studies*, ed. Kobe University Earthquake Reconstruction Assistance Platform, 60–72. Kyoto: Minerva Shobo. (In Japanese).

Toyoda, T. 2016. The Framework of International Cooperation for Disaster Management and Japan's Contribution. In *Asian Law in Disasters*, ed. Y. Kaneko et al., 315–328. Abingdon: Routledge.

Tsukui, S. 2012. *Great Disasters and Law*. Tokyo: Iwanami-shoten. (In Japanese).

UNDRR (United Nations Office for Disaster Risk Reduction). 2015. *Sendai Framework for Disaster Risk Reduction 2015–2030*. Geneva: UNDRR. https://www.undrr.org/publication/sendai-framework-disaster-risk-reduction-2015-2030.

UNISDR (United Nations International Strategy for Disaster Reduction). 2015, 2016. *Terminology*. Geneva: UNISDR. https://www.unisdr.org/we/inform/terminology.

UNISDR (United Nations International Strategy for Disaster Reduction). 2017. *Build Back Better: In Recovery, Rehabilitation and Reconstruction*. Geneva: UNISDR. https://www.unisdr.org/files/53213_bbb.pdf.

World Bank. 2018. *KOBE Creative Reconstruction*. Washington DC: World Bank. http://documents.worldbank.org/curated/en/663101525354320401/Kobe-creative-reconstruction.

Yamanaka, S. 2018. Genealogy of Disaster Recovery from the Viewpoint of Changing Principles: A Structural Analysis of Individualism versus Collectivism in Reconstruction. *Studies in Disaster Recovery and Revitalization*, 10: 1–37. (In Japanese).

Yamasaki, E. 2016. Legislation to Support Disaster Victims in Japan. In *Asian Law in Disasters*, ed. Y. Kaneko et al., 163–177. Abingdon: Routledge.

CHAPTER 4

Patterns of Risk Management Policies and Systems in South Korea: Special Reference to Water-Related Disaster Management

Seungho Lee

INTRODUCTION

The chapter will shed light on the patterns of disaster risk management policies and projects in South Korea, with special reference to water-related disaster risk management policies and systems from the 1960s to the present. The study discusses the institutional framework, concerned ministries and bureaus, and their responsibilities, and policy implications of national disaster risk management in the country.

Particular attention is paid to flood risk management policies, because water-related disasters such as floods have given the most detrimental impacts on to the country among various natural disasters since the 1960s. Water-related disasters are the most common type of natural disaster not only in South Korea but also in the world. The Center

S. Lee (✉)
Graduate School of International Studies, Korea University,
Seoul, South Korea
e-mail: seungholee@korea.ac.kr

© The Author(s), under exclusive license to Springer Nature
Singapore Pte Ltd. 2021
Y. Jing et al. (eds.), *Risk Management in East Asia*,
https://doi.org/10.1007/978-981-33-4586-7_4

61

for Research on the Epidemiology of Disasters (CRED) has provided statistics of natural disasters every year through the Emergency Events Database (EM-DAT) since 1988, and the most recent figures of disasters in 2018 indicate that there were 315 climate-related and geophysical disaster events, affecting 68 million people with the death toll of 11,804. Out of the 315 disaster events, 273 events, about 87%, were associated with water-related disasters, which encompass floods (127 events), storms (95 events), droughts and extreme temperatures (41 events), and wildfires (10 events). This is the reason why primary attention should be paid to water-related disasters in natural disaster risk management policies at the global level (CRED 2019a, b).

The occurrence of water-related disasters in South Korea shows a similar pattern over the last 10 years, especially heavily affected by typhoons almost every year. In the period between 2009 and 2018, the country had been affected by various types of natural disasters, including snow, wind wave, storm, typhoon, earthquake, and heat wave. The annual average amount of economic losses due to natural disasters reached over Korean Won (KRW) 150 billion (US$ 130 million), and water-related disasters that exclude earthquakes and heat wave events entailed approximately 97% of the total amount of economic losses (Ministry of the Interior and Safety 2019). This demonstrates the salience of water-related disaster risk management policies in order to ensure continuous socio-economic development and environmental sustainability in the country.

In this context, in-depth analyses will highlight flood risk-related structural measures, i.e., multi-purpose dams, embankment and levees and non-structural methods, i.e., flood insurance and flood prevention-related legal and institutional settings. Such analyses help delineate the extent to which an East Asian country like South Korea has increasingly been aware of the significance of risk and vulnerability against floods. Achievements and challenges derived from such experiences can be mirrored in the other developing countries of Asia and the Pacific.

Recognizing far-reaching impacts from flood events in recent few decades, the study provides the case study that highlights some of the most detrimental typhoons recorded in the country's disaster risk management history, Typhoon Rusa in 2002 and Typhoon Maemi in 2003. The case study not only unveils the extent to which the typhoons wreaked havoc to the country in terms of economic and human losses but also discusses the path to institutional reforms and policy shift toward more risk-aware and resilient policies.

The first part of the chapter discusses the concepts of disaster, disaster risk, and disaster risk reduction in order to have a good understanding of disaster risk management. In addition, the study sheds light on the national framework of disaster risk management of South Korea, having a close look at relevant strategies and plans. Attention will be placed on a variety of organizations that are involved in disaster risk management at the national, provincial, or municipal levels. Legal and regulatory settings are also evaluated. In the third part, the study explores the overview of water-related disasters in South Korea referring to various figures and statistics. The fourth part focuses on Typhoon Rusa in 2002 and Maemi in 2003 that devastated the country on a large scale, triggering massive amounts of economic losses and numerous casualties. A list of challenges and achievements will be explored regarding the case study. The patterns of the development of water-related risk management systems in South Korea will be discussed at the last part, particularly on institutional frameworks.

Disaster Risk Management

Prior to the discussion of disaster risk management, it is imperative to explore the meaning of disasters at the beginning. According to CRED in 2018, a disaster is referred to as 'a situation or event that overwhelms local capacity, necessitating a request at the national or international level for external assistance; an unforeseen and often sudden event that causes great damage, destruction and human suffering' (CRED 2018).

Kim and Sohn (2018) define a disaster by accommodating important elements from the Korean, Japanese, and US experiences and the UN International Strategy for Disaster Reduction (UNISDR). The definition of disaster is 'a status of community or nation's being seriously damaged by natural, technological or social cause and difficult to recover the damage with its own resources, requiring the whole community to cope together' (Kim and Sohn 2018). A disaster is understood as an unprecedented natural or anthropogenic event that a community or society has not easily coped with and requires tremendous levels of social capacity for overcoming far-reaching impacts on the society.

While a disaster encompasses not only natural but also human-induced or anthropogenic one in general, the study pays special attention to a natural disaster. Since the chapter provides the particular context of Korean experiences on disaster risk management, the study takes a look at the definition of natural disaster and human-induced or social accidents according to the Disasters and Safety Act in 2013. Natural disasters indicate disasters triggered by typhoon, flood, downpour, strong wind, wind and waves, tidal wave, heavy snowfall, lightning, drought, earthquake, yellow dust, red tide, ebb and flow, and other natural phenomena equivalent.

The act specifies social accidents that give damage beyond the scale, i.e., a fire, collapse, explosion, traffic accidents, chemical, biological, and radioactive accidents, environmental pollution incidents and other similar accidents. In addition, some social accidents cause serious damage such as the paralyzation of the state's critical systems, including energy, communication, transport, finance, medical treatment, and water supply. Korea's Infectious Disease Control and Prevention Act specifies a spread of infectious diseases and the Act on the Prevention of Contagious Animal Diseases pinpoints an outbreak and spread of contagious animal diseases as social accidents (Kim and Sohn 2018).

Then, what is disaster risk? Disaster risk is 'a function of the probability of occurrence of a hazard of varying severity in a particular location, the people and assets situated in that location and therefore exposed to the hazard, and the level of vulnerability of those people and assets to that hazard.' Critical is a good level of understanding of the interrelatedness between the exposure, hazard, and vulnerability of the population, livelihoods, infrastructure, and systems. By doing so, a society can decrease disaster risk by lessening the exposure of the current generation and infrastructure and safeguard prosperity for the future (ADB 2018).

One of the fundamental principles in disaster risk management is Disaster Risk Reduction (DRR). According to the UNISDR (2019), the DRR is defined as 'the concept and practice of reducing disaster risks through systematic efforts to analyze and reduce the causal factors of disasters.' Relevant examples are decreasing exposure to hazards, reducing vulnerability of people and property, good management of land and the environment, and enhancing preparedness and early warning for adverse events (UNISDR 2019). Disaster risks can be decreased by the following methods: (1) reducing the hazard; (2) reducing the vulnerability of the elements at risk; (3) reducing the amount of the elements at risk; and (4) increasing the degree of coping capacity.

At the similar token, disaster risk management primarily aims to reduce possible risks related to all sort of disasters, depending upon structural and non-structural measures. Structural measures are any physical infrastructure to reduce or avoid possible impacts of hazards, including engineering measures and construction of hazard-resistant and protective structures and infrastructure. Examples of non-structural measures include policies, awareness, knowledge development, public commitment and methods and operating practices, such as participatory mechanisms and the provision of information, which can lessen risk and related impacts (van Westen 2015).

The system or framework of disaster risk management varies at the local, national, regional, and global levels, and this study introduces the situations of disaster risk management system in South Korea. As of 2019, it is the Ministry of the Interior and Safety which is responsible for the overall administration of the nationwide disaster risk management or response according to the Disasters and Safety Act (2004, last revision 2015). The ministry takes full responsibility for supervising and coordinating the initial response, rescue and first aid operations by operating the Central Disaster and Safety Countermeasure Head Quarters (CDSCHQ). A coordinating role is given to the Prime Minister if there is a need for government-wide responses confronted with a major disaster.

Together with the ministry, the Crisis Management Center under the National Security Council in the Blue House (President's Office) serves as a coordinating and control tower tackling national crises. The hierarchical system of disaster risk management in the country is composed of various bureaus and agencies at different levels depending upon normal times and emergency situations.

Organizations in normal times include disaster risk management agencies, disaster management supervision agencies, emergency rescue agencies, emergency rescue, and relief support organizations. In addition, committees at various levels from the central, metropolitan (like Seoul, Busan, Daejeon, Ulsan, and Incheon) or provincial, prefectural, to district take responsibility for discussing and make decisions on issues related to disaster and safety management (Kim and Sohn 2018).

All phases of disaster management activities are in the hands of disaster management agencies, and these are national administrative agencies, local governments, local administrative agencies, and public institutions and organizations. Disaster management supervision agencies are involved in responding to various natural and social disasters, and for instance,

66   S. LEE

the Ministry of Environment is in charge of environmental pollution accidents, and disasters in schools and school facilities should be dealt with by the Ministry of Education. Table 4.1 illustrates different disaster management supervision agencies by disaster or accident types.

Life rescue, first aid, and other measures to protect the lives and property of people are in the hands of emergency rescue agencies when a disaster strikes or is expected to occur. The agencies involved in these activities are fire headquarters (HQs) and coast guard HQs under the Ministry of the Interior and Safety, City or Province fire HQs, and city, prefecture or district fire stations, and regional HQs of the Korea Coast Guard and coast guard stations. Human resources, installations, equipment, and operations should be ready for emergency and rescue and relief services in these organizations (Kim and Sohn 2018).

Whereas a disaster triggers chaotic situations in communities, responses to the disaster should neatly be coordinated between different levels and

Table 4.1   Disaster management supervision agency in South Korea by disaster or accident type

Supervising agency	Disaster and accident types	Supervising agency	Disaster and accident types
Ministry of the Interior and Safety	Pipe utility conduit disaster Fire and hazardous material accent, ship and ferry accident on river Great fire at multi-use facility Disaster or accident caused by flood (except for tidal wave), earthquake, volcanic activity, lightning and drought, not belonging to other disaster management authorities Accidents at a major government facility	Ministry of Land, Infrastructure and Transport	Pipe utility conduit disaster High-speed railway and road tunnel accident Land cargo transport accident Subway and aircraft accident Air transport paralysis and navigation safety facilities obstacle Multi-cluster building collapse disaster and accident not belonging to another disaster management authority

(continued)

4 PATTERNS OF RISK MANAGEMENT POLICIES AND SYSTEMS ... 67

Table 4.1 (continued)

Supervising agency	Disaster and accident types	Supervising agency	Disaster and accident types
Ministry of Trade, Industry and Energy	Gas supply and leakage accident Oil supply accident Nuclear safety accidents (including outages due to strikes) Accident of electric power Accident in dam for power generation	Ministry of Environment	Disaster or accident caused by flood and drought Environmental pollution accident on water quality Accident involving drinking water (incl. local waterworks) Drinking water (limited to wide-area waterworks) accident Dam accident supervised by the ministry Hazardous chemical leak accident Algae outbreak (limited to green algae), Yellow dust
Ministry of Oceans and Fisheries	Algae outbreak (limited to red algae), tidal wave Environmental pollution accidents in the marine sector Marine vessel accident	Ministry of Education	Accidents at schools and school facilities
Ministry of Science and ICT	Cosmic radio disaster, information communication accident, electric wave interference of GPS	Financial Services Commission	Financial computing and facility accidents
Ministry of Agriculture, Food and Rural Affairs	Livestock disease Reservoir accident	Ministry of Justice	Accidents at a correctional facility

(continued)

Table 4.1 (continued)

Supervising agency	Disaster and accident types	Supervising agency	Disaster and accident types
Ministry of Health and Welfare	Infectious disease Healthcare accident	Ministry of Culture, Sports and Tourism	Accidents at stadiums and venues
Korea Forest Service	Forest fire Landslide	Ministry of Foreign Affairs	Overseas accident
Nuclear Safety and Security Commission	Nuclear Safety accident Radiation leakage accidents in neighboring countries	Ministry of Employment and Labor	Large-scale human accidents at workplaces
Cultural Heritage Administration	Cultural property accident	Ministry of National Defense	Accidents at defense facilities

Source Modified based on Kim and Sohn (2018, 52–53)

sectors of public agencies. As for South Korea, the Central Safety Management Committee plays a pivotal role in coordinating such a complexity of disaster risk management works, which is overseen by the Prime Minister. In line with the committee, there are several coordinating mechanisms in work during the disaster period: (1) the Safety Policy Coordination Committee, chaired by the Minister of the Interior and Safety; (2) the Central Disaster Broadcasting Consultative Committee, led by a person appointed by the Minister of Science and ICT; and (3) the Central Private-Public Cooperative Committee, overseen by the Vice Minister of the Interior and Safety. In addition, such a multilayered governance system of disaster risk management requires a civilian representative to advise, consult, deliberate or decide disaster and safety management issues.

At the regional and local levels, similar committees are organized and in operation during a disaster period, such as a Municipal or Provincial Safety Management Committee, a City, Prefectural or District Safety Management Committee, a City or Provincial Disaster Broadcasting Consultative Committee, and a City, Prefectural or District Disaster Broadcasting Consultative Committee.

A disaster often results in emergency situations where all the possible resources should be mobilized and allocated for affected areas and communities. National-level agencies include the Central Disaster and

Safety Countermeasure Headquarters (CDSCHQ) which is chaired by the Ministry of the Interior and Safety, and the Central Disaster Management Headquarters (CDMHQ), led by the head of relevant disaster management supervision agency. Such a system, however, has been criticized in terms of operational efficiency, because the Minister of the Interior and Safety might not be able to play a spearheading role in making significant decisions in collaboration with other ministers, i.e., the Minister of Strategy and Finance, and the Minister of Education who are recognized as the level of vice president in the country.

As Bae (2019) maintains, the operational efficiency of the system would enhance if the head of the CDSCHQ became the Prime Minister (Bae 2019). Although the Prime Minister leads the Central Safety Management Committee for coordination, the committee serves as an entity to provide a policy suggestion or advice only without the mandate or capacity to implement relevant policies. Therefore, there has been a continuous call for the Prime Ministry leading the CDSCHQ.

Additionally, the Central Emergency Rescue Control Group (CERCG) is involved in emergency activities, and the head of the central fire headquarters for disaster takes the leading role on land whereas the chief of the Central Rescue Center for disaster is in charge of emergency situations at sea.

Responses to disasters at the local levels show a strong feature of top-down structure in Korea's public administration system. Provincial governors and mayors are often leading disaster and safety countermeasure groups whereas local emergency rescue control groups are engaged in relevant activities that are chaired and participated by local fire stations (Kim and Sohn 2018). Figure 4.1 summarizes the hierarchical disaster risk management and response system in South Korea.

Looking into the disaster response process of the country, the Ministry of the Interior and Safety is fully responsible for organizing and running response meetings by initiating response, rescue and first aid operations and coordinating intergovernmental disaster response activities. This case is only associated with a disaster within the country. It is the Ministry of Foreign Affairs which takes responsibility if a disaster concerning Korean citizens occurred overseas as observed in the case of the Danube Boat Accident which killed 19 Koreans and one Hungarian on 29 May 2019 (Bae 2019; BBC 2019). Responses to radioactive disasters are in the hands of the Nuclear Safety and Security Commission, leading the Central Disaster and Safety Countermeasure HQs.

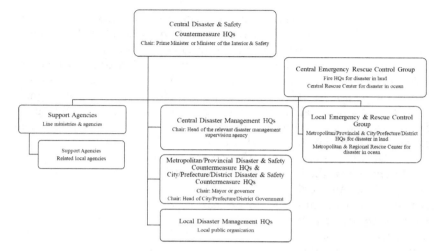

Fig. 4.1 Disaster risk management and response organizations in South Korea (*Source* Modified based on Kim and Sohn 2018, 56; Korean Society of Hazard Mitigation 2012, 21)

Mayors or provincial governors and the head of a city, prefecture or district have to establish their own CDMHQ and begin to coordinate response and recovery operations. In collaboration with this, the disaster management supervision agency should work together. Local disaster management HQs function as an action team of CDMHQ in disaster areas (Kim and Sohn 2018; Korean Society of Hazard Mitigation 2012).

It is necessary to shed light on disaster response plans for having a better understanding of disaster risk management system in South Korea. The architecture of the disaster response planning in the country comprises three parts: (1) the Standard Risk Management Manual; (2) the Working-level Manual for Risk Response; and (3) the Manual for Actions-at-scene. There were 32 kinds of standard risk management manuals, 254 working-level manuals for risk response, and 5032 kinds of manuals for actions-at scenes in May 2017. The Standard Risk Management Manual embraces roles and responsibilities of relevant bureaus and agencies involved in disaster risk management at the national level, which is also associated with the guidelines for preparing the Working-level

Manual for Risk Response. This manual often involves a number of relevant ministries and agencies in a major disaster event, such as typhoon and drought, and in general, is prepared by the Ministry of the Interior and Safety.

The Working-level Manual for Risk Response describes measures and procedures for responding to actual disasters in accordance with the functions and roles of disaster management supervision agency and support agencies. The manual is taken care of by related support agencies, designated by the Standard Risk Management Manual. Agencies that are responsible for implementing disaster response activities are linked to the Manual for Actions-at-scene which delves into the step-by-step actions to be taken at a disaster scene. Local governments (city, prefectural, and district levels) are allowed to develop their own Manuals for Actions-at-scenes.

Together with the manuals, it is worth taking a closer look at the Action Plans for Disaster Response by Function (Article 43.5 of the Enforcement Decree of the Disasters and Safety Act). The action plans specify 13 functions for disaster response, which adequately reflect essential principles and activities as written below.

1. Managing disaster situation
2. Supporting emergency livelihood stabilization
3. Supporting emergency communications
4. Emergency restoration of facilities damage
5. Restoring damaged energy supply facilities
6. Supporting disaster management resources
7. Traffic countermeasures
8. Supporting medical and disinfection services
9. Environmental arrangement at disaster scenes
10. Supporting and managing volunteer work
11. Maintaining social order
12. Searching, rescuing and emergency support at disaster areas
13. Publicity of disaster management.

In a nutshell, the primary two pillars of disaster response plan in South Korea include three levels of manuals and 13 functional action plans. Particular roles and responsibilities of major response ministries and agencies are described and summarized in the manuals. 13 functional action plans delineate the process of each relevant institution's functions in accordance with its roles and responsibilities (Kim and Sohn 2018).

Overview of Water-Related Disasters in South Korea

This section focuses on water-related disasters in South Korea, especially flood. Korea's efforts to harness flood events over a few decades provide food for thought on what should be necessary in the field of disaster risk management and illustrates the lessons learned for overcoming challenges in disaster risk management systems of the country.

A significant feature over the last half century is emerging risks and threats triggered by climate change, which has fundamentally shaken assumptions and modelings of hydrology and weather patterns, thereby making disaster risk management more difficult. It should be critical to take into serious consideration climate change-affected factors in water-related disaster risk management in the country. A series of climate change-driven phenomena have become a new norm, including increased precipitation, decreased days of precipitation, and an upsurge of short-term, and localized heavy rainfall.

The frequency of localized heavy rain, which reaches 30 mm per hour or more, had increased at 37%, from 60 times in the 1980s to 82 times from 2000 to 2018. For example, the total amount of localized heavy rainfall in Dongducheon City, Gyeonggi Province was recorded at 449.5 mm per day and in Moonsan City, Gyeonggi Province, 322.5 mm per day on 27 July 2011 whereas the Gwanak-Gu, Seoul witnessed 113 mm on the same day. In 2011, there were large-scale landslide accidents, which were triggered by localized heavy rainfall in the Woomyeon Mountain, Seoul and Chuncheon City, Gangwon Province. These flood disasters stem mainly from a change in rainfall characteristics. Compared with the last three decades (1976–2015), a chance of future 100-year frequency maximum precipitation by region can increase more than twice.

It is necessary to have a good understanding of major characteristics of water resources in South Korea prior to the introduction of the statistics on water-related disasters. An average annual precipitation in the country reached 1299.7 mm from 1986 to 2015, whose level is 1.6 times the global average, 813 mm. The high population density is attributed to per capita precipitation, 2546 m^3 per annum, only one-sixth of the global average, 15,044 m³. There is a big gap of variation of precipitation between seasons and years, and in particular, a wide range of seasonal variation in precipitation has brought about a frequent outbreak of extreme flood and drought events throughout history. Figure 4.2 explicitly illustrates the concentrated average annual precipitation from June to September in the period from 1986 to 2015, which accounts for 68%. In particular, vast amounts of precipitation from July to August are as large as 44% of the total amount of annual average precipitation in the same period.

In addition, there is a large gap between regions, river basins and estuary areas in terms of precipitation, which leads to a high degree of vulnerability to extreme floods and droughts. For instance, whereas the southwestern parts of the country show higher levels of average annual precipitation up to 1728 mm, Jeju Island and Ulleng Island, the middle parts of the country display the level of annual average precipitation down to 1240 mm in the Geum River Basin over the past three decades (Kim et al. 2018).

Take a look at statistics on water-related disasters in the country, excluding drought. Figure 4.3 indicates economic losses caused by a

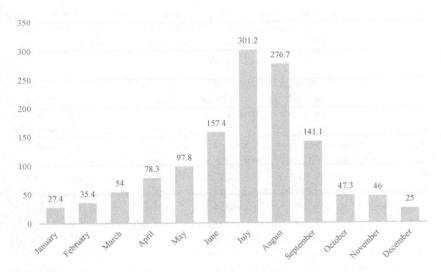

Fig. 4.2 Annual precipitation history of South Korea between 1986 and 2015 (Unit: mm) (*Source* Kim et al. 2018, 2)

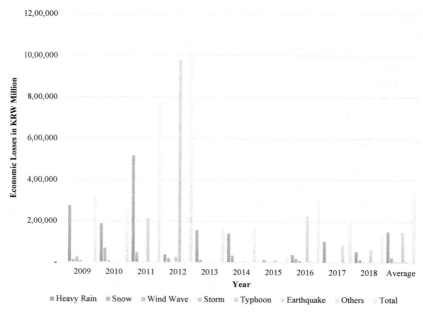

Fig. 4.3 Economic losses caused by natural disasters of South Korea in recent 10 years (Unit: KRW Million) (*Remarks* *others primarily indicate heat waves and relevant costs. *Source* Ministry of the Interior and Safety 2019, 12)

variety of natural disasters from 2009 to 2018. The most damaging disasters are something to do with hydrological and climatological ones, including snow, wind wave, storm, and typhoon. Heavy rain and typhoons accounted for over 88% of the annual average financial damage from water-related disasters, and if adding the other hydrological and climatological ones, the total contribution of water-related disasters to economic losses is as large as over 97%. Considering such tremendous impacts caused by water-related disasters, primary foci of natural disaster risk management are primarily on how to harness potential damage and threat engendered by typhoon, torrential rainfall, and flashflood (Table 4.2).

Numerous flood events in South Korea from 1945 to 2007 hit hard major urban and industrial areas, and a total of 17 typhoons entailed serious damage to the country (Kim et al. 2007). For example, with regard to the flood event in September, 1990, some of the riverine

Table 4.2 Economic losses caused by natural disasters of South Korea in recent 10 years (Unit: KRW Million)

Types/year	2009	2010	2011	2012	2013	2014	2015	2016	2017	2018	Average
Heavy rain	276,735	189,041	517,080	37,404	156,409	141,414	1256	37,867	103,613	53,800	151,462
Snow	13,873	69,339	47,108	19,808	11,219	32,239	13,489	19,720	85	14,032	24,082
Wind wave	26,152	7359	293		44		345	8761	617	2823	4639
Storm	7638	182		25,999	922	94	4031			7	3887
Typhoon			213,956	976,906	1671	5262	13,886	226,301		64,200	150,218
Earthquake								11,628	86,713		9834
Others[a]										7	0.7
Total	324,398	265,921	778,437	1,060,117	170,265	179,009	33,007	304,277	191,028	134,869	344,123

Remarks [a]others primarily indicate heat waves and relevant costs
Source Ministry of the Interior and Safety (2019, 12)

areas along the Han River within the Seoul Metropolitan Area and the Gyeonggi Province were flooded, 163 people were killed or missing, and around 187,265 people were evacuated from flood-prone areas due to heavy rainfall. Economic losses related to property damage were estimated at over KRW 520 billion (US\$ 500 million). More than 400 mm of torrential rain were poured over a few days in the Suwon City, Gyeonggi Province, and the total amount of economic losses was estimated at KRW 330 billion (US\$ 303 million) (Kang et al. 2013a; Kim and Sohn 2018).

Table 4.3 reviews the 10 most detrimental typhoons in the trajectory of flood management in South Korea from 1925 to 2006. Among them, the two most intense flood events stem from Typhoon Rusa 2002 and Typhoon Maemi 2003. In addition, Typhoon Ewiniar in 2006 wreaked havoc to the country by resulting in economic losses worth US\$ 380 million. In the summer monsoon season of 2006, the total volume of rainfall in the Han River Basin was recorded as large as 717.3 mm, which was regarded as the largest total amount of rainfall in the summer monsoon season in the river basin since 1973.

Distinguishable features observed from Table 4.2 are, first, the diminishing number of human casualties, and second, the increasing value of economic losses over the same period of time. Such phenomena can occur due to socioeconomic factors, such as urbanization and industrialization, and natural factors, i.e., climate change and its relevant effects. These factors have appeared to intensify the magnitudes of flooding and property damage. In addition, primary causes for flood damage between 2004 and 2007 can be attributed to an increase of flood discharges, which were exacerbated by heavy rainfall and urbanization, inadequate channel capacities, mediocre river management, unsystematic institutional settings, and improper disaster prevention facilities (Kang et al. 2013b).

Case Studies

Typhoon Rusa in 2002 and Typhoon Maemi in 2003 are the most devastating typhoons recorded in the history of flood management in the country. Typhoon Rusa in 2002 landed in the peninsular in 2002, causing insured losses of US\$ 5.59 billion. Typhoon Maemi devastated the southern part of the country in 2003 and triggered insured losses of US\$ 4.59 billion (Kang et al. 2013b; Kim et al. 2007). Table 4.4 displays a list of the most damaging typhoons in South Korea between the 1950s to the 2000s.

4 PATTERNS OF RISK MANAGEMENT POLICIES AND SYSTEMS ... 77

Table 4.3 Summary of damage from top 10 typhoons in South Korea from 1925 to 2006, ranked by loss of lives and by property damage

Rank	Ranking according to loss of lives			Ranking according to property damage		
	Typhoon	Period	Death Toll (Persons)	Typhoon	Period	Property damage[a] (US$ 1000 million)
1	3693	28 August 1936	1232	Rusa	31 August–1 September 2002	5.59
2	2353	11–14 August 1923	1157	Maemi	12–13 September 2003	4.59
3	Sara	15–18 September 1959	846	Olga	23 July–4 August 1999	1.08
4	Bete	18–20 August 1972	550	Selma	15–16 July 1987	0.60
5	2560	15–17 July 1925	516	Jenis	19–30 August 1995	0.55
6	1427	7–13 September 1914	432	Ewiniar	9–10 July 2006	0.38
7	3383	3–5 August 1933	415	Gladis	22–26 August 1991	0.32
8	Selma	15–16 July 1987	345	Yani	26 September–1 October 1998	0.28
9	3486	20–24 July 1934	265	Prapiroon	23 August–1 September 2000	0.25
10	Rusa	31 August–1 September 2002	246	Jun	31 August–4 September 1984	0.25

Remark [a]Property damage converted to the monetary value of 2006
Source Kang et al. (2013b, 424)

There are differences between the two monstrous typhoons. The amount of precipitation of Typhoon Maemi reached just 50% of that of Rusa. Typhoon Rusa in 2002 heavily impacted on river bank areas in many parts of the country through heavy rainfall, thereby engendering

78 S. LEE

Table 4.4 The most devastating typhoons in South Korea from the 1950s to the 2000s

Year	Typhoon	Economic losses (US$ Million)	Maximum rainfall (mm/d)
1959	Sarah	Not available	Not available
1987	Thelma	530	Not available
1991	Gladys	260	600
2000	Prapiroon	560	247
2000	Saomai	890	491
2002	Rusa	6700	871
2003	Maemi	4800	432
2004	Megi	270	322
2006	Ewinar	201	265
2007	Nari	164	300
2012	Bolaven and Tenbin	543	244
2012	Sanha	312	405
2016	Chaba	195	220

Source Updated based on Kim et al. (2007, 18), and Ministry of Environment (2019, 65)

many riverine areas inundated. No major reports were given about inundation cases beyond embankments of rivers related to Typhoon Maemi in 2003. Typhoon Rusa in 2002 is dubbed as a wet typhoon whereas Typhoon Maemi in 2003 is categorized as a dry typhoon.

Typhoon Rusa accompanied large amounts of rainfall together with the maximum wind speed of 56.7 m/s, and the historic concentrated rainfall was recorded in the Gangreung City of the Gangwon Province, estimated at 870.5 mm, which was about 60% of the total amount of annual average rainfall in the city. The typhoon claimed 321 casualties, and over 63,000 people had to be evacuated.

The most serious damage caused by Typhoon Maemi 2003 stemmed from strong winds, estimated at 60 m/sec. The level of maximum rainfall was estimated at 453 mm, which was not as large as the one by Typhoon Rusa in 2002. Numerous affected areas were close to industrial areas. Over 130 people were killed, and approximately over 10,000 people had to leave their homes and properties (Kim 2006a, b; Kim et al. 2007; Kim and Sohn 2018).

The bitter typhoon experiences turned out to be a window of opportunity for water and disaster risk managers in South Korea to reflect flood management systems about preparedness, response and recovery policies and measures. These emblematic events also became a turning point for experts, government authorities, and the public to recognize the risk of large-scale typhoons, torrential rainfall, and flashflood, which would occur more frequently than before due to climate change.

Confronted with a number of challenges by the typhoons, there was the societal mood of the urgency to reform existent institutional frameworks and enhance physical infrastructures and introduce more efficient and innovative scientific and socioeconomic policies and plans. There were four invaluable lessons in the post-Rusa and Maemi periods.

The first lesson is the problematic governmental systems to cope with flood disasters, especially associated with slow relief measures for the people affected by Typhoon Rusa in 2002. While the public anger against the governmental incapability still remained strong in the following year, Typhoon Maemi in 2003 devastated the country. Surprisingly inefficient evacuation policies and measures were found in many affected areas and heavily criticized by the general public, which led the government to take into serious account the reform of the whole system of disaster risk management. The government was determined to enhance relief and evacuation systems and began to operate the special task force for planning multifaceted flood mitigation measures under the Office of the Prime Minister. Such a policy shift signifies the empowerment of disaster risk management related authorities and steps up the preparedness for protecting the general public with detailed guidelines and regulations, especially for evacuation and relief (response and recovery).

As the second lesson, there was a growing recognition that climate change-driven adverse impacts should carefully be considered for establishing flood prevention and protection measures (physical and non-physical infrastructures). Prior to the new millennium, flood management ministries and research institutions had not focused on complex and multifaceted challenges triggered by climate change. Related policies and measures against flood events were often ineffective in terms of protecting people and economic assets. After the typhoons, the Korea Meteorological Administration decided to improve its weather forecasting systems by introducing cutting-edge technologies and super computers as well as more flexible and site-specific forecasting systems reflecting climate change. The two typhoons unfortunately forced people to be aware of risk and uncertainty accompanied by climate change and were the opportunity to take into serious consideration upcoming impacts caused by climate change, which might be even worse if there would be no preparation to hedge the flood risk.

Third, the typhoon cases unveiled the lack of readiness and preparedness of the Korean society to tackle such large-scale typhoons or flood events. The government had been strongly committed to establishing a good network of infrastructures in mainstreams and tributaries of the Four Major Rivers (the Han, the Geum, the Nakdong, and the Youngsan-Seomjin Rivers). However, natural disaster risk management policies and systems were not necessarily able to follow the speed of urbanization and industrialization, which began to intensify and scale up from the 1960s to the 1990s. An encroachment of the built environments to riverine areas enlarged flood-prone areas in cities and suburban areas, and the rapid urbanization and the emergence of numerous industrial complexes along rivers since the mid-1990s had exacerbated the situations. Flood prevention facilities and infrastructures were not adequately in place, which resulted in inundation and flooding in many parts of the country.

The fourth lesson from the two typhoon experiences is closely linked to the policy shift toward flood prevention policies and measures. Prior to the typhoons, more weight had been put on sophisticated regulations and guidelines about the declaration of special disaster zones and provision of compensation to the affected people by water-related disasters, such as typhoons, torrential rainfall, and flashflood. In addition, the central government made a quick move toward the distribution of supplementary budget bill that would enable local governments to make a quick recovery as well as make short-term and long-term investment for building a variety of facilities and infrastructures against possible flood events.

Such recovery-focused policies and financing support had caused the vicious cycle of flood damage every year, since there would be very little investment or political commitment to any systematic or coherent policies for preventing future flood events. Rusa and Maemi made people rethink about previous flood risk management policies, i.e., recovery-focused flood management policies and felt the urgency to emphasize the preparedness and prevention measures against water-related disasters. The total amounts of R&D investment for flood prevention technologies and systems were substantially increased, and a good set of relevant regulations and guidelines was introduced for strengthening flood prevention policies and plans at the central and local governments (Kim et al. 2007).

Institutional Framework Against Water-Related Disasters in South Korea

This section discusses the institutional framework on water-related disasters in the country. There are the nine national-level laws: (1) Natural Disaster Countermeasure Law; (2) Small Stream Maintenance Law; (3) Disaster and Safety Management Basic Law; (4) Basic Water Law; (5) River Law; (6) Dam Construction and Support for Adjacent Areas Law; (7) Sewerage Law; (8) Land Planning and Use Law; and (9) Construction Law. These laws accompany their own plans, which are overseen by related ministries. The Ministry of the Interior and Safety is in charge of dealing with disaster risk management issues, and relevant laws are the Natural Disaster Countermeasure Law, the Small Stream Maintenance Law, and the Disaster and Safety Management Basic Law.

The Ministry of Environment takes the overall responsibility for tackling water-related disasters, particularly flood, and is concerned about the implementation of the Basic Water Law, the River Law, the Dam Construction and Support for Adjacent Areas Law, and the Sewerage Law. In addition to these laws, the ministry is the competent agency in implementing the Basic Water Law which was created in May 2019, which plays a leading role in taking case of all kinds of water resources management issues. The Ministry of Land, Infrastructure and Transport is in charge of the Land Planning and Use Law and Construction Law and responsible for establishing the National Land Comprehensive Planning (Kang 2017).

Table 4.5 visualizes flood-related ministries, laws, and plans. The Ministry of the Interior and Safety manages natural disasters as a whole via the three national-level plans, i.e., the Storm and Flood Damage Reduction Comprehensive Plan, the Small Stream Maintenance Plan, and the National Safety Management Basic Plan. The Ministry of Environment specifies its roles in tackling flood-related matters through a myriad of associated plans, such as the National Water Resources Management Basic Plan, the Water Resources Long-Term Comprehensive Plan, the River Maintenance Basic Plan, the River Basin Comprehensive Flood Management Plan, the Long-term Dam Construction Plan, and the Sewerage Maintenance Basic Plan. Establishing the National Land Comprehensive Plan is in the hands of the Ministry of Land, Infrastructure and Transport.

Based on the understanding of flood risk management in South Korea, it is necessary to pay close attention to the flood management system,

82   S. LEE

Table 4.5   Flood-related ministries, laws, and plans in South Korea

Ministry	Law	Plan
Ministry of the Interior and Safety	Natural Disaster Countermeasure Law Small Stream Maintenance Law Disaster and Safety Management Basic Law	Storm and Flood Damage Reduction Comprehensive Plan Small Stream Maintenance Comprehensive Plan National Safety Management Basic Plan
Ministry of Environment	Basic Water Law River Law Dam Construction and Support Adjacent Areas Law Sewerage Law	National Water Resources Management Basic Plan Water Resources Long-Term Comprehensive Plan River Maintenance Basic Plan River Basin Comprehensive Flood Management Plan Long-term Dam Construction Plan Sewerage Maintenance Basic Plan
Ministry of Land, Infrastructure and Transport	Land Planning and Use Law Construction Law	National Land Comprehensive Plan

Source Modified based on Kang (2017, 37)

which clarifies relevant agencies and entities and their roles in order to reduce vulnerability and mitigate damage caused by typhoons, heavy rainfall, and flashflood. As discussed above, the Ministry of Environment is responsible for flood risk management in the country and closely work together with relevant ministries and agencies, such as the Ministry of the Interior and Safety, and the Ministry of Land, Infrastructure and Transport. In addition, the Korea Meteorological Administration collaborates with the ministry by providing hydrological data through its monitoring stations and customized and detailed precipitation forecast services based on super-computer modelings (Kim et al. 2018).

There are the four Flood Control Centers in the Four River Basins which undertakes scientific and systematic data collection and analyses of water resources in each river basin. The centers are committed to preventing possible flood damage to people and properties by providing flood forecast and warning services to localities in each river basin. As observed earlier, one of the success factors to decrease flood damage is associated with the commitment of the government to make vast amounts of investment in establishing a systematic network of multi-purpose dams that have been capable of harnessing disastrously strong typhoons and historically heavy rainfalls. Flood prevention dams have been able to protect human lives and invaluable economic properties and have served as a sound platform with which local economies have taken off.

Since the construction of the Seomjin River Dam in 1964, the first multi-purpose dam, there are a total of 20 multi-purpose dams, 54 water supply dams (domestic and industrial water supply), 15 hydropower dams, and 17,401 agricultural water supply dams in the Four Major River Basins as of 2018 (Ministry of Environment 2019). Table 4.6 displays the overall situations of dams and the details of multi-purpose dams are shown in Table 4.7.

In addition to such well-networked multi-purpose dams, the government has made considerable amounts of investment in reducing flood risk in local streams as well as major river basins through river maintenance works (embankments and levees), and therefore, inundations near large rivers have decreased. Cutting-edge technologies and engineering methods have been introduced in order to refurbish the Four Major Rivers, considering possible magnitudes and frequencies of flood. However, climate change has become a game changer, which has put up side down research outcomes and forecast through super-computer modelings, and requires more flexible and site-specific, structural, and non-structural measures.

Table 4.6 Specifications of dams in South Korea

Items	Total	Multi-purpose dams	Water supply dams	Hydropower dams	Agricultural water supply dams
No.	17,490	20	54	15	17,401
Capacity (million m^3)	13,708.2	9170.0	536.3	992.8	3009.1
Share (%)		66.9	3.9	7.2	22.0

Source Ministry of Environment (2019), 98

Table 4.7 Specifications of multi-purpose dams in South Korea

River basin	Multi-purpose dam (Completion year)	Basin area (km²)	Data		Total capacity of reservoir (million m³)	Installed capacity of power station (MW)	Enterprise effect	
			Height (m)	Length (m)			Flood control (million m³)	Water supply (million m³/year)
Han River	Soyang (1973)	2703	123	530	2900	200	500	1213
	Chungju (1986)	6648	97.5	447	2750	412	616	3380
	Hoengseong (2002)	209	48.5	205	86.9	1.3	9.5	119.5
Nakdong River	Andong (1977)	1584	83	612	1248	91.5	110	926
	Imha (1993)	1361	73	515	595	51.06	80	591.6
	Hapcheon (1989)	925	96	472	790	101.2	80	599
	Namgang (2003)	2285	34	1126	309.2	14	269.8	573.3
	Miryang (2002)	95.4	89	535	73.6	1.3	6	73
	Gunwi (2012)	87.5	45	390	48.7	0.5	3.1	38.3
	Gimcheon-Buhang (2014)	82.0	64	472	54.3	0.6	12.3	36.3
	Bohyun Mountain (2014)	32.61	58.5	250	22.11	1.414	3.49	14.87

4 PATTERNS OF RISK MANAGEMENT POLICIES AND SYSTEMS ... 85

River basin	Multi-purpose dam (Completion year)	Basin area (km²)	Data		Total capacity of reservoir (million m³)	Installed capacity of power station (MW)	Enterprise effect	
			Height (m)	Length (m)			Flood control (million m³)	Water supply (million m³/year)
Guem River	Daechung (1981)	4134	72	495	1490	90.8	250	1649
	Yongdam (2006)	930	70	498	815	26.2	137	650.43
Youngsan-Seomjin River	Seomjin-River (1965)	763	64	344.2	466	34.8	32	350
	Junam (1992)	1010	58	330	457	1.44	60	270.1
	Junam Regulation (1992)	134.6	99.9	562.6	250	22.5	20	218.7
Etc.	Buan (1996)	59	50	282	50.3	0.193	9.3	35.1
	Boryeong (2000)	163.6	50	291	116.9	0.701	10	106.6
	Jangheung (2007)	193	53	403	191	0.8	8	127.8

Source Ministry of Environment (2019, 100)

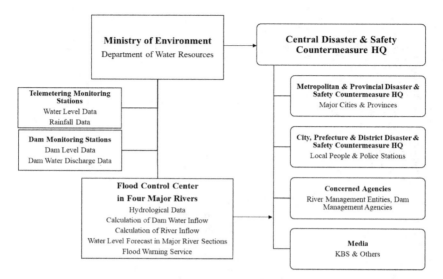

Fig. 4.4 Flood warning dissemination system in South Korea (*Source* Modified based on Ministry of Environment 2019, 257)

Non-structural measures can reduce susceptibility to flood risks and related possible damage, and the examples are the early flood warning systems, the zoning of flood-prone areas, the relocation of residents and buildings which are located in flood-prone areas, and flood insurance. Also, authorities are recommended to train local people to be familiar with flood prevention strategies and concepts, such as awareness, avoidance, alleviation, and assistance associated with flood management. It is imperative for the central government and local governments to work together for the decrease of flood risk being clearly aware of the six stages of flood management: (1) prevention; (2) mitigation; (3) preparedness; (4) response; (5) recovery; and (6) reconstruction (Kang et al. 2013b).

It is useful to delve into the process of flood warning system in South Korea as primary preventive methods against flood. At the central level, the Department of Water Resources in the Ministry of Environment is in charge of flood risk management through the Four Flood Control Centers in the Four Major Rivers. The centers collect data on rainfall, hydrological statistics, dam reservoir level, and dam water discharge and analyze and calculate dam water inflow and river water flow together with forecasting the water level in major river sections. On the basis of the outcomes, the centers provide forecast warnings at various levels, i.e., the Central Disaster and Safety Countermeasure HQs at the central government and various disaster and safety countermeasure HQs at diverse localities, local people, police stations, dam operating agencies, and media companies, including the Korea Broadcasting System, which is the primary agency in disseminating flood-related information to the general public (Ministry of Environment 2019). Figure 4.4 shows the flood warning dissemination system in South Korea.

CONCLUSIONS

The chapter has appraised the patterns of risk management policies and systems in South Korea with special reference to water-related disaster management. Among various types of natural disasters in the world and South Korea, water-related disasters account for around 90% in 2018, which confirms the salience of sound management of water-related disasters in every country, particularly South Korea that has often been affected by typhoons, torrential rainfall, and flashflood.

Although people are intuitively aware of the risk of natural disasters depending upon particular natural circumstances, it is not necessarily common to observe that communities are well equipped with relevant institutional and structural policies and measures for protecting human lives as well as economic assets. An array of mega trends, such as urbanization, population growth, and industrialization, has incrementally left many parts of human settlements in the world vulnerable to natural disasters, especially water-related disasters. It is imperative to be highly aware of disaster risk and be committed to establishing disaster risk management strategies and programs in every country.

A good practice of natural disaster risk management in Asia and the Pacific is South Korea's commitment to tackling natural disasters based on its strong top-down nature and the combination of institutional settings and physical infrastructures. Under the auspices of the Minister of the Interior and Safety, the Central Disaster and Safety Countermeasure Headquarters serves as a control tower to administer all the natural disaster-related issues in close collaboration with related ministries and different levels of local authorities.

The majority of available resources for natural disaster management in the country is concentrated on how to harness water-related disasters, especially flood. The data on flood events in several decades explicitly unveil not only the vast scale of human losses as well as economic losses thanks to typhoons, torrential rainfall, storm and flashflood, and landslides but also the gradual decrease of human losses and the exponential growth of economic losses. Challenges caused by urbanization and industrialization in the country are formidable, compounded by climate change-driven adverse impacts.

The experiences of the two typhoon cases, Rusa in 2002 and Maemi in 2003, imply the fundamental policy shift of the country toward more people-centered, climate change-considered, socioeconomic aspects-factored, and prevention and preparedness focused policies and measures. The lessons have been learned, and those challenges have been accommodated and dealt with. Yet, there is still large room to be improved in water-related risk management systems, in particular, with regard to non-structural measures and institutional settings, i.e., integration of relevant laws and regulations, and coordination of various ministries, bureaus, and authorities at the central and local levels.

South Korea has been dedicated to creating a systematic network of multi-purpose dams that are at the forefront preventing flood damage. The system of flood prevention and forecasting demonstrates cutting-edge technologies and engineering skills to hedge the risk of flood events. In addition, non-structural measures against flood events have played a significant role in decreasing the risk of flood, such as the early flood warning system, the zoning of flood-prone areas, the relocation of residents and buildings, and flood insurance.

Disasters are always with us and force people to be aware of consequences if disaster risks are not properly taken care of. The case of South Korea has become a useful benchmark for its neighbors as well as countries in other parts of the world in terms of how to cope with water-related disaster risk with institutional and structural capacity. As the case of South Korea implies, a good degree of state capacity for disaster risk management has never been established without bitter experiences of trials and errors.

REFERENCES

Asian Development Bank. 2018. *Understanding Disaster Risk for Advancing Resilient Development—Knowledge Note*. Asian Development Bank, Manila.

Bae, Jaehyun. 2019. Limitations and Improvement Measures for the Command-and-Control System of National Disaster Response in South Korea. National Assembly Research Service, No. 88. 17 December, 2019, 1–10. www.nars.go.kr. Accessed 26 Dec 2019.

BBC. 2019. Danube Boat Accident: Danube Boat Accident: More Bodies Found as Vessel Is Raised in Hungary. BBC News, 11 June 2019. www.bbc.co.uk. Accessed 26 Dec 2019.

Centre for Research on the Epidemiology of Disasters. 2018. *Annual Disaster Statistical Review 2017*. Brussels: CRED.

Centre for Research on the Epidemiology of Disasters. 2019a. *Disasters 2018: Year in Review*. Brussels: CRED.

Centre for Research on the Epidemiology of Disasters. 2019b. *Natural Disasters 2018*. Brussels: CRED.

Kang, B.S. 2017. Suggestions for a River Basin Urban Flooding Countermeasure Plan. Presented at the 1st Urban Flooding Forum, 6 April 2017. Seoul, Korea Water Resources Association, 25–52.

Kang, H., H. Moon, H. Kim, Y. Kim, J. Ahn, I. Yang, M. Park, B. Kim, and C. Jung. 2013a. A Study on Policy Measures to Formulate National Water Security System. Korea Environment Institute (in Korean).

Kang, M.G., H.S. Jeong, J.H. Lee, and B.S. Kang. 2013b. Assessing National Flood Management Using a Sustainable Flood Management Framework. *Water Policy* 15: 418–434.

Kim, T. 2006a. Typhoon Rusa. National Archives of Korea. http://www.archives.go.kr. Accessed 10 Feb 2018.

Kim, T. 2006b. Typhoon Maemi. National Archives of Korea. http://www.archives.go.kr. Accessed 10 Feb 2018.

Kim, Y., and H. Sohn. 2018. *Disaster Risk Management in the Republic of Korea*. Singapore: Springer.

Kim, S., Y. Tachikawa, and K. Takara. 2007. Recent Flood Disasters and Progress of Disaster Management System in Korea. Annals of Disaster Prevention Research Institute, Kyoto University, No. 50B, 15–31.

Kim, H.Y., C. Shin, Y. Park, and J. Moon. 2018. Water Resources Management in the Republic of Korea: Korea's Challenge to Flood & Drought with Multi-purpose Dam and Multi-regional Water Supply System. Inter-American Development Bank Technical Note, 1566, IDB, Ministry of Environment, and K-water.

Korean Society of Hazard Mitigation. 2012. Disaster Management. Seoul, Goomi Book.

Ministry of Environment. 2019. Water and Future. Daejeon City, Ministry of Environment and K-water.

Ministry of the Interior and Safety. 2019. *Statistical Yearbook of Natural Disasters 2018*. Sejong City, the Ministry of the Interior and Safety.

UNISDR. 2019. What is Disaster Risk Reduction? UNISDR Webpage. https://www.unisdr.org/who-we-are/what-is-drr. Accessed 9 Dec 2019.

van Westen, Cees. 2015. Use of risk information for disaster risk management. International Institute for Geo-Information Science and Earth Observation. UN University, Lecture Slides.

PART II

Participatory Risk Management

CHAPTER 5

The Deliberative Option: The Theoretical Evolution of Citizen Participation in Risk Management and Possibilities for East Asia

Cuz Potter

INTRODUCTION

Risk analysis has historically been the province of technical experts. As a rational approach to addressing uncertainty, risk analysis has relied on the assessments of highly trained scientists, the decision making of risk management specialists, and the sophisticated communication practices of trained risk communicators (Yoe 2012). In some cases, this is still a pertinent approach. Contrary to some world leaders' resistance to expert knowledge, the sudden emergence of a crisis situation, like the contemporary COVID-19 pandemic, require immediate decision making and a reliance on technical expertise for efficient and effective action. Many other risk analyses, like the use of GMO crops and climate heating, do not have such pressing time schedules. Therefore, more time can be taken to delve into the issue, assess potential impacts, and incorporate social

---

C. Potter (✉)
Division of International Studies, Korea University, Seoul, South Korea
e-mail: cuzpotter@korea.ac.kr

© The Author(s), under exclusive license to Springer Nature
Singapore Pte Ltd. 2021
Y. Jing et al. (eds.), *Risk Management in East Asia*,
https://doi.org/10.1007/978-981-33-4586-7_5

values. This is necessary for at least two reasons. First, many issues in risk analysis do not have clearly definable, scientifically proven impacts—or at least include hotly contested scientific findings. That is, they often involve scientific uncertainty that cannot be resolved before decisions must be made. Second, risk management decisions must navigate conflicting and often irreconcilable values. For instance, as the COVID-19 pandemic wears on, governments must determine when to lift restrictions on movement and gathering. They must weigh the risks to public health and to economic activity, among other concerns. Restarting economic production too soon may lead to a resurgence, and waiting too long may cause irrecoverable damage to incomes. As a result of the uncertainty and value judgments involved, decisions must be made that fall within stakeholders' risk tolerance level and that address social values. Contemporary post-empiricist theory argues that robust decision making in the face of scientific and value uncertainty requires time and a reliance on citizen participation.

This primarily historico-theoretical chapter employs Weber's (1978) notion of social action to explore how citizens might become more involved in this second class of risk analysis and decision making. Weber identifies four types of social action: instrumentally rational, value rational, affectual, and traditional. Instrumentally rational action refers to action taken to achieve an end on the basis of expected causes and effects. While Weber's discussion offers the possibility that the end of social action can be rationally calculated, as in the case of profit maximization, more typically instrumentally rational social action refers to the means employed to achieve an end. In political decision making that end is typically a value rational end, which is pursued for its own sake, as in moral and aesthetic values. The remaining types of social action do not feature prominently in this chapter, but they will reappear at the end. The first of these is affectual social action, which is taken on the basis of an emotional state. The second is traditional action, which is taken on the basis of long repeated practice.

Though there are elements of value rational and instrumentally rational action in all spheres of risk analysis, they can be roughly divided into risk management and risk assessment, respectively. Risk management is a decision making process that deals primarily with value rational action. Risk assessment is a knowledge generation process that can be associated with instrumentally rational action.

This chapter first argues that the history of theory—and to some extent practice—in environmental risk assessment can be characterized as a twofold shift in citizens' and experts' role. Citizens' role has moved from the margin as passive recipients of instrumentally rational expert decision making to active arbiters of value rational ends and contributors to instrumentally rational means, while experts' role has moved in the opposite direction. That is, though citizens' involvement in risk analysis was initially in providing goals to be pursued by experts, they now are seen as critical contributors to risk assessment, and though experts were initially considered unalloyed arbiters of truth, their authority has been diminished and they are now seen as well-informed advisors. The chapter then introduces a number of techniques for more directly incorporating citizen viewpoints in decision making processes, ranging from telephone polls to consensus conferences. It finally offers an example of robust citizen participation in Korea called a "Participatory Survey" that has been touted as a Korean model for deliberative polling (The Public Deliberation Committee on Shin-Gori Nuclear Reactors No. 5 & 6 2017, 108).

Evolution of Theories of Expert and Citizen Decision Making

Four phases in the evolution of environmental risk analysis can be identified: unitary expertise, distributed expertise, unitary participation, and distributed participation. This evolution embodies an ongoing fragmentation of expertise and decision making. In the period of unitary expertise, experts served as unitary problem solvers addressing a singular public interest. The complexities of social problems, however, demonstrated first that teams of experts representing multiple disciplines were required, constituting the phase of distributed expertise. As citizens meaningfully questioned experts' findings, fragmentation increased. First, citizens found competing experts with alternative interpretations of risk assessment findings, who argued against government and industry experts in favor of the citizens' interests, which were newly perceived as fragmented. This ushered in a phase of unitary participation and was embodied in advocacy research. Now, in a period of distributed participation, citizens themselves have gotten involved in conducting research through participatory research collaborations with specialists. Each of these phases is

Table 5.1 Typology of risk analysis approaches

			Instrumentally rational			
			Citizen		*Expert*	
			Unitary	Fragmented	Unitary	Fragmented
Value rational	Citizen	*Unitary*			unitary expertise	distributed expertise
		Fragmented		distributed participation		unitary participation
	Expert	*Unitary*			unitary expertise	distributed expertise
		Fragmented	unitary participation			unitary participation, distributed participation

Source Author

explored below through the lens of their approaches to instrumental rationality, value rationality, and stakeholder interests.

These phases are depicted in Table 5.1. Each phase appears twice in order to capture the relationship between instrumentally rational and value rational processes as well as the role of citizens and experts in those processes.

Unitary Expertise: The Rise of Technocracy

At the core of the mid-twentieth-century height of neopositivist approaches to policy making lay a unitary form of technocratic expertise. Rapid social change around the turn of the twentieth century had brought levels of complexity to decision making that challenged the United States' ideals of democratic practice. As Dewey (1946), Lippman (1922), and others argued, the typical layperson was unable to fully understand the complexities of national and international issues sufficiently to participate effectively in democratic decision making processes. The Progressive movement thus pushed for greater reliance on technocratic expertise, referred to here as *unitary expertise*, in making policy decisions. Their success gave experts a newfound authority that in essence inverted Weber's distinction between instrumental rationality and value rationality. While Weber positioned value rationality and goal setting at the heart of decision making and instrumental rationality as a tool for implementing decisions, the neopositivist approach places the instrumental rationality of scientific reason at the heart of decision making, even subordinating value rational decisions to its analytical methods.

During this phase, risk management and policy making relied on the strategy of narrow expertise addressing a singular public interest. The epistemological basis of instrumental rationality in this phase was synonymous with neopositivism and the scientific method. Neopositivism holds that knowledge is comprised of sensory experience interpreted through logic and reason, rather than emotion or belief (Putnam 2004). The transparency of sensory experience and the immutability of logic and reason thus positioned neopositivist science as possessing privileged access to an objective truth, giving technical experts unprecedented authority to dictate reality (cf. Foucault 1991). Their authoritative role was bolstered by the phenomenal engineering achievements of the late nineteenth and early twentieth centuries, like electrification and medical advances, that employed neopositivist scientific practices (Hobsbawm 1997; Kaika and Swyngedouw 2000). This understanding of the scientific method as instrumentally rational underlay the dominance of the rational planning approach during this period and its ongoing influence in policy making in general and risk management in particular.

Rational planning classically posits that citizens share a singular and identifiable common interest, that problems can be clearly identified, and that the scientific method can produce genuine solutions. Rational planning presumes that the public shares a singular common interest: the "public good". Practitioners believe that despite superficial disagreements, rational practice can identify the public's true, underlying interest. This public value might be identified through a careful application of science and reason, as it often was in early socialist states, or through democratic processes that reveal the "true will of the people". Once an overriding value is identified and goals accordingly set, rational planners employ the scientific method to develop and analyze the complete set of possible solutions to the technical problems of achieving those goals (Klosterman 2003). Thus, the value rational ends of the public are considered to be unitary and distinct from the epistemic values of reason, logic, and the scientific method embraced by technical experts.

98   C. POTTER

Distributed Expertise: Wicked Problems Demand Collective Problem Solving

Faith in the ability of singular experts to successfully resolve social problems weakened after the mid-twentieth century. Though the assiduous application of rational planning and technical expertise to society's conflicts and challenges had resolved some simpler problems like hygiene, many more complex problems did not appear to be dissipating. Rittel and Webber (1973) highlighted the (US) public's discontent with professional expertise in their essay on "wicked problems", where they contrasted the "definable, understandable, and consensual" problems that were comparatively easily resolved (156) with those problems that are ill-defined, untestable, and interdependent. The latter are of course "wicked" because they do not admit of clear definition or solution, yet must be addressed anyway. For example, crime reduction is an impossibly complex goal to achieve. Crime rates are related to macroeconomic performance, technological change, racial discrimination, neighborhood and household poverty, education, and so on. All of these factors can impact crime rates directly, indirectly, or in tandem with other factors, making it impossible to clearly define an addressable problem or to know when progress has been made.

Because wicked problems involve so many disparate factors, Rittel and Webber argued that the best solution to handling them was harnessing interdisciplinary teams of experts as a form of *distributed expertise*. While they still held the epistemic value of neopositivist approaches to policy management and hence continued to endorse the scientific method and rational planning as instrumently rational means for achieving public goals, they acknowledged that social issues could not be addressed by individuals with a narrow field of expertise working in isolation from other types of experts. By bringing distributed expertise together into teams, they hoped to regain leverage over complex problems.

Rittel and Webber also recognized that the rational approach faces difficulties in identifying policy goals. Despite implementing rational strategies for identifying desirable outcomes of policy intervention, they reported that "goal finding is turning out to be an extraordinarily obstinate task" (157). This difficulty does not appear to have diminished their faith that there is a common public good that can be identified; it only highlighted the previously misguided approaches to policy making.

Unitary Participation: Expertise Politicized

However, it soon became clear to scholars and much of the public that the difficulties in identifying common goals lie not only in a fragmented population at large but also in technical experts' own fragmented interests. As public distrust of technical experts continued to grow, it became apparent that technical experts and their employers often have interests that conflict with those of the more general population. The tobacco industry, for example, has a long history of using expertise to obfuscate the health risks from smoking tobacco in order to avoid regulation (Brandt 2012). Even though experts may actively work for citizens' benefit, their policies or products have often had negative rather than positive impacts, like school busing and trickle-down economics, calling their very expertise into question (Fischer 2000). Fischer also suggests that experts are typically middle-class knowledge elites and, as such, they reflect narrow interests. On one hand, as just suggested, they represent and protect the interests of their employers and existing social systems in general since doing so will protect their own interests, most particularly their interest in earning a comfortable income. Additionally, middle-class experts tend to embody middle-class values, which are not necessarily the same as those of the more populous working class.

This realization led to the generalized politicization of expertise. As both Beck (1992) and Fischer (2000) relate, civil society groups began to employ the services of experts to counter the claims of government and industry experts, especially in the environmental and epidemiological fields. This produced a phase of *unitary participation*, a bottom-up form of risk communication in which civil society groups identify and defend their own interests.

Civil society groups employed competing expertise to argue on their behalf. This practice came to be called advocacy research, which Fischer (2000, 38) describes as an "attempt to transcend the 'value-neutral' ideology of expertise by explicitly anchoring research to the interests of particular interest groups and to the processes of political and policy argumentation in society generally" and functioning much like a lawyer advocating for her clients (Davidoff 1965). Like the previous two phases, the instrumentally rational means of marshaling expertise remained that of the neopositivist scientific method. However, value rational goals were often seen to be competing. Technical experts were no longer understood

100   C. POTTER

to be pursuing the public good, and, indeed, the very notion of a singular public good came into question.

Distributed Participation: Post-Positivism Levels the Playing Field

The advocacy research approach that informs the unitary participation phase still privileges expertise and the language of experts. It also adopts traditional research methods, which exclude citizen input. But the emergence of post-positivist science (also called post-empiricism) in recent decades has pushed theory to consider new possibilities. As described by Fischer (2000), post-positivism denies neopositivism's claims to a privileged access to truth. Even the most rigorous of the hard sciences engage in highly interpretive practices (Latour 1999; Latour and Woolgar 1986). Scientists must invent machines to translate reality into codified output (like pH levels), which are subsequently translated, for example, through selected mathematical formulae into graphs or regression analyses and interpreted in light of existing theories. Accepting this interpretive practice as fundamental to science, post-positivism positions science, especially social science, as one of many possible accounts of reality. Other accounts of reality are typically based in other forms of knowledge and knowing. Schon (1983), for instance, demonstrates how tacit knowledge cannot be codified and transmitted linguistically but must be developed through practice and interaction. Others have made similar claims for emotional knowledge (Zembylas 2007), religious knowledge (Barbey et al. 2005), and other forms of indigenous knowledge (Barnhardt and Kawagley 2005). The post-positivist approach does not deny the value of science. In fact, the rigor of the scientific method is perceived to produce strong knowledge claims. This is primarily because of post-positivism's belief that theoretically coherent knowledge claims that demonstrate consistency with empirical findings deserve stronger consideration in policy debate than inconsistent and contradictory beliefs that hold up poorly to empirical verification. Despite this privileging of scientific claims, the goal of post-positivism is to capture and incorporate the multiplicity of theories that bear on an issue of concern.

The post-positivist approach levels the playing field between citizens and experts, setting the stage for a much more participatory form of policy making and risk management. It positions experts as specialized citizens and citizens as experts. As discussed above, technical experts bring their own values and interests to their presentation and interpretation of reality. Additionally, the competing expertise identified above shows that scientific claims to indisputable truth are untenable by highlighting the indeterminacy of contemporary science, the existence of disagreements, and the evolution of scientific knowledge (cf. Kuhn 1970). Thus, scientific analysis can serve at best as policy advice, as informed opinion, rather than as objective, technical policy solutions, and experts can no longer claim privileged status in policy debate (Fischer 2000, 42).

Fischer (2000) goes on to argue that citizens, on the other hand, have a much greater capacity for participation in complex, technical decision making than they are typically given credit. First, citizens are very often specialists themselves. They may not specialize in the field in question, but the analytical skills and knowledge they have developed in their own fields serve amply to facilitate the learning and analysis required to make decisions in other fields. Second, citizens possess *ordinary knowledge*, "knowledge that does not owe its origin, testing, degree of verification, truth, status, or currency to distinctive...professional techniques, but rather to common sense, casual empiricism, or thoughtful speculation and analysis" (Lindblom and Cohen 1979, 12). While such knowledge may lack the robustness and precision of the scientific method, ordinary knowledge often transcends the narrow specializations of experts and integrates across disciplines, which is vital to addressing the interconnected components of wicked problems. One important subset of ordinary knowledge is *local knowledge*. Citizens possess unparalleled knowledge of their local contexts. They know their neighborhoods, their towns, their local traditions, and their social practices, better than any outside expert. Though this knowledge is generally tacit and oral—rather than explicit and written—there is nothing inherent in the medium of communication that discredits the utility of such knowledge. Thus, citizens possess essential knowledge and a genuine capacity for participating in sophisticated risk management.

The post-positivist approach, in a sense, reasserts Weber's distinction between instrumental and value rationality while undermining it. On one hand, post-positivism diminishes the authority of experts and subordinates instrumental rationality to value rational decision making. Because technical expertise by nature cannot provide unassailable proof of empirical findings or the efficacy of particular risk management solutions and because experts only consider narrow aspects of complex situations, their instrumentally rational suggestions must be subordinated to value rational (i.e., political) decision making about acceptable risks and desired outcomes. On the other hand, post-positivism argues that value and instrumental rationality infuse each other. Neopositivism's instrumental rationality itself embodies a set of values, like "efficiency" and "falsifiability", that lead it toward reducing wicked problems to tractable problems and implementing technical solutions, rather than social and political solutions (Fischer 2000; Putnam 2004). Meanwhile, the value rational impetus behind citizens' decision making is recognized as having a base in tacit ordinary knowledge. Thus, the distinction between value rational and instrumentally rational, while still useful, emerges blurrier through the post-positivist lens.

Post-positivism recognizes policy making and risk management to be not simply a technical construction, but also a social and political construction. It is a technical construction insofar as scientific knowledge helps decision makers understand the context of their decisions. But because stakeholders' haggling over a given policy's normative goals demonstrates that policy decisions are ultimately normative, value rational decisions, it is evident that policy making is ultimately a political construction. Finally, it is a social construction for at least two reasons. First, knowledge is socially constructed (Berger and Luckmann 1967). Second, knowledge is applied in the context of social practices. That is, localized social practices are instrumental in shaping effective policies. A policy that may work well in one context may not work in another (Potter 2019).

Since the post-positivist approach strives to integrate social, political, and technical constructions by leveling the playing field between citizens and experts, it thus promotes new forms of research and decision making. The most popular family of strategies, called "participatory research" or "action research", rely on the theoretical assumption that human beings are co-creators of their own reality through participation (Fischer 2000, 175). Drawing on Friere (1973) and Kurt Lewin (Argyris and Schon 1978), participatory research and action research see "intervention as an approach to theory-building, and...theory-building as a guide to intervention" (322). This approach involves a wide range of stakeholders (experts and non-experts) from the beginning in developing theories that inform their collective intervention in the situation in question. Collective theory building in this case incorporates not only the technical knowledge of experts but also the ordinary knowledge of citizens. After the intervention has been made for a suitable period, these theories are then reconsidered and reformulated to better explain the unfolding of events and provide a basis for future intervention. This approach embraces the open-ended nature of wicked problems while offering a strategy for addressing them.

This post-positivist approach is at the core of a current phase of thinking about risk management and policy making, which can be referred to as the *distributed participation* phase. While previous phases relied on the positivist scientific method as a source of instrumental rationality in risk management, the distributed participation phase adopts the post-positivist approach of drawing on a range of forms of rationality and knowing in order to more comprehensively understand the policy issue at hand. In particular, it advocates for the incorporation of citizen input from the earliest stages of research and analysis through participatory research practices. This phase localizes value rationality in at least two ways. First, the distinction between instrumental and value rational is blurred, localizing forms of instrumental rationality in the socioeconomic and cultural interests of stakeholders and localizing value rationality in different forms of knowing. Second, this phase emphasizes the importance of ordinary local knowledge in conducting research and developing responses. In localizing and leveling forms of instrumental and value rationality, distributed participation embraces the reality of competing interests that seek to shape policy. While many practitioners strive for an ideal of reaching collective consensus through dialogue, the fundamental understanding is that interests are competing and even radically opposed but not necessarily irreconcilable (Forester 2009). The challenge is to discover and co-create forms of governance that recognize difference and promote reflective learning (Forester 1999).

Table 5.2 summarizes this evolution of theoretical approaches to risk analysis with regard to their instrumentally rational and value rational

Table 5.2 Characteristics of risk analysis approaches

Phase	Instrumental	Value	Interests
Unitary expertise	Neopositivism	Epistemic	Singular
Distributed expertise	Neopositivism	Epistemic	Singular
Unitary participation	Neopositivism	Competing	Competing
Distributed participation	Post-positivism	Localized	Competing

Source Author

orientations as well as their conception of the interests of stakeholders. The general transition is one of broadening. Beginning with a reliance on the neopositivist notion of a singular truth, unitary expertise demonstrates a narrow understanding of social problems as tractable and the public interest as singular. As neopositivist claims weaken and technical experts demonstrate their commitment to specific value orientations, knowledge and value claims fragment and express themselves through competing interests.

POST-POSITIVIST PRACTICE

Implementing post-positivist participatory research approaches in practice can be complicated, expensive, and time-consuming, especially when addressing risk management and public administration that goes beyond narrow, small-scale local concerns. Decision making by experts tends to be more efficient in the short run because the number of participants is limited and the scope of issues considered is narrower. Participatory processes, meanwhile, involve a wider range of stakeholders with a wider range of possibly incompatible interests, and coordinating many stakeholders and resolving disagreements involves much more to-and-fro (Forester 1989). However, dependence only on technical decision makers often generates controversies that reopen debate and extend the overall time required to implement policies effectively (Callon et al. 2009; Forester 2009). Participatory advocates claim that organized participation avoids later controversies by more accurately reflecting the public's will, increasing legitimacy, and securing more citizen buy-in when implementing new policies (Fischer 2000). This section introduces a range of approaches that aim to incorporate increasing levels of citizen participation without consuming too many resources: polling, focus groups, public inquiries, citizen's panels and juries, deliberative polling, and consensus conferences.

Polling

The simplest approaches involve telephone-based surveys. Experts poll citizens and use their responses in formulating policy, marginally softening the distinction between expert and citizen. According to Fischer (2000), in the first variant pollsters directly call a large, representative sample of the population (typically 1000–1500 people). Prior to the phone interview, the poll takers provide basic information that lays out an issue and different positions. Phone interviews then allow respondents to express themselves more fully than they could on a simple questionnaire. This approach, however, assumes that citizens can reach a conclusion on an issue in a brief time on the basis of a simplified presentation.

A variant on this approach is the "televote", which gives citizens the opportunity to consume the printed literature at their leisure and discuss it with those around them before voting for an opinion. Televoting has been critiqued for limiting choices, which oversimplifies participants' opinions, and for allowing survey designers to influence outcomes through their choice of framing and voting options.

Focus Groups

Focus groups will be familiar to academics, political consultants, and marketing specialists. Though sometimes as large as 25 or more people, they typically involve five to twelve people. Focus group meetings may begin with a presentation (a new product, a political commercial, a proposal), to which participants indicate their approval or disapproval in real time using clickers or another device. Regardless of whether this introductory exercise is employed, the main activity is an open-ended discussion. A facilitator encourages participants to share any feelings, thoughts, ideas, or reactions they have and then discuss the ideas as a group.

Focus groups have at least four advantages. First, being small-scale, they are relatively easy to organize and comparatively inexpensive. Second, they offer a reasonably representative set of stakeholder views. Third, focus groups allow for the emergence of unanticipated topics and the construction of new ideas. Because focus groups are open-ended (as opposed to surveys, polls, referendums, and the like), participants often introduce ideas or concerns that organizers had not previously considered and that can open up new policy directions. Finally, because focus groups are discussions, participants not only share their own initial opinions but also co-create collective understandings of an issue that may identify and solidify unrealized or inchoate stakeholder interests.

Focus group findings can then be used by experts and politicians in decision making. Though far from citizen control over decision making, focus groups represent a form of consultation (Arnstein 1969) that can

106 C. POTTER

constructively inform and guide decision making, potentially leading to more socially desirable outcomes. They also create an opportunity for citizens to interactively "discover" and build their own opinions on an issue, testifying to their capacity for evaluating complex issues.

Public Inquiries

Public inquiries represent a step toward more open citizen participation. While focus groups are tightly controlled processes, public inquiries create conditions that may facilitate independent citizen action. Public inquiries are official reviews of acts or events that are initiated by a government body. Though some inquiries are mandated through legislation, typically civil society actors will formally request an inquiry into an issue of concern. If the relevant government body decides to conduct the inquiry, then a variety of techniques are employed to collect and evaluate information. The findings are then expected to shape political decision making.

Perhaps the most famous inquiry is Thomas Berger's Mackenzie Valley Pipeline Inquiry. In 1974 the Government of Canada commissioned Berger to investigate the social, economic, and environmental impacts of a proposed gas pipeline through northern Canada. Over three years, Berger interviewed experts, business people, local residents (especially indigenous peoples), government officials, and other stakeholders and represented a landmark effort to formulate a comprehensive analysis that seriously considered the views of indigenous peoples. The final report concluded that the pipeline would be highly damaging and should not be built. Though not obliged to do so, the government heeded the report's findings and canceled the project. The findings also opened up new policy approaches to address longstanding conflicts in the regions, especially land claims and environmental conservation (Nishihata 1977).

While the Pipeline Inquiry is known for its comprehensiveness and its success, inquiries too often function more as window dressing than decision making. Citizen participation is typically weak, functioning as a unidirectional means for stakeholders to share their thoughts and concerns without any power to make decisions. Thus, though politicians may give lip service to the findings, politicians often ignore them in actual decision making. Instead, inquiries often serve as tools for obtaining citizen acceptance of a project. If the findings have an impact, it tends to be quite limited (Callon et al. 2009). However, even the very process of bringing citizens and civil society groups together can cultivate civic organization and result in unanticipated political action. That is, if an inquiry addresses a controversial topic, the process itself may galvanize citizens and spark social organization, indirectly creating representative political forces capable of influencing future decision making.

Citizens' Panels

Citizens' panels originated in Europe and have since spread to other parts of the world, including the US, where they are referred to as "citizens' juries". While the previous approaches emphasize the extraction of views and opinions from citizens, citizens' panels strive to create conditions for citizens to explore and debate an issue in depth, taking on the role of citizen experts.

Citizens' juries gather twelve to twenty-four citizens for three to five days under the guidance of a moderator. Sometimes multiple panels are convened simultaneously to increase the robustness of the findings. Participants are randomly and representatively selected from among the broader population, are exempted from their regular work obligations, and are typically compensated for their time, much the same as serving on a trial jury in the US. A moderator works with each panel to keep the discussion moving and to resolve conflicts of opinion, if possible. Despite the presence of a moderator, participants are allowed a great deal of leeway in deciding on the procedural rules and agenda. The moderator ensures that relevant experts are on hand, and participants are encouraged to consult with them on any factual questions they may have. The extra time they have and their access to experts allows participants to develop a much deeper understanding of an issue than they can through the previous forms of participation. After debating the issue, a report of the findings and recommendations are prepared and submitted to the pertinent government body (Fischer 2000).

Deliberative Polling

The next approach to be presented here was developed by Fishkin and combines the representative sampling of simple polling with the robust deliberation of the small group approaches like citizens' panels. Though they strive to combine large-scale sampling with in-depth exploration, deliberative polling, also known as deliberative opinion polling, remains

108   C. POTTER

largely in the hands of the experts that organize the process (Fischer 2000). Deliberative polling places emphasis on how opinions change through the deliberative process. By evaluating how deeper reflection on an issue leads to the co-creation of knowledge and changes participants' view of the issue, decision makers can adopt more informed positions and develop strategies for effectively communicating those decisions. "An ordinary opinion poll models what the public thinks, given how little it knows or pays attention. A deliberative poll models what the public would think if it had a more adequate chance to assess the questions at issue" (Fishkin 1993).

To achieve this end, deliberative polling begins with a baseline poll, a large-scale, representative sample survey of a population's views on a particular topic. A representative subset of those polled are selected to participate in a weekend-long conference. Fishkin (2009, 26) believes that the smaller scale motivates participants to invest in the process by convincing them that their opinions really do matter, a feeling that often gets lost in large-scale voting practices. Textual materials are provided to each individual invited to participate directly and to the public at large through various distribution outlets. The weekend functions much like a collection of citizens' panels, in which the participants both join large plenary sessions and are broken up into small groups, where a moderator facilitates discussion and inquiries of available experts. These discussions are typically broadcast on television or online. After the weekend, the original sample is again polled and changes in citizens' opinion are evaluated by the experts and presented to decision making bodies as reflecting the views of an engaged and informed population.

Consensus Conferences

Consensus conferences (also known as "citizen conferences" and "publiforums") reflect the highest degree of citizen participation of approaches presently in use in large-scale decision making. A more robust version of citizens' panels, consensus conferences were first introduced in Denmark in the 1980s. Like the other approaches, consensus conferences work to identify public opinion around a technical or scientific issue with inconclusive evidence and normative implications. However, consensus conferences grant participants more time to explore an issue and even more control over the research agenda.

Ordinarily, a team of academics works as a steering committee for months ahead of time to compile themes, information on stakeholder organizations, and training sessions for participants. Participant selection parallels that of citizens' panels. But rather than meeting for three to five days, consensus conference participants come together over at least three weekends. The first weekend is given over to training sessions designed to familiarize participants with the technical and social issues at hand. They are given extensive reading materials to consider before the next meeting. Having developed some expertise, participants use the second weekend to explore the issue and ask the steering committee about any considerations they might have, like legislative frameworks, medical treatments, etc. The steering committee strives to address these questions and provide additional reading materials. The main output of the second weekend, however, is a set of questions that the citizens will ask the experts. During the conference proper, typically a public four-day affair, the citizens interrogate the experts. By this point, the citizens have developed a fairly robust level of expertise on the issue and the experts often include civil groups who are not themselves necessarily recognized as "experts" in the more formal sense, blurring the lines between citizens and experts. Toward the end of the conference, the group of citizens withdraw to draft their opinion of the question they were asked. Finally, a press conference is held for the citizens to share their conclusion with the media and thereby the government and the populace at large (Callon et al. 2009; Fischer 2000).

The Nuclear Option

In this final section, the paper presents a variant example of deliberative polling in the Republic of Korea. This account is drawn primarily from The Public Deliberation Committee on Shin-Gori Nuclear Reactors No. 5 & 6's *Results of Participatory Surveys for Public Deliberation on Shin-Gori Nuclear Reactors No. 5 & 6* (2017).

The role of nuclear power has long been a point of contention in South Korea. The Korean Peninsula's lack of fossil fuel reserves led to the early adoption of nuclear power as a route to energy security. While opposition to nuclear power in South Korea grew with the global environmental opposition movement, the fate of the Fukushima Daiichi Nuclear Power Plant in the wake of the Tohoku earthquake and subsequent tsunami in 2011 brought these concerns to the forefront of public attention. The shock of Korea's largest ever earthquake in 2016 further amplified public fears of nuclear disaster and thus their perception of risk (Jang 2017).

Responding to these concerns, Moon Jaein, a presidential candidate in 2017, pledged to create a "safe" Korea and to halt construction of two new reactors, the Shin-Gori Nuclear Reactors 5 and 6. However, by the time Moon had been elected and taken office, a contract for the construction of these reactors had been signed, their construction was almost a third completed, and significant government funds had been invested. Amidst the heated debate over the future of the reactors' construction, President Moon halted construction, announced his intention to achieve societal consensus on the issue, and formed a committee to do so in July 2017. The practice adopted for establishing that societal consensus was a variant of Fishkin's deliberative polling.

First, a steering committee of nine members was created that included a chairperson and two members selected from each of the following fields: humanities and social sciences, science and technology, research and statistics, and conflict management. Nuclear power and energy experts were deliberately excluded from the committee, since its purpose was to establish a fair deliberative process. To ensure that the committee represented a range of perspectives and were acceptable to organized stakeholders, eight academic associations and research institutes were asked for a list of three candidates for each field. Civil society groups and institutions with clear positions both opposed to and in favor of nuclear power and were then given the opportunity to disqualify any proposed candidates. The final eight members were selected from a pool of 17 candidates with the additional goal of balancing both the age and gender of its members. The committee members were broken up into four subcommittees for coordinating legal matters, polling, deliberate processes, and communication. Their selection was not without some controversy. Opponents of resuming construction opposed the inclusion of employees of government-funded research institutions under the fear that they would represent the government's opinion in setting the agenda, while proponents argued that they would contribute meaningfully. The disagreement never abated but was abandoned after the government found no legal basis for restricting their participation and freedom of expression. To build robustness, the committee was supplemented by a range of experts from academia, the private sector, and the public sector. To ensure transparency, the committee's discussions were made publicly available and an independent review committee based at Seoul National University was established to evaluate and report on the entire process.

Double sampling was adopted to establish a representative sample of citizens, and represents a significant change to Fishkin's approach. The steering committee claims that this approach is more statistically robust than Fishkin's because its sample size is larger and more representative. First, a random sample of 20,000 registered adult residents stratified by region, age, and gender was given a baseline telephone survey that included questions about their views on resuming construction. A random sample of 500 respondents from the almost 6000 first survey respondents who had expressed a willingness to participate was stratified by age, gender, and opinion on resuming construction on the reactors and were invited to take part in the "critical deliberation program". Following the precise percentile breakdown of public opinion reflected in the large survey, roughly 37 percent of participants were initially in favor of resuming construction, 28 percent were opposed, and 36 percent reserved judgment. Nearly half the sample was male and half female. And age groups were more or less evenly distributed with a slight bias toward those over 40-years-old. This distribution constitutes not only a representative sample but also a reasonably balanced sample that was initially inclined *away* from the President's official position, suggesting an absence of attempts to influence the outcome. However, it should be noted that residents local to the construction site, who stood both to obtain employment and to bear the risks, were not given any additional weighting in the sampling.

The critical deliberative program took place over roughly a month in the early fall of 2017. Selected participants attended a four-hour orientation on deliberative processes, where they were provided with a 70-page factual information sourcebook prepared in conjunction with experts representing both proponents and opponents of construction. Two of the sourcebook's four chapters were written by the steering committee, while proponents and opponents wrote one chapter each, which were offered in reverse order for half the sourcebooks to further reduce bias in presentation. The partisan chapters were also reviewed by the opposing side and a group of experts with regard to the facts presented. In the case of disagreement, the experts' opinions were reflected in footnotes. The materials were supplemented by an online learning component, through which participating citizens could view videos on the subject and access forums for online discussion and communication with experts from both sides prior to the general forum. These materials were also prepared by both sides based on their arguments in the sourcebook with facts and sources reviewed by experts. They were also given a brief additional survey to establish a baseline for comparing the final outcome by identifying their position on, interest in, and level of knowledge about the construction project and nuclear power more generally.

On October 13–15, 2017, 471 of the 500 invited participants took part in a general forum. Prior to any other activity, participants were given a third survey to again measure their views, collect additional demographic information, and determine the impact of the sourcebook and online materials. Then, the forum was divided into four main sessions. The first three sessions consisted of a general discussion of the pros and cons of resuming reactor construction, including safety, environmental impacts, and energy supply. The fourth session involved final presentations, a small group decision on the issue, and a discussion of strategies for fostering social acceptance of their decision. Each session involved presentations by both proponents and opponents, small group discussion, and a question and answer period. Presentation order was designed in coordination with both sides to promote fair representation. The small groups consisted of nine to ten members each facilitated by moderators, who were considered to be conflict management experts, were drawn from a variety of fields, and had undergone two training sessions on maintaining neutrality and fostering deliberation. The moderators' role was to be as minimal as possible and to allow members to autonomously drive their own discussions. In addition to discussing the issue among themselves, each small group identified one question each for the proponents and opponents of resuming construction. Of these, ten of the most frequently asked questions for each side were selected for a two-minute response, two-minute rebuttal, and one-minute rebuttal response. After the sessions were complete, a final survey was implemented to determine participants' final opinion on resumption and future construction, their political attitudes, level of understanding of the issue, and assessment of the process.

Though this critical deliberative program effectively mimicked deliberative polling, the steering committee also incorporated a supplementary program for the wider Korean public to foster both awareness and public debate. This program consisted of seven regional public debates, five television debates, and a "Future Generation Debate". The regional debates included balanced presentations on the issue, a wider ranging discussion, and a question and answer period for the audience. The televised debates involved academic supporters of both sides of the argument in a variety of contestation-oriented formats. The Future Generation Debate invited over one hundred students from twenty high schools in Seoul to listen to two academics present the suspension and resumption arguments, followed by questions from the students, and small group discussions moderated by high school students who had received a short training session.

In this case, the deliberative polling strategy fulfilled the claims made for it by Fishkin. As shown in Table 5.3, deliberation appears to have shifted the opinion of the participating citizens. After reading the materials initially provided, those in favor of resuming construction had risen from 37 percent to almost 45 percent, those opposed had increased from 28 percent to just over 30 percent, and about 25 percent remained undecided. After the general forum, the final poll showed that roughly 60 percent of those with a final decision were in favor of resuming construction and 40 percent were opposed. As participating citizens learned more about the issues involved, their opinions shifted. Though those with clear opinions initially maintained those positions, 2.2 percent of the participants changed their position from resuming construction to stopping construction, while 5.3 percent changed in the opposite direction. Initially, undecided participants divided more or less evenly between the two camps with a slight bias toward supporting the resumption of construction. This demonstrates that education and deliberation can indeed shift public opinion. It should be noted that the key factors in final decision making were slightly different. Though virtually all participants emphasized safety as an important concern, proponents of resuming

Table 5.3 Percent change for and against resuming construction by survey

Population	Survey	For	Against	Undecided
General survey (N = 20,000)	1st	36.6	27.6	35.8
Participatory deliberation group (N = 471)	1st	36.6	27.6	35.8
	3rd	44.7	30.7	24.6
	4th	57.2	39.4	3.3
	Final	59.5	40.5	–

Source Author

114 C. POTTER

construction were more likely to consider economic factors, while opponents emphasized environmental concerns. And the importance of these factors shifted marginally over the entire process, again demonstrating the impact of education and deliberation.

Participants were also asked about the future of nuclear power in South Korea. While participants were in favor of resuming construction, a majority were in favor of scaling back nuclear power generation in the future, while a third supported maintaining current levels of generation and ten percent advocated for expansion. Policy recommendations were also made for safety and renewable energy mix. Though this process was non-binding, acceding to the clear expression of public opinion, President Moon initiated the resumption of construction of the Shin-Gori 5 and 6 reactors (Yonhap News Agency 2017), but canceled existing orders for six more.

CONCLUSION: A CONCERN

This Korean model of deliberative polling, which has been dubbed a "Participatory Survey" (The Public Deliberation Committee on Shin-Gori Nuclear Reactors No. 5 & 6 2017, 108), demonstrates the potential for much greater and more direct citizen participation in risk analysis. Rather than relying on singular experts attempting to define and address a social problem in the putative social interest through instrumental rationality under the unitary expertise model, the Korean experience highlights the ability of citizens to bring their own expertise to bear on complex social issues involving scientific uncertainty and conflicting values. That is, citizens have proven themselves capable of integrating instrumental and value rational social action.

Such success suggests a wider scope for citizen involvement in future decision making. However, some theorists and practitioners urge even higher levels of citizen participation. Drawing on Habermas's notion of the "ideal speech situation" shorn of power relations (Habermas 1984), they argue that deliberative democratic processes can lead to consensus decisions through rational debate and co-learning. The difficulties of achieving this goal at the regional or national scale may be prohibitive (Fainstein 2000), but they may be accessible at the local scale. Japan, for instance, has a decades-long history of consensus-based deliberative decision making at the local scale through *machizukuri*, a form of neighborhood planning (Hein 2001; Satoh 2020).

5 THE DELIBERATIVE OPTION ... 115

These examples show that higher levels of citizen participation are possible, effective, and meaningful. It is also hoped that they generate optimism about introducing more robust deliberative practices. This chapter, however, ends with a note of caution. The healthy contextualization of technical expertise and the realistic recognition of neopositivism's limits appears to have led many citizens and decision makers to disavow scientific expertise altogether. Climate change denialism, for example, stems from a refusal to accept scientific evidence and expertise as legitimate. This anti-scientism has been amplified as globalization has undermined existential security and challenged long-held beliefs. The result has been a rise in populism and traditionalism (Barber 1995), a reassertion of Weber's affectual and traditional social action. These non-rational approaches to setting value rational goals threaten to override instrumentally rational social action by undermining the co-creation of knowledge that is at the heart of deliberative practice.

REFERENCES

Argyris, Chris, and Donald A. Schon. 1978. *Organizational Learning: A Theory of Action Perspective*. Reading: Addison-Wesley.

Arnstein, Sherry R. 1969. A Ladder of Citizen Participation. *Journal of the American Institute of Planners* 35 (4): 216–224.

Barber, Benjamin. 1995. *Jihad vs. McWorld*. New York: Times Books.

Barbey, Aron, W. Lawrence Barsalou, Kyle Simmons, and Ava Santos. 2005. Embodiment in Religious Knowledge. *Journal of Cognition and Culture* 5 (1–2): 14–57.

Barnhardt, Ray, and Angayuqaq Oscar Kawagley. 2005. Indigenous Knowledge Systems and Alaska Native Ways of Knowing. *Anthropology & Education Quarterly* 36 (1): 8–23.

Beck, Ulrich. 1992. *Risk Society: Towards a New Modernity*. Thousand Oaks: Sage Publications Ltd.

Berger, Peter L., and Thomas Luckmann. 1967. *The Social Construction of Reality: A Treatise in the Sociology of Knowledge*. Garden City, N.Y.: Anchor Books.

Brandt, Allan M. 2012. Inventing Conflicts of Interest: A History of Tobacco Industry Tactics. *American Journal of Public Health* 102 (1): 63–71.

Callon, Michel, Pierre Lascoumes, and Yannick Barthe. 2009. *Acting in an Uncertain World: An Essay on Technical Democracy*. Translated by Graham Burchell. Cambridge: The MIT Press.

Davidoff, Paul. 1965. "Advocacy and Pluralism in Planning." Edited by Scott Campbell and eds (2003) Susan S. Fainstein, *Journal of the American Institute of Planners* (Oxford) 31 (4): 331–338.

Dewey, John. 1946. *The Public and Its Problems: An Essay in Political Inquiry.* Chicago: Gateway Books.

Fainstein, Susan. 2000. New Directions in Planning Theory. *Urban Affairs Review* 35 (4): 451–478.

Fischer, Frank. 2000. *Citizens, Experts, and the Environment: The Politics of Local Knowledge.* Durham: Duke University Press.

Fishkin, James S. 1993. *Democracy and Deliberation: New Directions for Democratic Reform.* New Haven: Yale University Press.

Fishkin, James S. 2009. *When the People Speak: Deliberative Democracy and Public Consultation.* Oxford New York: Oxford University Press.

Forester, John. 1989. *Planning in the Face of Power.* Berkeley: University of California Press.

Forester, John. 1999. *The Deliberative Practitioner: Encouraging Participatory Planning Processes.* Cambridge: The MIT Press.

Forester, John. 2009. *Dealing with Differences: Dramas of Mediating Public Disputes.* New York: Oxford University Press.

Foucault, Michel. 1991. Governmentality. In *The Foucault Effect: Studies in Governmentality*, ed. Graham Burchell, Colin Gordon, and Peter Miller, 87–104. Chicago: University of Chicago Press.

Friere, Paulo. 1973. *Pedagogy of the Oppressed.* New York: Continuum.

Habermas, Jugen. 1984. *The Theory of Communicative Action.* Boston: Beacon Press.

Hein, Carola. 2001. Toshikeikaku and Machizukuri in Japanese Urban Planning: The Reconstruction of Inner City Neighborhoods in Kobe. *Jahrbuch Des Deutsches Institut Fur Japanstudien* 13: 221–252.

Hobsbawm, Eric. 1997. *The Age Of Capital: 1848–1875.* London: Abacus.

Jang, Se Young. 2017. "South Korea's Nuclear Energy Debate." *The Diplomat* (October).

Kaika, Maria, and Erik Swyngedouw. 2000. Fetishizing the Modern City: The Phantasmagoria of Urban Technological Networks. *International Journal of Urban and Regional Research* 24 (1): 120–137.

Klosterman, Richard E. 2003. Arguments For and Against Planning. In *Readings in Planning Theory, 2nd*, ed. Scott Campbell and Susan S. Fainstein, 86–101. Oxford: Blackwell.

Kuhn, Thomas. 1970. *The Structure of Scientific Revolutions.* Chicago: University of Chicago Press.

Latour, Bruno. 1999. *Pandora's Hope: Essays on the Reality of Science Studies.* Cambridge: Harvard University Press.

Latour, Bruno, and S. Woolgar. 1986. *Laboratory Life: The Construction of Scientific Facts*. Princeton: Princeton University Academic Press.

Lindblom, Charles, and David K. Cohen. 1979. *Usable Knowledge: Social Science and Social Science Problem Solving*. New Haven: Yale University Press.

Lippman, Walter. 1922. *Public Opinion*. New York: Harcourt, Brace & Co.

Nishihata, Jesse. 1977. "The Inquiry Film: A Report on the Mackenzie Valley Pipeline.".

Potter, Cuz. 2019. Just Like Korea in the 1970s? Policy Transfer and the Fiction of Familiarity. *International Development and Cooperation Review* 11 (4): 21–36.

Putnam, Hilary. 2004. *The Collapse of the Fact/Value Dichotomy and Other Essays*. Cambridge: Harvard University Press.

Rittel, Horst W. J., and Melvin M. Webber. 1973. "Dilemmas in a General Theory of Planning." 4:155–169.

Satoh, Shigeru. 2020. *Japanese Machizukuri and Community Engagement*. New York: Routledge.

Schon, Donald A. 1983. *The Reflective Practitioner: How Professionals Think in Action*. New York: Basic Books.

The Public Deliberation Committee on Shin-Gori Nuclear Reactors No. 5 & 6. 2017. *Results of Participatory Surveys for Public Deliberation on Shin-Gori Nuclear Reactors No. 5 & 6*. Research report. Citizens' Group for Participatory Deliberation on the Construction of Shin-Gori Nuclear Reactors No. 5 & 6, October 20.

Weber, Max. 1978. *Economy and Society: An Outline of Interpretive Sociology*. In *and Claus Wittich*, ed. Guenther Roth. Berkeley: University of California Press.

Yoe, Charles. 2012. *Primer on Risk Analysis: Decision Making under Uncertainty*. New York: CRC Press.

Yonhap News Agency. 2017. "Proposed Resumption of Nuclear Reactors to Delay Moon's New Energy Policy." *The Korea Herald* (October).

Zembylas, Michalinos. 2007. Emotional Ecology: The Intersection of Emotional Knowledge and Pedagogical Content Knowledge in Teaching. *Teaching and Teacher Education* 23 (4): 355–367.

CHAPTER 6

Participation Willingness and Interactive Strategy in Collaborative Risk Governance

Chun-yuan Wang and Yanyi Chang

INTRODUCTION

Over the last decade, disasters have continued to cause major damage and casualties, which has severely affected people, communities, and governments. It is estimated that at least 700,000 people have been killed, more than 1.5 million have been injured, and 23 million have been left homeless, with economic losses of more than USD $1.3 trillion. In other words, the impact of disasters on human life has become increasingly severe (Karimova 2016, 177). In order to effectively face the challenge of disasters, the United Nations held the second World Conference on Disaster Reduction (WCDR) in Kobe, Japan from January 18 to 22, 2005. The conference passed the Hyogo Declaration, which discussed

---

C.-y. Wang
General Education Center, Department of Police Administration,
Central Police University, Taoyuan, Taiwan
e-mail: g885422@seed.net.tw

Y. Chang (✉)
Department of Public Administration, Chung Hua University,
Hsinchu, Taiwan

© The Author(s), under exclusive license to Springer Nature
Singapore Pte Ltd. 2021
Y. Jing et al. (eds.), *Risk Management in East Asia*,
https://doi.org/10.1007/978-981-33-4586-7_6

119

the role of the government and the need for stakeholders to participate in disaster reduction. These participants should include governments, regional organizations, international organizations, financial institutions, the private sector, non-governmental organizations (NGOs), and the scientific sector (Jan 2013, p. 76). After this WCDR conference, the academic community has gradually paid attention to the topic of collaborative disaster governance, and related studies have explored and discussed collaboration (Kapucu 2008), network management (Moynihan 2009), and public-private partnership approach to disaster prevention and response (Chowdhury 2011; Medury 2011).

In March 2015, the United Nations Third World Conference on Disaster Risk Reduction (WCDRR) proposed the Post-2015 Framework for Disaster Risk Reduction. This framework aims to achieve the following outcome over the next 15 years: the substantial reduction of disaster risk and losses in lives, livelihoods, and health and in the economic, physical, social, cultural, and environmental assets of persons, businesses, communities, and countries. To attain the expected outcome, the following goal must be pursued: prevent new and reduce existing disaster risk through the implementation of integrated and inclusive economic, structural, legal, social, health, cultural, educational, environmental, technological, political, and institutional measures that prevent and reduce hazard exposure and vulnerability to disaster, increase preparedness for response and recovery, and strengthen resilience (UN 2015, 12).

As more and more diverse actors participate in the process of public governance, the concept of collaborative governance has also received increasing attention. Kooiman (1993) considered that in the process of policy implementation, no single actor can possess sufficient knowledge to deal with increasingly complex issues; therefore, new governance requires public and private sector collaboration to form different networks, share responsibility, power, and capacity so that the best results of policy can be achieved. However, when we look into the actual operation of collaborative disaster management, does it always work so smoothly?

On May 12, 2008, an 8.0 magnitude earthquake struck Sichuan province in Mainland China, killing nearly 70,000 people and injuring hundreds of thousands. The government and non-governmental organizations rushed to the disaster area for relief. According to Tong and Zhang (2012), although social mobilization led to more than 300 non-governmental organizations that went to the front line to participate in disaster relief after the disaster, the number of volunteers involved reached about 3 million. Optimists think that 2008 was "the first year" of China's civil society. Nevertheless, the reality is that by April 2009, there were probably fewer than 50 non-governmental organizations in the disaster area and less than 50,000 volunteers. In addition, on February 6, 2016, a 6.4 magnitude earthquake occurred in the early morning of Kaohsiung's Meinong District in Taiwan, causing many buildings in Tainan City to collapse. The collapse of the Weiguan Jinlong Building in Tainan City saw the worst causalities in this earthquake. During the rescue process, the Tainan City Government and civilian rescue organizations continued rescue efforts day and night collaboratively. However, a few days later, the media reported that there was a problem in the interaction and communication between the Tainan City Government and one rescue team, which caused more than 160 members of the rescue team to be dismissed directly from the search and rescue site (ETtoday 2016).

These cases point to the main questions of this research: Why do actors in disaster governance want to participate? What factors may affect the willingness of actors to participate? How do these factors affect the interaction strategies between different actors? In order to strengthen the disaster risk governance capabilities at the township (town, city, and district) level, the National Disaster Prevention and Response *Committee* submitted a "Disaster Prevention and Protection Project" (DPPP) that was approved by the Executive Yuan. This project includes three phases which is from 2009 to 2013, 2014 to 2017, and 2018 to 2022. The Ministry of the Interior provides this project with financial assistance and technical experience to assist local governments in disaster prevention and rescue operations. The current plan for the third phase is to "build resilient communities." Based on the policy of collaborative risk governance, this article explores the main factors in community participation and the relationship between the motivation of community members' participation and the interaction strategies of relevant government agencies. This chapter first reviewed the literature on collaborative risk governance and participation motivation, then defined different strategies for collaborative network management, and finally collected data for analysis through in-depth interviews and made some recommendations based on the findings.

Participation Willingness and Interactive Strategy in Collaborative Risk Governance

Under the critical challenge of increasing risks and increasing disaster scale, it is necessary to engage in collaborative risk and disaster governance. Kapucu et al. (2010) argued that when a catastrophic event occurs, a large amount of communication and coordination capabilities are required between the public sector, nonprofit organizations, and private organizations. For emergency management, it is necessary for government to have excellent ability to assess and adapt, and be able to make decisions flexibly to increase the coordination and trust of the diverse responding agencies. Demiroz and Kapucu (2015) provided some policy tools for collaborative disaster management, such as insurance mechanisms, outsourcing, and collaborative public management, and call for concerted use of these governance methods in the field of emergency disaster management. They realized that contemporary society has become more and more complicated, and the damage caused by a disaster requires public, private and non-profit organizations to work together.

Smith and Toft (1998) considered that at the core of risk analysis, the issue of governance is important. Facing the challenges of the complex environment, the public sector needs to be trained to deal with uncertainty within the multi-organizations and communicate with stakeholders to manage this uncertainty. The current multi-organizational and multi-sector operating environment of the government needs to design new coordination-oriented strategies. Collaborative governance has gradually become an obvious interest in related research fields and can complement the traditional hierarchical governance and market governance models, and also mitigate the complexity of public issues and strengthen responsiveness. In this governance process, collaboration between the public and private sectors is not limited to a single model, but needs to be viewed as a systematic process (Bang and Sorensen 1999, 329; Grimsey and Lewis 2004; Stoker 1998, 18–26). Emerson, Nabatchi, and Balogh (2012) explored the integrated framework of collaborative governance and proposed the concept of "Collaborative Governance Regime"(CGR). They defined collaborative governance as a process of public policy construction that enables people to participate in what was previously difficult, participate in setting the boundaries of public organizations, and achieve public purposes that cannot be accomplished otherwise. These collaborations are not limited to formal government-initiated activities and should also include non-governmental stakeholders. It also involves partnerships among government, the private sector, and civil society.

The literature has pointed out that collaborative governance can be time-consuming and full of uncertainty. Once successful, collaborative governance can increase government accountability and citizen participation, and can be implemented consistently by subordinate units. However, successful cooperative governance is usually difficult to achieve, which always depends on creating a climate of prudence, promoting trust, shared commitment, mutual accountability, and willingness to share risks. Stakeholders must be reassured that everyone involved in the process has an equal opportunity to influence decisions and believe that these decisions may have an impact on problem-solving (Johnston et al. 2011).

In other words, collaborative governance is not necessarily a short-term solution to public problems, and there are still many problems to be overcome during this period. For example, Tseng (2011) considered that the organizational form of public-private partnerships happens to be in a "twilight zone" in the public and private spheres, and collaborative behavior is deeply affected by so-called "conflicting institutional logic." The results of the study show that there are three main factors that make synergy a "reluctant partner": (1) from the authoritative sharing policy claim, gradually returning to the inertia of dominant power" in the public sector; (2) from adhering to the belief in flexible negotiation and mutual adaptation, gradually returning to restrictions of discretion and contract rigidity; and (3) from the original contract design concept of risk transfer and risk dispersion, gradually devolving into risk transfer and risk avoidance for the public sector. As Johnston et al. (2011) pointed out previous studies have largely ignored the "when and how" in facing challenges in joining group actions.

Therefore, the first step in effective collaborative governance should be to shape an "enthusiastic" environment. Public participation means working together and active participation in political, economic, and cultural life (Sarokhani 1991, 521). Participation also refers to conscious and voluntary involvement in decision-making and planning to meet social needs and goals. Citizen participation is described as a path that extends from citizen incompetence to delegated power and citizenship. The first stage states that no form of participation is indicative of public manipulation. There are three levels in the middle stage, which handle the transmission and reception of information without guaranteeing the implementation of opinions or recommendations. This means a one-way approach. The third phase involves partnerships, empowerment and citizenship control, citizen monitoring, and completing urban management tasks (Berner et al. 2011; Khoshdel and Bakhshan 2015).

Participation is a key factor in achieving development goals, especially urban development goals. Kapucu (2013) addresses the impact of disaster management on the level of community participation, and explains that the federal government plays an important role in disaster recovery. He believes that knowledge of disaster recovery is ignored by disaster management, and applied research at this stage is seriously lagging behind. Some scholars discuss the response part of collaborative governance in disaster management, such as Thailand's flood disaster policy after 2011, which includes different levels of government management and stresses the importance of people's participation in flood management. In other words, flood disaster management involves the transmission of information (Raungratanaamporna et al. 2014). Besides, the more citizens participate in urban affairs, the more successful the urban development plan will be. As a result, vulnerable social groups will benefit from citizen participation. A fundamental change in municipal management is the transition to participatory management. Participatory management focuses on voluntary citizen collaboration and involvement, with the aim of using citizens' ideas, suggestions, innovations, and skills to solve organizational problems (Khoshdel and Bakhshan 2015).

It is worth noting that the fundamental problem for actors in collaborative governance is still motivation and willingness to participate. Studies have shown that there is a great deal of willingness to influence citizen participation. For example, Moynihan (2003) considers administrative costs and instrumental benefits. The former includes direct administrative costs, self-interested administrative costs, decision-making processes, and the costs of decision outcomes; the latter includes more targeted and effective plans, innovative ideas, and acceptance of public decisions. Emerson et al. (2012) pointed out the importance of shared motivation in collaborative governance. They considered that shared motivation is a self-reinforcing cycle that consists of four elements: mutual trust, mutual understanding, internal legitimacy, and shared commitment. The first element is the development of mutual trust. Over time, all parties work together to understand each other and prove to each other that they are reasonable, predictable, and reliable. Trust enables people to transcend their personal, institutional, and jurisdictional frameworks to understand the interests, needs, values, and constraints of others, which also forms the second element of common motivation: mutual understanding. This development can progress to the third factor—that is, the perception of legitimacy of interpersonal authentication. Finally, informal interpersonal trust and reciprocity norms further strengthen the legitimacy and effectiveness of the motivation for collaboration.

Collaborative governance of diverse participants naturally involves the process of network interaction. Fountain (1994, 273) mentioned that "the network perspective offers both rich descriptive capacity and rigorous methodologies for study of both micro- and macro-level organizational and inter-organizational phenomena of great importance to public management." According to O'Toole (1997, 45) mentioned "Networks are structures of interdependence involving multiple organizations or parts thereof, where one unit is not merely the formal subordinate of the others in some larger hierarchical arrangement."

Regarding how different actions in the collaborative process can effectively shape-related strategies from the managerial perspective, it has been a key issue in academic discussions recently. As pointed out by Liu (2006), because the network participants have invested considerable time and resources in the network, no one wants to see the negotiation process fail. Therefore, public managers need to master the meaning and strategies of network management, make good use of management strategies, and let the network perform its due effects. In addition to the advantages of network management itself, network managers must also have a certain degree of ability in management projects such as negotiation, mediation, risk analysis, trust building, and collaboration. However, in the process of network management, there are many complex members and factors, and it is impossible and time-consuming to reach a complete consensus among all personnel, so managers also need to consider the cost of complex governance procedures (Herranz Jr. 2006).

Researchers have crafted four types of network strategy based on a behavioral perspective valued and later applied by scholars, including activation, framing, mobilization, and synergy. The following is the specific content (Agranoff and McGuire, 2001; McGuire and Agranoff, 2014):

1. Activating: Network activating means actioners or organizations would like to lead the interactions and operations of the network. These actors may stand on the edge of the network, so they change their position in the network via an activating strategy, such as offering motivation or resource exchange. Activating resources

should identify the participants and shareholders among networks, as well as the knowledge of developers. All benefits should be included in networks.

2. Framing: When the efficiency of a network is not ideal, framing would be the management tool to form the networks, which includes the establishment of networking regulations, influencing their common perceptions and morals, and changing participants of networks' perspectives. Participants' feelings could be shaped and quickly generate a non-productive network by framing, which could generate conscious change.

3. Mobilizing: The managers of networks should motivate individual members to commit to joint undertakings and also make them fulfill their promises. As a result, mobilizing needs a view of the strategic whole and a shared capability of attaining the goal. Mobilizing should put more emphasis on human relations components such as motivating, inspiring, and inducing commitment.

4. Synthesizing: It emphasizes that one plus one should be bigger than two. This effect can bring about cooperation and learning among diverse participants. Some network management-related studies point out that synergy can enhance the conditions and generate an interactive network for participants by creating a conducive environment. Managers should combine different participants, goals, and morals to realize the goals of network strategy.

In addition to network strategies, information and knowledge sharing is also a significant factor in actors' interaction in collaborative risk governance. For example, in Taiwan's disaster management system, information sharing in the public and private sectors at different levels of the network is important (Kuo et al. 2015). Wu and Chang (2018) considered the perspective of disaster management, resource integration, and knowledge sharing to be important parts of the disaster governance mechanism.

DPPP and Disaster Resilience

Taiwan's natural environment faces many challenges, including global climate change, the impact of excessive urban and rural development, and the occurrence of various major accidents. Therefore, after the Disaster Prevention and Protection Act was passed in 2000, government agencies adjusted and revised plans and related laws and regulations that can respond to contingency and adaptation at any time. Data has been collected and integrated from natural disasters (such as earthquakes, landslides, and flooding) over the past two decades, which will ensure effective disaster mitigation, prevention mechanisms, and decision-making support systems. Since 2009, the Ministry of the Interior has implemented of the Disaster Prevention and Protection Project (DPPP) at 135 townships (town, city, and district). Based on the DPPP, Phase 1 in 2009–2013 and Phase 2 in 2014–2017 all focused on the principles of the priority (in high-risk potential and vulnerable areas) and the construction of collaborative organizations by using scientific research results to conduct regional disaster investigation, assessment, and analysis (RDEC 2013, 1, 4).

The third phase of the DPPP (2018–2022), promoted by the National Fire Agency of the Ministry of the Interior, focuses on building resilient communities. The plan emphasizes that community should coexist with environmental risks. The resilient community is this plan defined as "The risk of disasters cannot be completely avoided, and the community may still be affected by disasters. However, the promotion of resilient communities can reduce the impact of disasters and quickly recovery during impact." The goals of promoting resilient communities plan are (1) to raise awareness among the community about the crisis in disasters, (2) gather the community's centripetal force, encourage people to participate in disaster prevention work, cultivate their capacity to help themselves and help each other, and look forward to connecting neighboring units such as schools, volunteer groups, long-term care institutions, and even enterprises to participate together, (3) identify and assess potential disaster risks in the community, prioritize improvements based on community resources and capabilities, and implement them to strengthen community resilience, (4) promote community-based disaster prevention work through building resilient communities, and (5) resilient communities continue to operate autonomously after external resources are reduced (National Fire Agency 2018).

The Sendai Disaster Reduction Framework mentioned "Disaster risk reduction requires an all-of-society engagement and partnership. It also requires empowerment and inclusive, accessible and non-discriminatory participation, paying special attention to people disproportionately affected by disasters, especially the poorest. A gender, age, disability, and cultural perspective should be integrated in all policies and practices, and women and youth leadership should be promoted. In this context, special attention should be paid to the improvement of organized voluntary work of citizens" (UN 2015, 13). In short, the third phase of DPPP is to promote through wide and diversified channels to raise people's awareness of risk (disaster prevention) so that they can attach importance to disaster prevention, and then encourage people to participate in disaster prevention and relief work; promote and integrate civil volunteer groups, invite enterprises to participate in disaster prevention and direct the energy of self-assistance, mutual assistance, and public assistance to local governments to make up for their lack of human and other resources. That is, through the participation and partnership of society, we can strengthen the promotion of various DPPP work projects (National Fire Agency 2018).

In order to understand the participation willingness and interaction strategies of multiple actors in collaborative risk governance, this research focused on DPPP and conducted in-depth interviews with local government officials and community leaders. The interviewees are shown in Table 6.1.

Table 6.1 List of in-depth interviews

Code	Organization	Interviewees	Time/Location
A	Disaster Management Office, OOO City Government	Executive Secretary OOO	Jan. 31, 2020 Southern Taiwan
B	OOO District, Tainan City Government	Village Chief OOO	Feb. 13, 2020 Southern Taiwan
C	OOO District, Tainan City Government	Village Chief OOO	Feb. 13, 2020 Southern Taiwan
D	OOO District, Tainan City Government	Village Chief OOO	Feb. 13, 2020 Southern Taiwan
E	OOO District, Tainan City Government	Village Chief OOO	Feb. 13, 2020 Southern Taiwan
F	OOO District, Hsinchu City Government	Village Chief OOO	Feb. 24, 2020 Northern Taiwan
G	OOO District, Hsinchu City Government	Village Chief OOO	Feb. 25, 2020 Northern Taiwan
H	OOO District, Hsinchu County Government	Village Chief OOO	Mar. 05, 2020 Northern Taiwan
I	Disaster Management Office, OOO City Government	Executive Secretary OOO Specialist OOO Section Director OOO	Mar. 09, 2020 Central Taiwan (Focus group)

Source The authors

DPPP is expected to promote 126 resilient communities in 22 counties and cities across Taiwan, for which 2018 was the planning and preparation period and was promoted in 2019. In other words, at the time of these interviews, the Village Chiefs already had one year of experience. This chapter interviewed a total of seven community leaders in four counties and cities in the northern, central, and southern districts of Taiwan. Among them, there is one first-elected Village Chief, and several with more than 10 years or even 20 years of experience were re-elected. Among the local government interviewees were senior civil servants from the Disaster Management Offices in south and central Taiwan. During the interviews, most of the interviewees were also very pleased to know that academic research has focused attention on this topic. Each interview was about one hour on average. The interviewees provided many ideas and opinions that not only helped answer the research questions for this chapter, but also enabled the DPPP to perform smoother in the next few years.

PARTICIPATION AND COLLABORATION IN DPPP PROJECTS

Risk Awareness and Citizens' Participation in Risk Governance

If risks are not recognized at the initial stage, subsequent risk assessment and management practices will operate poorly; therefore, the first step in risk management is to be aware of the risks (Koller 2007; Wang 2012). In an environment full of uncertainty and various risks, the new risk philosophy is to develop "governance mechanisms" under the concept of "shared-risk"(Comfort 1999). Under the concept of risk governance, various diverse actors must have the ability to assess, analyze, coordinate, integrate, and deal with risks. This involves risk awareness, administrative mobilization, and laws and regulations. At all levels such as infrastructure, it depends on the collaboration of actors. In recent years, natural disasters such as typhoons and earthquakes have occurred frequently in Taiwan, which have caused many losses. In these cases, the government and community leaders communicated to awaken the risk awareness of the community and help them participate in risk governance.[1]

---

[1] The citizens are probably already aware of the risks from these major disasters. They want to do it but they don't know where to start. That's why we have such a plan (DPPP) and teams come in. (Interviewee A)

In addition to being hit by typhoons and rainstorms every year, the political and economic center of Taiwan, Taipei City, also faces sudden fires, earthquakes, epidemics, and various other disasters. Since citizens face the risk of natural disasters, it is important for citizens to have basic knowledge of how to prevent and prepare to disasters. In order to strengthen citizens' disaster coping knowledge and resilience, the Taipei City Fire Department has issued a "Citizens' Disaster Prevention and Preparedness Manual," which contains knowledge about how to deal with earthquakes, typhoons, fires, and other disasters (Taipei City Government 2016). There is of course no way to get all citizens to participate in the disaster preparedness network with just one manual. Of course, there is no way to allow all citizens to participate in the disaster preparedness network based on a manual. Therefore, the Taipei City Government joined the DPPP project from 2018.

After one year of planning and preparation, four communities in Taipei have participated in DPPP since 2019. During the planning and preparation period, willingness to participate in DPPP was investigated. A questionnaire was administered which addressed three basic issues. The first issue was the cognition of the community environment. Participants were asked: What kinds of disasters does the community worry about most? Are there plans to prepare for these disasters? Is the community vulnerable or not? The second topic is the current situation of disaster preparedness in the community. Participants were asked: Is there a Neighborhood Watch team or a volunteer group in your community? Has the community done disaster education and training? Has the community conducted escape and sheltering drills? Third, participants were asked if they were willing to participate in the DPPP in 2019. There were a total of 191 respondents willing to participate in the DPPP community, of

The people have asked that they should not be flooded. It is possible that they can help you faster drainage, then it is already very good. It is possible to use Typhoon Morakot or the 0823 flood standard for drainage, but you also have no way of knowing what standards to use to avoid flooding. (Interviewee B)

After the 0206 earthquake in 2016, the community realized that this Houjia fault is closed to our community and has been looking at the community's own disaster prevention and relief response, which should be very important. (Interviewee C)

This community was originally a vulnerable area to flooding, so for the safety of the people. Most of the residents in our community are relatively old. Young people live in urban buildings. Old houses [often encountering flooding] house old people. (Interviewee E)

whom 159 completed the response to the questionnaire and other related issues. The Taipei City Fire Department then selected four communities to participate in DPPP based on the standards (Taipei City Disaster Prevention Info Website 2019).

In summary, the willingness of the community to participate plays a very important role. The community is facing the problem of aging population and insufficient resources; however, the community is currently facing risks from natural disasters, and insufficient input from young people. Therefore, DPPP helps to connect different actors to work on building resilient communities together. The planning and implementation process DPPP has implied the driving force of the CGR framework proposed by Emerson et al. (2012), which is shared motivation; specifically, the wake-up of community risk awareness can be described as such shared motivation.

Participation, Multi-level Governance, and Translational Leaders

There are at least four types and scopes of collaborative governance: internal governance, horizontal intergovernmental governance, vertical intergovernmental governance, and cross-sectoral collaborative governance (Chen 2004). Vertical inter-government governance can be practiced through hierarchical control, communication and coordination, etc.; however, from the perspective of the community, each citizen makes their own decision on whether to participate. In the process of urbanization and urban governance, young and middle-aged people usually spend more time on work and family; in other words, those who are willing and have time to participate in community activities are naturally older.[2] The government is leading the plan, but the community is understaffed. In

---

[2] When worked with several buildings in the community to do fire drills, only a few want to participate without incentive. When contacted the building residents, there were no more than ten persons to join. Life and property are important to them, but no one wants to participate (always no time in week days or even in the weekend). The incentive turns into giving away gifts. (Interviewee D)

There are also many members belonging to the elderly, because during the daytime, the elderly will be invited to participate (the training course of resilient community), and young people go to work. Most of the community volunteers or participants have already retired. The older people rarely use computers. (Interviewee G)

This is the same situation when the National Fire Agency promoted fire prevention. Many people who came to participate are elderly or retirees. (Interviewee I-1)

addition to the government's investment plan and manpower, different levels government also need to invest manpower support. From the interviewees' responses, it is apparent that community leaders are also playing the critical and transforming role of disaster management in the building of resilient community.

Recent research has emphasized the role and function of translational leaders in building a resilient community. They can integrate various disparate networks, opinions, and knowledge systems into a harmonious whole. These translational leaders also promote adaptive governance during the process—that is, the integration of formal systems and informal networks to promote the capacity to respond to risk. The community's collaborative risk governance system can be divided into more subsystems. Of course, the role of translational leaders is not only limited Village Chiefs.[3] Each system and subsystem needs to create the role of translational leader for more resilient systems (Wang 2019; Zolli and Healy 2012).

In addition to the support of the government plan, the use of computer documents and the sharing of knowledge and information are even more important for the chief of the resilient community. Resilient communities also have relevant courses to train community members to recognize the importance of disaster information and knowledge. When the community faces a disaster or crisis, the neighboring universities will also support the community.

In summary, through resilience community training courses and making good use of human resources in the community, it will help create more synergistic risk governance and translational leadership roles. In the DPPP, including the Village Chiefs, the university teams, district offices, and municipal city or county government disaster management offices can all play important roles.

---

[3] The education levels of the Village Chiefs are also uneven. Almost everything in planning and organizing activities now requires paperwork, so people who can do paperwork are also very important. The community needs some volunteers, such as calling on some retired civil servants. (Interviewee B)

Because [collaborative team] there are partners from National Central University, as well as from the fire department. (Interviewee H)

Since the Morakot Typhoon in 2009, some problems have come out. Everyone started asking for better disaster prevention. However, many of the civil servants resigned the positions of disaster management officers within one or two years, and they changed to a new civil servant to start again. Therefore, the entire disaster prevention system was not built up at all. Fortunately in recent years, there is DPPP, and the collaborative partner in this city is Fengjia University. (Interviewee I-1)

The Community's Willingness to Participate and the Network Management Strategies

Koppenjan and Klijn (2004) viewed the network as a more unstable social relationship between interdependent actors. Interactions between networks are generally as complex as the interests of actors and policy concepts, so their corresponding solutions must also be different. In other words, when network participants have different motivations, interests, or cognitions, of course their interaction strategies will also be more diverse, which will affect the effectiveness of interaction. In DPPP, since the first phase has been invited by the city/county government, fire department, or district office with the villages willing to participate in the promotion of resilient community, naturally facilitating the community providing incentives or activating strategy to induce resource exchange. The formation of a synthesizing interactive strategy that emphasizes the learning or cooperation of multiple participants has been also found in this chapter.[4]

Take Taipei City as an example. After the implementation of DPPP in the four major communities in Taipei City in 2019, there will be a meeting involving the Taipei City Fire Department, the District Office, the Village Chief, and the collaborative team from academia. Then, through the enlightenment start-up activities, the complex professional knowledge or disaster prevention information is converted into common knowledge that residents can easily absorb through easy-to-understand text or schematic diagrams, and residents have a more intimate and vivid understanding of the potential disasters facing the community. After that, the community environmental exploration, disaster prevention, and relief issues countermeasures were discussed, and disaster prevention and relief units or organizations were established in the community (Taipei City Disaster Prevention Info Website 2019).

---

[4] In the beginning, there are several selected criteria. The first is to value the community's willingness to participate. The willingness part probably accounts for the first priority. (Interviewee I-2)

Last year, the city government held a meeting about DPPP then. Being a new Village Chief, I wanted to learn and then brought this resource into OO Village and let the people know some prevention, common sense, and knowledge in all aspects before and after the disaster. At the meanwhile, the DPPP can provide some resources to help the community improve the situation of floods. (Interviewee G)

For disaster management, the willingness of the community to invest is critical. The above-mentioned interviews and the example of the implementation of the DPPP process in Taipei City show that the willingness to participate contributes to the activation of network interaction and the application of comprehensive strategies. For example, the application for the plan by the Village Chief is also an investment of the community to reduce risks, which will bring resources to the community and also help to establish network partnership. The participation of community members can promote the strengthening and exchange of network relationships. The implementation of DPPP in Taipei City also reflects that the willingly participating communities have strong motivation to learn about disaster management.

Conclusion

With the rise of governance, this concept has also greatly influenced the philosophy of risk. The most important aspect is that with the participation of multiple stakeholders, risk governance no longer emphasizes "control," like traditional risk management; instead, it is inter-governmental and cross-sectoral. In other words, building a resilient community is not about creating a zero-risk community, but how quickly the community can respond to the impact of risks and disasters and make better preparations for the future. From the example of DPPP in Taiwan, it can be successfully practiced through collaborative risk governance. Besides, communication, coordination, integration, and cooperation have already become the core values of risk governance. That is to say why different actors participate in the network of risk governance and how to interact with each other have become important factors affecting the effectiveness of collaborative risk governance. In this chapter, through in-depth interviews, the key factors to collaborative risk governance can be explored. This chapter believes that in collaborative risk governance, the willingness of participation, the sharing of information and knowledge, and the interaction strategies of network actors are very influential to the collaborative outcomes.

This research adopted Taiwan's DPPP as an example. It shows that it is not easy to plan and executive such a long-term three-phased project which is more than 10 years. This shows that different ruling parties in Taiwan have agreed that it is important and meaningful to work together

6 PARTICIPATION WILLINGNESS AND INTERACTIVE ... 135

to improve disaster prevention and relief capabilities in the community. In addition, increasing motivation and willingness to participate in the community can often have a positive impact on promoting resilient communities. In particular, the willingness to participate will affect the results of the actor's interactive strategy of activating and synthesizing. On the one hand, the higher willingness to participate in DPPP will naturally not exclude new network actors, such as university partner teams or government officials, and the participants will be more able to accept the results discussed by multiple participants. On the other hand, a higher willingness to participate also helps to improve learning motivation, and thus achieve the effect of mutual learning and mutual growth in a synthesized strategy. Therefore, continuous training, education, communication, and the design of incentive structures to ensure the willingness of participation will be the goals that can be sustained in the next stage for collaborative risk governance.

REFERENCES

Agranoff, R., and M. McGuire. 2001. Big Questions in Public Network Management Research. *Journal of Public Administration Research and Theory* 11 (3): 295–326. https://doi.org/10.1093/oxfordjournals.jpart.a003504.

Bang, H.P., and E. Sorensen. 1999. The Everyday Maker: A New Challenge to Democratic Governance. *Administration Theory & Praxis* 21 (3): 325–341. https://doi.org/10.1080/10841806.1999.11643381.

Berner, M.M., J.M. Amos, and R.S. Morse. 2011. What Constitutes Effective Citizen Participation in Local Government? Views from City Stakeholders. *Public Administration Quarterly* 35 (1): 128–163. doi:https://doi.org/10.2307/41804544.

Chen, C.W. 2004. Administrative Accountability: Strategies to Strengthen Local Governance Capacity. *Journal of Policy Research* 4: 23–46. (in Chinese). https://doi.org/10.7070/pr.200405.0023.

Chowdhury, M.R. 2011. Bridging the Public-Private Partnership in Disaster Management in Bangladesh. In *Community Disaster Recovery and Resilience*, ed. D.S. Miller and J.D. Rivera, 395–422. New York, NY: CRC Press.

Comfort, L. 1999. *Shared Risk: Complex Systems in Seismic Response.* UK: Emerald Group Publishing Limited.

Emerson, K., T. Nabatchi, and S. Balogh. 2012. An Integrative Framework for Collaborative Governance. *Journal of Public Administration Research and Theory* 22 (1): 1–29. https://doi.org/10.1093/jopart/mur011.

ETtoday. 2016. The Chinese Search and Rescue Team Looks Like Part-Time Jobs? City Government: Official Command is not accepted. *ETtoday,* Feburary

14. Accessed 20 Sept 2019. https://www.ettoday.net/news/20160214/647 056.htm.

Fountain, J.E. 1994. Comment: Disciplining Public Management Research. *Journal of Policy Analysis and Management* 13 (2): 269–277. https://doi.org/10.2307/3325012.

Grimsey, D., and M.K. Lewis. 2004. *Public Private Partnerships: The Worldwide Revolution in Infrastructure Provision and Project Finance.* Northampton, MA: Edward Elgar.

Herranz Jr, J. 2006. Network Management Strategies. Working Paper No. 2006-01. Daniel J. Evans School of Public Affairs, University of Washington, Seattle, WA.

Jan, C.Y. 2013. The Disaster Reduction Dtrategy in Taiwan: Decision-Making, Community, Collaborative Accountability, and Information. *Fudan Public Administration Review* 10: 76–79. (in Chinese).

Johnston, E.W., D. Hicks, N. Nan, and J.C. Auer. 2011. Managing the Inclusion Process in Collaborative Governance. *Journal of Public Administration Research and Theory* 21 (4): 699–721. https://doi.org/10.2307/41342601.

Kapucu, N. 2008. Collaborative Emergency Management: Better Community Organising, Better Public Preparedness and Response. *Disasters* 32 (2): 239–262. https://doi.org/10.1111/j.1467-7717.2008.01037.x.

Kapucu, N. 2013. Collaborative Governance and Disaster Recovery: The National Disaster Recovery Framework (NDRF). In US. *Disaster Recovery,* 41–59. Tokyo: Springer. https://doi.org/10.1007/978-4-431-54255-1_3.

Kapucu, N., T. Arslan, and F. Demiroz. 2010. Collaborative Emergency Management and National Emergency Management Network. *Disaster Prevention and Management* 19 (4): 452–468. https://doi.org/10.1108/096535610 11070376.

Kapucu, N., and F. Demiroz. 2015. A Social Network Analysis Approach to Strengthening Nonprofit Collaboration. *The Journal of Applied Management & Entrepreneurship* 20 (1): 87–101. https://doi.org/10.9774/GLEAF. 3709.2015.ja.00007.

Karimova, T. 2016. Sustainable Development and Disasters. In *Research Handbook on Disasters and International Law,* ed. S.C. Breau and K.L. Samuel, 177–203. UK: Edward Elgar Publishing.

Khoshdel, M.K., and Y. Bakhshan. 2015. Measuring Willingness to Participate and the Factors Affecting Citizen Participation (Case Study on Citizens in the 20th Municipal District of Tehran). *Mediterranean Journal of Social Sciences* 6(3 S2): 155. https://doi.org/10.5901/mjss.2015.v6n3s2p155.

Koller, G.R. 2007. *Modern Corporate Risk Management: A Blueprint for Positive Change and Effectiveness.* Boca Raton, FL: J Ross Publishing.

Kooiman, J. 1993. Governance and Governability: Using Complexity, Dynamics, and Diversity. In *Modern Governance: New Government-Society Interactions*, ed. J. Kooiman, 35–48. Newbury Park, CA: Sage.

Koppenjan, J.F.M., and E.H. Klijn. 2004. *Managing Uncertainties in Networks: A Network Approach to Problem Solving and Decision Making*. London: Routledge.

Kuo, M.F., C.Y. Wang, Y.Y. Chang, and T.S. Li. 2015. Collaborative Disaster Management: Lessons from Taiwan's Local Governments. In *The Road to Collaborative Governance in China*, ed. Yijia Jing, 147–170. New York, NY: Palgrave-Macmillan.

Liu, I.C. 2006. The Research of Public Network Management and Its Performance Evaluation. *Public Administration and Policy* 42: 107–142. (in Chinese).

McGuire, M., and R. Agranoff. 2014. Network Management Behaviors. In *Network Theory in the Public Sector: Building New Theoretical Frameworks*, ed. R. Keast, M.P. Mandell, and R. Agranoff, 137–156. New York, NY: Routledge.

Medury, U. 2011. Building Disaster-Resilient Communities: The Public-Private Partnership Approach. In *Community Disaster Recovery and Resilience*, ed. D.S. Miller and J.D. Rivera, 423–445. New York, NY: CRC Press.

Moynihan, D.P. 2003. Normative and Instrumental Perspectives on Public Participation Citizen Summits in Washington D.C. *American Review of Public Administration* 33 (2): 164–188. https://doi.org/10.1177/027507400325 1379.

Moynihan, D.P. 2009. The Network Governance of Crisis Response: Case Studies of Incident Command Systems. *Journal of Public Administration Research and Theory* 19: 895–915. https://doi.org/10.2139/ssrn.1311597.

Nation Fire Agency. 2018. The Introduction of Promoting Resilient Community. http://pdmcb.nfa.gov.tw/dc/intro. *Nation Fire Agency*, June 1. Accessed 11 Dec 2019.

O'Toole, L.J. 1997. Treating Networks Seriously: Practical and Research-Based Agendas in Public Administration. *Public Administration Review* 57 (1): 45–52. https://doi.org/10.2307/976691.

Research, Development and Evaluation Commission, the Executive Yuan (RDEC). 2013. *The Benefit Evaluation and Policy Recommendations of the Five-Year Term Disaster Prevention and Protection Project*. Taipei City: RDEC. (in Chinese).

Raungratanaamporna, I-soon, P. Pakdeeburee, A. Kamiko, and C. Denpaiboon. 2014. Government-Communities Collaboration in Disaster Management Activity: Investigation in the Current Flood Disaster Management Policy in Thailand. *Procedia Environmental Sciences* 20: 658–667. https://doi.org/10.1016/j.proenv.2014.03.079.

Sarokhani, B. 1991. *Encyclopedia of Social Sciences*. Tehran: Keyhan Publications.

Smith, D., and B. Toft. 1998. Risk and Crisis Management in the Public Sector: Editorial: Issues in Public Sector Risk Management. *Public Money & Management* 18 (4): 7–10. https://doi.org/10.1111/1467-9302.00133.

Stoker, G. 1998. Governance as Theory: Five Propositions. *International Social Science Journal* 50 (155): 17–28. https://doi.org/10.1111/1468-2451.00106.

Taipei City Disaster Prevention Info Website. 2019. The Final Reports of Communities Disasters Prevention. *Taipei City Disaster Prevention Info Website*, October 25. https://www.eoc.gov.taipei/News/Details/b1d32bc5-20bc-4b32-8c9c-f222dbf323f4. Accessed 2 June 2020. (in Chinese).

Taipei City Government. 2016. The Mayor Concerns About Disaster Prevention and Pays Attention to the Citizen Disaster Prevention Manual. *City Press Release*, March 1. https://www.gov.taipei/News_Content.aspx?n=F0DDAF49B89E9413&sms=72544237BBE4C5F6&s=C2D2CAECDE11E71F. Accessed 2 June 2020. (in Chinese).

Tong, X., and H. Zhang. 2012. *Emergency Management in China: Theory, Practice, Policy*. Beijing: Social Science Press. (in Chinese).

Tseng, K.-C. 2011. Becoming Reluctant Partners? An Institutionalist Explanation on a Futile Case of Public-Private Partnerships (PPPs). *Taiwan Democracy Quarterly*, 8(4): 83–133. https://doi.org/10.6448/tdq.201112.0089. (in Chinese).

United Nations. (UN). 2015. Sendai Framework for Disaster Risk Reduction 2015–2030. *United Nations (UN)*, June 1. https://www.preventionweb.net/files/43291_sendaiframeworkfordrren.pdf. Accessed 15 June 2019.

Wang, C.Y. 2012. Do Plans Ever Keep Up with Changes? A Study on the Impact of Risk Factors on Strategic Management in Taiwan local government. *Soochow Journal of Political Science* 30(3): 109–159. https://doi.org/0.6418/SJPS.201209.0109. (in Chinese).

Wang, C.Y. 2019. *Collaborative Disaster Governance: The Building of Resilient System and Network Management Strategy*. Taipei City: Wu-nan Culture Enterprise. (in Chinese).

Wu, W.N., and S.M. Chang. 2018. Collaboration Mechanisms of Taiwan Nonprofit Organizations in Disaster Relief Efforts: Drawing Lessons from the Wenchuan Earthquake and Typhoon Morakot. *Sustainability* 10 (11): 4328–4342. https://doi.org/10.3390/su10114328.

Zolli, A., and A.M. Healy. 2012. *Resilience: Why Things Bounce Back*. New York, NY: Simon and Schuster Paperbacks.

PART III

Risk Management in a New Era

CHAPTER 7

Postmodern Risks: The Fourth Industrial Revolution in East Asia

Daniel Connolly

INTRODUCTION

East Asia and the rest of the world are facing an era of unprecedented technological disruption known as the Fourth Industrial Revolution, or 4IR. This term refers to a series of innovative new business models and digital technologies which are widely anticipated to drive unprecedented economic growth in the twenty-first century. The revolutionary consequences of the 4IR stem from phenomenal increases in automation and connectivity, which are enabling the creation of distributed networks dedicated to the rapid digitalization, distribution, and application of unprecedented volumes of real-world data, a process known as the Physical-Digital-Physical Loop (PDP). These new technologies and business models are expected to dramatically alter how our economies, political systems, and societies work (Schwab 2016; Schwab and Davis 2018). To maintain economic competitiveness, South Korea, China,

---

D. Connolly (✉)
Division of International Studies, Hankuk University of
Foreign Studies, Seoul, South Korea
e-mail: danielc@hufs.ac.kr

© The Author(s), under exclusive license to Springer Nature
Singapore Pte Ltd. 2021
Y. Jing et al. (eds.), *Risk Management in East Asia*,
https://doi.org/10.1007/978-981-33-4586-7_7

141

142   D. CONNOLLY

and Japan have all embarked on ambitious government-led initiatives to implement the Fourth Industrial Revolution.

Although the 4IR is often described as creating infinite possibilities for the human species, each previous industrial revolution has transformed humanity's risk landscape, with some hazards fading away and new ones emerging. Therefore, in an era of private and government-led efforts to engineer the next industrial revolution, it is urgent for scholars to question how this new paradigm will affect the nature of risk in the twenty-first century.

This chapter begins by introducing the origins and development of the 4IR concept and then situates it in relation to mainstream approaches to risk management. On one hand, the greatly enhanced data processing capacity of 4IR business models and technologies promise to solve many of the challenges facing human societies and will greatly facilitate the management of many natural and human-made risks. However, there is a dark side to the 4IR because it is creating new types of *postmodern technological hazards* that threaten the mental integrity and autonomy of human individuals and groups. These hazards, which arise from phenomenal advancements in datafication and predictive analytics as well as new business models that seek to control human behavior, depart significantly from traditional forms of physical risk associated with technological assemblages.

In the second half of the chapter, these emerging hazards are illustrated by zooming in and examining cases of fake news and digital addiction in South Korea, one of the world's most connected societies. Although these cases are only precursors of 4IR hazards, they highlight some of the key challenges that stakeholders have in conceptualizing and responding to postmodern risks. These cases also underscore how the systemic erosion of human autonomy and agency through distributed technological interventions is already happening and that the 4IR may have existential consequences for contemporary societies as well as future generations.

What is the Fourth Industrial Revolution?

The Fourth Industrial Revolution is talked about more often than it is defined. Indeed, policymakers are sometimes caught using the term without a clear understanding of what it means, such as the widely publicized failures to explain the 4IR by UK Labour leader Jeremey Corbyn in 2016 and Deputy President Mabuza in South Africa in 2019 (Colson

2016; Head 2019). Further complicating matters, the term Fourth Industrial Revolution coexists with several other terms covering the same set of processes such as *Industry 4.0, convergence,* and *digital transformation.* An additional complication is the tendency of the popular media to focus on individual technologies, such as the *AI revolution* or the *Cloud Computing revolution.* This complex mix of hype and overlapping terminologies, in the words of one business consultant, has created a twofold challenge: "What exactly is Industry 4.0 and how do we sift through the B.S. to find the facts?" (Durand 2018).

The first step is going back to the term's origins. The classical definition of the Fourth Industrial Revolution was first put forward by Klaus Schwab in his 2016 book of the same name, which envisioned human history as a series of economic and technological paradigm shifts beginning with the development of steam engines in the nineteenth century. The second industrial revolution, which Schwab dates from the late nineteenth to the early twentieth centuries, consisted of electrification and mass production. The third industrial revolution, which started in the 1960s, saw the creation of the Internet and automated production but is already transitioning into a new stage of human development. According to Schwab (2016), the 4IR is a paradigm shift characterized by rapid technological change that will witness the blurring of physical, digital, and biological boundaries. In a later book, he elaborated that the 4IR is being driven by twelve clusters of new and emerging technologies, including quantum computing, blockchain, virtual reality, and artificial intelligence (Schwab and Davis 2018).

However, Schwab did not create the 4IR concept out of a vacuum; rather, he adapted it from the earlier concept of Industry 4.0, which was pioneered by the German government in its 2006 high-tech plan. Industry 4.0 was originally far more limited in scope than the 4IR because it focused on the creation of a "brave new world of decentralized, autonomous real-time production" by applying new technologies to the manufacturing sector (Germany Trade & Invest 2014, 4). Moreover, even as recently as 2014, the term was little known outside of the German language (Lasi et al. 2014). Although early Industry 4.0 documents also spoke of a fourth industrial revolution, it was conceptualized narrowly as a revolution in production. Schwab's key contribution was extrapolating how these processes of automation and networking were restructuring all of society, not just the factory.

Today, the terms 4IR and Industry 4.0 are used nearly synonymously to refer to the technological transformations occurring in workplaces and the rest of society. But broadening the term and using it beyond its original engineering milieu has come at a significant cost in clarity. The 4IR has alternatively become shorthand for technological innovation, disruption, and economic opportunities, which is probably why many policymakers struggle to define what the term means. Ultimately, the 4IR is used in so many contexts, by so many actors, that it risks becoming an empty signifier (see Cammaerts 2013). However, by going back to the engineering and technical literature that first spawned the 4IR concept we can gain a firmer grasp of what it is and how it is radically restructuring our world.

Unlike earlier industrial revolutions, the 4IR does not consist of a single technology; rather, it consists of a complex intermeshing of hardware and techniques such as big data analytics, the Internet of Things (IoT), cloud computing, machine learning, and autonomous machines, to name only a few prominent examples. In this regard, the 4IR can be classified as a combined-system revolution rather than a single-system revolution (see Hundley 1999). This means that the 4IR cannot be easily understood by merely assessing the intrinsic features and limitations of its underlying technological systems.

Instead, the 4IR needs to be understood as a conceptual shift in how organizations collect, share, and use data. Identifying the 4IR as a new philosophy not only helps anticipate shifts in how organizations are restructuring themselves but also helps explain how technological change, such as the lower cost and miniaturization of microchips or the emergence of cloud computing, which initially enabled this new thinking about data, is now also being driven and reinforced by it. Viewing the 4IR as a philosophy has the additional advantage that it moves our focus away from speculative and indeterminate debates about the intrinsic nature of the underlying technologies and instead focuses our attention on the purposes of these assemblages.

The purpose of the 4IR is simple: to make better decisions by utilizing previously untapped sources of data. As such, the 4IR is perhaps best understood as a civilian variant of the Revolution in Military Affairs (RMA), which ambitiously attempted to use new digital technologies to remove the fog-of-war from military operations (see Connolly 2019). The method by which the 4IR seeks to create better decision-making can be conceptualized as a datafication cycle. This cycle, which is referred to in the engineering literature as a Physical-Digital-Physical Loop (PDP) (Daecher et al. 2018), consists of three interlocking stages which are described below.

The first stage is *datafication*, or the digitalization of real-world objects and processes. Early proponents of Industry 4.0 envisioned networking all the machinery in a factory to create a cyberphysical system that could be monitored in real-time (Wang et al. 2016). Today this digitalization has spread into all parts of our lives, including the scanning of old library books and famous works of art, or Google's ambitious attempt to continuously map and visualize the human geography of the entire planet (Coyle 2006; Bernardini et al. 2002; Gorelick et al. 2017). Additionally, the evolution of the Internet from a read-only technology to a read-write platform has fueled a phenomenal increase in datafication, which now includes information on human preferences and behavior. Social media platforms, such as Facebook, have effectively encouraged people to voluntarily upload vast volumes of their textual, photographic, and video data for free. In 2012, for example, Facebook reported that it was "ingesting" 500 terabytes of data each day (Constine 2012). The miniaturization of sensors and the proliferation of smart devices has made self-digitalization a prominent feature of contemporary social life (Neff and Nafus 2016).

The vastly expanded technological capacity to capture and archive digital traces is just the beginning. The second element of the 4IR consists of the safe and secure *distribution* of this data within and between organizations. This is often referred to as horizontal and vertical integration (Petrillo et al. 2018, 9). At the engineering level, theorists of the 4IR focus on the need for interoperability through common standards and celebrate the potential of new technologies, such as 5G and blockchain, to facilitate connectivity (Tapscott and Tapscott 2016; The Institute of Internal Auditors 2019). Augmented and virtual reality, by creating high-fidelity representations of data, are also celebrated in the literature for conveying information more accurately than other methods (Yuen et al. 2011). However, many 4IR advocates also stipulate that there is a strong need for institutional changes and new mindsets to enable the sharing of information. Kelly (2018), for instance, argues that corporate management in the 4IR must focus on cultivating decentralized flows of information, a radical departure from the hierarchical control of data seen in traditional business models.

Ultimately, the purpose of this data collection and transmission is the facilitation of *decision-making* that alters the real-world. This also requires institutional reform aimed at creating decentralized organizations where decisions can be made rapidly by local actors instead of a centralized and distant leadership. This is expected to result in heightened levels of efficiency, productivity, and flexibility (Petrillo et al. 2018, 12). As illustrated by theoretical work on the observation-orientation-decision-action time loop (OODA), individuals and organizations that process data faster and make more accurate decisions have a competitive edge over their rivals (Boyd 2007). Smart factories, for example, are celebrated for being able to customize products in real-time based on consumer demand (Burke et al. 2017). An important technological innovation at this stage of the datafication cycle is the growing tendency to outsource decisions to autonomous systems. An Industry 4.0 brochure boasts "industrial machinery no longer simply processes the product, but that the product communicates with the machinery to tell it exactly what to do" (Germany Trade & Invest 2014, 4). A frequent example of this in the engineering literature is predictive maintenance by machines that anticipate when a component is going to wear out and order a replacement before the breakdown occurs.[1]

The 4IR datafication cycle and associated technologies combine historically unprecedented leaps in connectivity and automation to allow faster and more accurate decision-making. They also allow data collection, transmission, and decision-making to be folded into autonomous or semi-autonomous systems that are distributed horizontally rather than arranged in hierarchical structures. These attributes are truly revolutionary because they have the potential to transform economies, political systems, and societies. As we will discuss below, they also transform our conceptualizations and management of risk.

Positive and Negative Impacts of the 4IR on Risk Management

According to Lupton (1999) there are several major approaches to understanding risk. The governmentality approach highlights the role of experts and normalization processes in categorizing "at risk" populations. The second is the risk society approach, which focuses on explicating the structural shifts in the contemporary world that contribute to the globalization of complex risks such as climate change and financial crises. The third and most dominant approach is the technoscientific perspective that is narrowly concerned with empirically measuring and calculating risk.

These approaches can be understood as a spectrum with social constructivist perspectives at one end and scientific realism at the other. Leveraging these divergent approaches can help us identify the positive as well as negative consequences of the 4IR.

Positive Impacts

The techniques and technologies of the 4IR have the clearest utility from the technoscientific perspective of risk management. In his classic work on industrial accidents, Perrow (1984) argued that disasters occur because large socio-technical organizations are too complex for hierarchical decision-makers to accurately understand what is happening. However, the 4IR's central premise is that new approaches to data collection, storage, transmission, and application will make organizations more transparent and responsive. Moreover, decentralized decision-making can detect problems early and resolve them while they are still small. It is noteworthy that the key features of High Reliability Organization (HRO) identified in the literature (see Summerton and Berner 2003, 14–16), such as adaptive decision-making and multidirectional dataflows, are also attributes celebrated by proponents of the 4IR.

The 4IR's impact on risk management is best understood in relation to the datafication cycle. First, the accelerating digitalization and datafication of people and things allows better risk management because hazards are better measured, which means that risk probabilities can be calculated more accurately. Therefore, new data collection technologies, such as remote sensing, vastly improve our ability to understand natural and environmental risks (Gomez and Purdie 2016). Likewise, the datafication of human populations has practical benefits, as exemplified by researchers using social media posts to trace disease outbreaks (Gao et al. 2018).

Second, the secure and accurate sharing of this information within an organization will allow faster decisions and more effective responses to disasters or accidents when they do occur. This is exemplified by the recent partnership between the UN Human Rights Office and Microsoft to create an early warning system called Rights View, which will synthesize dataflows from a variety of public and UN sources so that UN officials can have a real-time picture of global human rights violations and emerging crises. As with predictive maintenance in a factory, the goal of this system is to use data to identify problems before they happen: "The

148   D. CONNOLLY

best intervention from the UN is one that stops the human rights crisis from occurring" (Ith 2017).

In fact, the growing use of autonomous machines and processes creates the promise of self-optimizing systems that can reduce risks for human users. Autonomous cars, for example, are expected to reduce worldwide traffic fatalities by 90%, which would potentially save ten million lives per decade (Fleetwood 2017, 532). Moreover, as sensors and computing power become more accessible, these self-adjusting systems could be tailored for individuals. An ambitious plan, outlined by computer researchers in 2015, would use extreme connectivity and real-time data to protect individual users. This is how they describe the system:

> Data from public IoT [Internet of Things] infrastructure like snapshots of individuals, position of patrol vehicles, vehicular and human traffic, weather conditions etc. is also collected at the cloud. Based on this consolidated data and historical profile of a woman, security decisions are taken for her. (Sehgal et al. 2015, 256)

In subsequent scenarios, the researchers describe the protective software automatically sending distress signals to the authorities if the user is attacked or recommending that a trip be canceled because of road conditions (Sehgal et al. 2015, 261).

The datafication cycle ultimately creates the possibility of digital twins. A digital twin is a real-time virtual model or simulation of a real-world process, machine, or organization. These digital representations are valuable for engineers because they allow the physical counterpart to be observed, controlled, and even simulated, thereby creating a fully functional cyber-physical system (Yun et al. 2017). For risk managers, digital twins are key innovations because they "deliver meaningful, actionable insights with powerful visualisations of risk and activity" (Menon 2019). For example, the basic premise behind predictive maintenance is that the collection and analysis of large amounts of real-time data can prevent catastrophic failures in complex systems (Wang 2016, 264). Thus, new datafication technologies of the 4IR are particularly exciting for insurance companies, which anticipate insurance becoming preventative rather than restorative. In the words of one insurance executive: "Wouldn't it be great if rather than sending a team of people to clear up after a flood, we were able to tell somebody they are beginning to have a leak?" (David Williams of AXA as quoted in Marketforce and TIBCO Software 2017,

8) In short, if calculating risk accurately is one of the "prime catalysts that drives modern Western society" (Bernstein 1998, 1), then the 4IR has the potential to propel humanity farther than ever before.

New Risks

Although the 4IR has clear advantages for managing risks from the technoscientific perspective, the risk society and governmentality approaches are less optimistic. Broadly classified as sociocultural theories of risk, these approaches are more critical of expert knowledge and emphasize how human interventions and subjectivities are important for creating as well as distributing risk in contemporary societies.[2] In other words, the technologies of the 4IR may enable us to better calculate existing types of risk but they may come at the cost of creating complex new hazards.

As a result, there are vocal groups of scholars and activists concerned about the negative consequences of the 4IR. A major point of contention is the risk of widespread technological unemployment due to automation.[3] There are also persistent concerns about the security implications of deeply interconnected societies, as one group of researchers explain: "Having everything attached to everything else in the IoT is going to monumentally increase the vulnerabilities present in any given network" (Xu et al. 2018, 93). Finally, another strand of activism focuses on the health-impact of radio-frequency electromagnetic fields, especially 5G networks. In fact, WHO's International Agency for Research on Cancer (2011) classified these fields as possibly carcinogenic for humans and subsequent researchers have linked them to a variety of biomedical effects, including metabolic and neurological changes, and miscarriages (see Di Ciaula 2018; Li et al. 2017).

These controversies underscore Beck's (1992, 29–30) observation that contemporary risk society is characterized by sharp disagreements between experts as well as between experts and civilians and that private sector actors and economic interests are increasingly important in creating and distributing new risks. Indeed, some of these emerging 4IR technologies are so economically important that governments, regulators, and companies may be incentivized to downplay risks. For example, one prominent corporation's effort to extol the commercial potential of 5G not only fails to mention possible health effects but recommends the doubling of the world's mobile base stations (Ericsson 2018).

Although economic disruptions and subtle but pervasive health consequences need to be considered, the rest of this chapter focuses on an entirely new category of risks being created by 4IR datafication cycles. These new hazards constitute an important gap in existing conceptualizations of risk because they are immaterial threats to human autonomy and agency rather than physical threats to human bodies or the environment. Although Ulrich Beck's conceptualization of risk society remains relevant for many features of the 4IR, namely the globalized nature of the new technologies, the discursive struggles between expert communities, and the role of subpolitics in shaping the implementation of these new systems, the risks he focused on are traditional ones—disease, environmental pollution, and industrial accidents (Beck 1992, 22–24, 27). Even emerging debates over electromagnetic fields fits securely in this tradition and are amenable to technoscientific calculative approaches, i.e., more empirical studies. But it is necessary to also examine a new category of *postmodern technological hazards* that threaten human decision-making and identity formation. These new threats are labeled as *postmodern* in this chapter because they represent an entirely new category of hazard that are digital rather than material. Although intangible, these risks are serious and require new theorizing by risk managers.

Put succinctly, 4IR datafication cycles are increasingly encompassing individuals and communities and these improvements in connectivity and automation have drastically expanded the technical capacity to manipulate human decision-making. These improvements are the result of two interrelated processes. First are technical improvements in collecting data on human cognition and mental processes, including MRI scanners and cameras capable of capturing individuals' micro-expressions and subcutaneous blood flows.[4] Second, the sharing of personal data, primarily through social media sites, has allowed the creation of large datasets that allow human behavior and personality to be systematically studied. In 2013, for example, researchers found that Facebook Likes, an easily accessible digital record of behavior, could be used to predict individuals' psychodemographic profiles, such as sexual preferences, race, and political affiliations (Kosinski et al. 2013).

This accelerating datafication of individuals, groups, and entire societies has facilitated the creation of increasingly accurate digital representations of large populations, thereby facilitating their manipulation. This is exemplified by Cambridge Analytica, a now-defunct consultancy that illegally used information from its partnership with Facebook to create personality profiles of millions of US citizens in 2016. These virtual models of people's personalities were then used to create tailored political advertisements (Hern 2018). Facebook itself admitted in 2014 that it manipulated the moods of a half million of its users both upward and downward by altering the content of their feeds in a mass experiment (Goel 2014). The project's researchers concluded that they had successfully demonstrated emotional contagion via networks and additionally observed that "online messages influence our experience of emotions, which may affect a variety of offline behaviors" (Kramer et al. 2014, 8790).

For scholars working from the governmentality approach, these new capacities for manipulation are viewed in the context of a long tradition of expert-led interventions in managing human populations. For example, a study on using social media digital footprints to predict personality types largely justifies itself by referring to the value of being able to individually tailor health care messages (Azucar et al. 2017, 151). However, what is changing in the 4IR is that these capabilities are proliferating. Rather than government bureaucracies and experts working to nudge people in the public interest, the private sector is at the forefront of attempts to use these new and emerging techniques to influence individual's purchasing habits (Wu 2017). As will be shown below in the case of Korea, these commercialized habit-forming technologies are already generating complicated and unique forms of risk.

Case Study—South Korea and New Risks from Emerging Technologies

Although the benefits and risks associated with the 4IR are global in scope, East Asia's prominent role in the development and implementation of digital technologies means that these effects will be felt in the region first. South Korea, especially, is one of the world's most connected societies. The country's position as an "Internet powerhouse" is attributed to strong government regulatory and policy support as well as a culture open to new technologies (Shin and Koh 2017, 37). The Korean government, eager to maintain its technological edge, has responded actively to the 4IR, which was a hot issue in the 2017 presidential election campaign. President Moon subsequently created a Presidential Committee on the Fourth Industrial Revolution (PCFIR) in August 2017. Currently, there are no fewer than thirteen government ministries implementing 4IR

152   D. CONNOLLY

initiatives (Sung 2018, 44). However, when these initiatives consider 4IR-related risks, they mostly focus on economic ones—especially the risks of not implementing this revolution—rather than the possibility of generating unique types of hazards.[5]

This section argues that Korea's highly connected society serves as a useful case study of the impact of new technologies. Specifically, two socio-technical issues in the country are identified as precursors of post-modern hazards created by the 4IR. First is the dissemination of fake news, best known because of the Druking scandal in 2018 but also exemplified by the country's infamous netizen culture. The contamination of information ecosystems, while reminiscent of the concept of "anxiety communities" (Beck 1992, 51), is a unique type of technological hazard and raises key concerns about distributed threats to mental integrity. The second example is the ongoing debate in Korean society over Internet addiction and children's access to online computer games, specifically the Shutdown Law of 2011, which attempted to create game curfews for children. Indeed, criticisms of online computer games foreshadow many of the key concerns raised by 4IR technologies, especially their focus on manipulating the emotional and cognitive states of users. In both examples, these new technological hazards are shown to have serious societal consequences, but key stakeholders lack consensus on how to define these hazards, assign responsibility, or devise appropriate policy responses.

Fake News and the Druking Controversy

The blurring of digital and physical spaces predicted by proponents of the 4IR is already attested to in the case of South Korean politics and society. The first wave of academic scholarship on the interpenetration of cyberspace and society was broadly optimistic about the potential of the Internet to increase peoples' agency and autonomy. In particular, the positive role of the Internet was highlighted in discussions of large citizen protest movements in Korea in 2002, 2008, and 2016. The Internet was celebrated for facilitating bottom-up communication between citizens and the government, politically empowering youth, and creating counter-public spheres for marginalized voices (Kim and Kim 2009; Choi and Cho 2017). For instance, in her work on Korean Internet activism, Kang (2016, 5) celebrates an emerging modality of social interaction in cyberspace called *captivation*, defined as the rapid dissemination of fascinating images, sounds, and information by users, which helps youth activists transcend traditional politics.

However, the rapid dissemination of fascinating hyperlinks described by Kang is also at the root of the fake news problem. Definitions of fake news vary considerably, but the concept is essentially grounded on the assumption that individuals' decision-making is susceptible to manipulation by false or misleading information.[6] Although fake news has always existed, it is particularly dangerous in networked societies because it spreads faster and farther and the immersive nature of new technologies makes it more persuasive.

The possibility of online spaces being contaminated was vividly illustrated by the Druking case in South Korea in early 2018. The incident centered on a blogger named Dongwon Kim, known by his online alias Druking, who confessed in May 2018 to manipulating public opinion during the 2017 presidential election, allegedly at the behest of a prominent member of the ruling Democratic Party of Korea. Druking admitted to using an automated program called King Crab to influence the ranking of tens of thousands of comments on Naver, South Korea's largest portal and search engine. In an interesting twist, Druking and his team did not generate fake news stories but instead altered the perceived popularity of comments beneath existing stories by manipulating Naver's sorting algorithm (Lee 2018). For this reason, he was not convicted of fake news or election interference but of unlawful computer interference of a business and sentenced to three and a half years in jail.[7]

In the aftermath of the controversy, legislators from various parties proposed laws to tackle fake news. By May 2018 there were nine different proposals to reform the Press Act and twelve proposals to alter the Information Communications Network Act (Moon 2018). These various proposals not only reflected the highly partisan nature of the debate but also the struggle to comprehensively define fake news. As pointed out by Choi (2018), a key gap in current regulations in Korea is the narrow definition of fake news as slanderous attacks on an individual's reputation. On one hand, Korean libel laws may be better able to deal with fake news than in many countries because it does not matter if the personal attacks are true or not, only that reputational damage occurs (Hayes 2015). On the other hand, this emphasis on personal reputations entirely overlooks the systemic nature of fake news, which can also be directed against collective identities, ideas, or even medical procedures, as exemplified by the case of online anti-vaccine campaigns.[8]

Another major challenge is the role of the private sector. A common element in these proposed laws was an attempt to outsource responsibility for combating fake news to businesses. However, Internet portals disagreed with policymakers on the nature of the problem and who had the ultimate responsibility for fixing it. The fact that online business models rely on the collection of personal data, user-generated content, and algorithmic sorting to maximize the popularity of this content makes attempts to regulate these practices highly contentious. Businesses especially disagreed with calls for out-linking, which would require portals to hurt their own business model by re-directing visitors back to the site where the news stories first originated (Moon 2018). Also, Internet intermediaries have a vested interest in avoiding being legally liable for online content (even though they profit from the traffic it creates) because it is extremely difficult to monitor and expensive to moderate. Thus, the Korean Internet Business Association has claimed that proposed regulations "encourages private censorship and imposes impossible duties on companies" (as quoted in Shim 2020).

These debates are a sharp reminder that it is a mistake to classify fake news only as a criminal or political problem. In fact, it is a direct but unintended consequence of the datafication of human emotions and the subsequent manipulation of these emotions by automated commercial systems. Therefore, there is a fundamental tension between the desire of businesses to refine their autonomous systems of persuasion and anti-fake news initiatives seeking to make them more transparent. Put another way, the same commercial techniques for making profits through *captivation* of online consumers are being repurposed as vehicles of fake news.[9]

This dilemma is being played out around the world. As is well known, Mark Zuckerberg, the CEO of Facebook, has had several highly publicized clashes with US policymakers regarding his platform's role in various fake news controversies (Hughes 2018). But the highly networked nature of Korean society makes incidents such as the Druking controversy a preview of the looming threats to mental integrity that can result from the contamination of virtual spaces in the 4IR. Commercial networks, designed to facilitate emotional contagion, are vectors of risk and profit, akin to the belching smokestacks of the First Industrial Revolution. And the problem is only going to get worse. As Bakir and McStay warn, "the potential to manipulate public sentiment via *emphatically-optimized automated fake news* is a near-horizon problem that could rapidly dwarf the contemporary fake news problem" (emphasis in original 2018, 2).

Digital Addictions

The Druking case illustrates how the manipulation of human decision-making is facilitated by the fusion of online and offline spaces and how governmental attempts to regulate online spaces are complicated by the commercial importance of these platforms. This leads to disagreements with the private sector on how to conceptualize and combat these new hazards. As we will see below, the case of computer game addiction in South Korea highlights a similar set of tensions.

Fake news is usually discussed in the context of politics, but the case of digital addictions serves as a reminder that threats to human agency will also occur in mundane areas of our daily lives because the 4IR is premised on using data to better understand the customer and tailor advertisements and content for them. In the private sector, this is referred to as *engagement*. This term is slippery to define but "embodies a sense of involvement" in the advertising media and the brand that is being advertised (Calder and Malthouse 2015, 3). In the past, engagement was focused on selling a physical product, but today, with the commodification of personal data, maximizing the consumers' engagement inside the game world or social media site is also profitable because it facilitates data collection. This data can then be traded, sold, or used to influence future purchasing habits.

Websites, computer games, and social media sites are the focus of cutting-edge research on techniques aimed at maximizing engagement, i.e., keeping customers watching, playing, or clicking. Furthermore, improvements in automation enable these platforms to adapt to users and personalize content in real-time (Varnali 2019, 1). This has resulted in growing concern about the emergence of digital addictions, variously classified as Internet addiction, smartphone addiction, or computer game addiction.[10]

As a highly digitalized society, Korea is increasingly affected by various forms of digital addiction and Korean scholars are at the forefront of research on this problem, especially regarding its impact on children. The Korean government created the Internet Game Addiction Scale (IGAS) as early as 2006 and current studies suggest that Internet game addiction may afflict anywhere between 13 and 30% of middle and high school youths.[11]

To control the social consequences of game addiction, the Korean Ministry of Gender Equality and Family implemented Article 26 of the

Youth Protection Act in November 2011. Also known as the Shutdown Law or the Cinderella Law, this prohibited children under the age of 16 from accessing online games between midnight and 6 a.m. Violators would face punishments of up to two years in jail or a fine of 10 million won (approximately US$ 8600). This law was supplemented in 2012 by a selective shutdown system established by the Ministry of Culture, Sports and Tourism that allowed parents to request gaming companies to establish individual restrictions on access to online games.

Nevertheless, it has proven difficult for government regulations to remedy the problem of digital addiction for several reasons. First, the manipulation of users' agency is subtle, difficult to quantify, and escapes easy classification. For example, some scholars question whether Internet or game addiction is even real.[12] Others suggest that the social and behavioral problems associated with Internet addiction are its causes rather than its symptoms (Jeon 2014). Moreover, there is a lack of consensus on the boundaries between game addiction and other forms of addiction involving the Internet or smartphones. Indeed, the definitional problems surrounding this issue were illustrated in the Korean case by the fact that mobile phone games or console games were not covered by the ban. Banning online PC games while leaving other forms of digital gaming unregulated was a particularly egregious oversight because Korea is one of the largest mobile gaming markets in the world, described by one study as a "mobile game wonderland" (Jin et al. 2013, 414). These debates surrounding definitions and the blurred boundaries between technologies are key reminders that the new risks of the 4IR are subtle and do not emanate from specific technologies; rather, they are a consequence of the overall datafication cycle.

A second problem is that much of this research and policymaking ignores the obvious fact that games are designed to be addictive. Although some scholars and policymakers distinguish between different types of games, such as social games or first-person shooters, they are mostly unreflexive about the fact that each iteration of these games is designed to be *more* addictive than the last. In fact, game designers are actively utilizing recent insights from the fields of cognitive and emotional sciences to keep users playing. Although these innovations cannot be fully explored here, one example is the finding that dynamically adjusting the difficulty of a game to fit each player's skill level can result in 9% more engagement (Xue et al. 2017). Another study found that providing more social-contextual information to players kept them playing longer (Kirman et al. 2010). In this way, incremental improvements in game design are making digital games ever more persuasive.

The third challenge is the commercial importance of games. Designers and companies are making games more addictive because doing so is profitable. The game industry is an important sector of the Korean economy, with game exports in 2018 totaling US$ 6.39 billion, a sizable 67% of Korea's total content exports (Choi 2019). As a result, the government is split between encouraging the industry and regulating it. Especially, the Ministry of Culture, Sports and Tourism is responsible for promoting Korean online games, which means that its attempts to deal with addiction diverge from the stricter approach adopted by the Korean Ministry of Gender Equality and Family (Lee and Kim 2017, 60). The game industry has also mobilized against shutdown systems, with the Korean Association of Game Industry (K-Games) arguing for the dismantling of government regulations and voluntary self-regulation by game companies (Kang 2015).

A final problem that needs to be emphasized is that these new risks to agency are often enjoyable for the victims, who do not even see themselves as victims. Unlike the risks caused by natural disasters or technological failures, the engagement created by digital technologies such as social media networks and computer games is pleasurable. Therefore, attempts to regulate these practices often face strong resistance by victims or vulnerable populations. Citizen groups in Korea, such as Cultural Action, have actively lobbied against the shutdown law on the basis that it was a violation of human rights.[13] But how much free choice will these victims have when they are accessing 4IR technologies that know them better than they know themselves? One is reminded of the case of a young Korean couple in 2009 who became so obsessed with a computer game that they left their infant to starve to death. The horrible irony was that the game they were playing was Prius Online, a game about raising a virtual baby. While it is tempting to attribute this to "poor self-discipline" (Wassom 2015, 312) we cannot ignore the fact that the gaming industry is a billion-dollar giant employing thousands of designers and academic researchers whose primary jobs are to craft addictive content.

Indeed, these trends show no sign of abating. Korea's struggles to define and react to post-physical hazards such as fake news and digital addictions are not aberrations but signs of the future. The data-rich business models and technologies of the 4IR are actively seeking to become more persuasive, pleasurable, and profitable, with a recent corporate report celebrating the potential of new technologies to create "a fundamental shift in how people will experience the world for generations to come. Soon, each individual will have their own reality, and every moment will represent an opportunity for companies to play a role in shaping it" (Accenture 2019, 5).

CONCLUSION

East Asia is still struggling with the legacies of earlier industrial revolutions, including rampant air pollution and unsustainable resource use. Fourth Industrial Revolution technologies and datafication cycles hold great promise for solving many of the pressing needs of the region, especially in South Korea which is a highly connected society and best positioned to maximize the benefits of these new technologies. Indeed, unprecedented datafication and processing speeds will enable many physical hazards to be better identified and mitigated.

However, every industrial revolution has drastically altered the nature of risks facing human populations. The 4IR will be no different. Although material threats to physical well-being are important to consider—perhaps future generations will look at our use of wireless devices as we look at our grandparents' use of asbestos for insulation—this chapter has focused on an entirely new category of risks arising from the technologies and business models of the 4IR. These postmodern technological hazards threaten human autonomy and mental agency because our minds and identities are increasingly vulnerable to being remotely read and manipulated because of unprecedented improvements in data collection, transmission, and processing. These interventions will often emanate from private sector technologies which are designed to be pleasurable and habit-forming. In South Korea, these challenges are already visible in the growth of fake news and digital addiction. In both cases, government agencies, users, and businesses have struggled to define these new hazards and respond effectively to them. Although these are serious social issues, they are only precursors of a deeper contradiction at the heart of emerging 4IR technologies and business models. On the positive side, the 4IR has the potential to help us understand and control the messy and chaotic world we live in. On the negative side, this control will be increasingly applied to our own minds and personalities.

NOTES

1. In fact, this function is now advertised for Tesla cars, see Alvarez (2019).
2. For more on the similarities between the two schools of thought see Lupton (2013, 37).
3. For more on this debate, see Autor (2015).
4. For an overview of the issues surrounding brain scanning technologies, see Blitz (2017).
5. The PCFIR, for example, frames its work in a very competitive tone ("Presidential Committee on the Fourth Industrial Revolution" 2019).
6. For a typology of fake news definitions, see Tandoc et al. (2018).
7. Appeals are still ongoing. For the original sentencing, see Moon and Park (2019).
8. In Korea, these online communities are known as ANAKI (Chang and Lee 2019, 2).
9. Of course, even truthful *captivation* can have dangerous unintended consequences, especially in highly networked societies (Choi and Oh 2016; Hong and Lee 2015).
10. For an overview of the concept, see Peper and Harvey (2018).
11. For more on these numbers, see Kim and Kim (2015, 369–370).
12. For an overview of this literature, see Hellman et al. (2013).
13. For more, see the group's Website https://culturalaction.org/ [in Korean].

REFERENCES

Accenture. 2019. *The Post-Digital Era Is Upon Us: Are You Ready for What's Next?* https://www.accenture.com/_acnmedia/PDF-94/Accenture-TechVision-2019-Tech-Trends-Report.pdf.

Alvarez, Simon. 2019. Tesla Cars Can Now Order Parts for Itself When in Need of Service Repair. *Teslarati*. https://www.teslarati.com/tesla-repairs-service-automatic-pre-order-parts/.

Autor, David H. 2015. Why are There Still So Many Jobs? The History and Future of Workplace Automation. *The Journal of Economic Perspectives* 29 (3): 3–30. https://doi.org/10.1257/jep.29.3.3.

Azucar, Danny, Davide Marengo, and Michele Settanni. 2017. Predicting the Big 5 Personality Traits from Digital Footprints on Social Media: A Meta-Analysis. *Personality and Individual Differences* 124: 150–159. https://doi.org/10.1016/j.paid.2017.12.018.

Bakir, Vian, and Andrew McStay. 2018. Fake News and the Economy of Emotions. *Digital Journalism* 6 (2): 154–175. https://doi.org/10.1080/21670811.2017.1345645.

Beck, Ulrich. 1992. *Risk Society: Towards a New Modernity*. London: Sage.

Bernardini, F., H. Rushmeier, I.M. Martin, J. Mittleman, and G. Taubin. 2002. Building a Digital Model of Michelangelo's Florentine Pieta. *IEEE Computer Graphics and Applications* 22 (1): 59–67. https://doi.org/10.1109/38.974519.

Bernstein, Peter L. 1998. *Against the Gods: The Remarkable Story of Risk*. New York, NY: Wiley.

Blitz, Marc Jonathan. 2017. *Searching Minds by Scanning Brains: Neuroscience Technology and Constitutional Privacy Protection*. Cham, Switzerland: Palgrave Pivot.

Boyd, John. 2007. Patterns of Conflict. Edited by Chuck Spinney, Chet Richards, and Ginger Richards. http://www.projectwhitehorse.com/pdfs/boyd/patterns%20of%20conflict.pdf.

Burke, Rick, Adam Mussomeli, Stephen Laaper, Marty Hartigan, and Brenna Sniderman. 2017. *The Smart Factory: Responsive, Adaptive, Connected Manufacturing*. Deloitte University Press. https://www2.deloitte.com/content/dam/insights/us/articles/4051_The-smart-factory/DUP_The-smart-factory.pdf.

Calder, Bobby J., and Edward C. Malthouse. 2015. Media Engagement and Advertising Effectiveness. In *Kellogg on Advertising & Media*, edited by Bobby J. Calder, 1–36. Hoboken, NJ, USA: Wiley. https://doi.org/10.1002/9781119198154.ch1.

Cammaerts, Bart. 2013. Banal Revolution: The Emptying of a Political Signifier. *Mediascapes Journal* 1 (1): 27–38.

Chang, Kyujin, and Soon Young Lee. 2019. Why Do Some Korean Parents Hesitate to Vaccinate Their Children? *Epidemiology and Health* 41: 1–10. https://doi.org/10.4178/epih.e2019031.

Choi, Min Sik. 2018. A Study of Online Service Provider's Fake Information Response and the Improvement of Legislation. *The Journal of Law of Education* 30 (3): 155–184. https://doi.org/10.17317/tjle.30.3.201812.155.

Choi, Moon-hee. 2019. S. Korea's Content Exports Total US$9.55 Bill in 2018. *Business Korea*. http://www.businesskorea.co.kr/news/articleView.html?idxno=34464.

Choi, Su Young, and Younghan Cho. 2017. Generating Counter-Public Spheres Through Social Media: Two Social Movements in Neoliberalised South Korea. *Javnost—The Public* 24 (1): 15–33. https://doi.org/10.1080/13183222.2017.1267155.

Choi, Yun Jeong, and Oh Hyungna. 2016. Does Media Coverage of a Celebrity Suicide Trigger Copycat Suicides? Evidence from Korean Cases. *Journal of Media Economics* 29 (2): 92–105. https://doi.org/10.1080/08997764.2016.1170020.

Colson, Thomas. 2016. Twitter Reacts to Jeremy Corbyn's 'Incomprehensible' Post. *Business Insider*. https://www.businessinsider.com/twitter-users-react-to-jeremy-corbyns-incomprehensible-tweet-2016-11.

Connolly, Daniel. 2019. Back to the Future? The Fourth Industrial Revolution's Impact on International Relations. *IIRI Online Series* 54 (November): 1–8.

Constine, Josh. 2012. How Big Is Facebook's Data? 2.5 Billion Pieces of Content And 500+ Terabytes Ingested Every Day. *TechCrunch*. http://soc ial.techcrunch.com/2012/08/22/how-big-is-facebooks-data-2-5-billion-pie ces-of-content-and-500-terabytes-ingested-every-day/.

Coyle, Karen. 2006. Mass Digitization of Books. *The Journal of Academic Librarianship* 32 (6): 641–645. https://doi.org/10.1016/j.acalib.2006.08.002.

Daecher, Andy, Brenna Sniderman, Jonathan Holdowsky, Mark Cotteleer, Monika Mahto, Timothy P. Hanley, et al. 2018. *The Industry 4.0 Paradox: Overcoming Disconnects on the Path to Digital Transformation*. Deloitte Insights.

Di Ciaula, Agostino. 2018. Towards 5G Communication Systems: Are There Health Implications? *International Journal of Hygiene and Environmental Health* 221 (3): 367–375. https://doi.org/10.1016/j.ijheh.2018.01.011.

Durand, Pete. 2018. Industry 4.0—What Does It Mean to Your Operations? *Automation World*. https://www.automationworld.com/factory/iiot/blog/13318945/industry-40what-does-it-mean-to-your-operations.

Ericsson. 2018. *5G Business Value: A Case Study on Real-Time Control in Manufacturing*. Stockholm, Sweden: Ericsson Consumer and IndustryLab Insight Report. https://www.ericsson.com/4aad73/assets/local/reports-papers/con sumerlab/reports/2018/5g_for_industries_report_blisk_27062018.pdf.

Fleetwood, Janet. 2017. Public Health, Ethics, and Autonomous Vehicles. *American Journal of Public Health* 107 (4): 532–537. https://doi.org/10.2105/AJPH.2016.303628.

Gao, Yizhao, Shaowen Wang, Anand Padmanabhan, Junjun Yin, and Guofeng Cao. 2018. Mapping Spatiotemporal Patterns of Events Using Social Media: A Case Study of Influenza Trends. *International Journal of Geographical Information Science* 32 (3): 425–449. https://doi.org/10.1080/13658816.2017.1406943.

Germany Trade & Invest. 2014. *Industrie 4.0 Smart Manufacturing for the Future*. Berlin. https://www.its-owl.de/fileadmin/PDF/News/2014-01-14-Industrie_4.0-Smart_Manufacturing_for_the_Future_German_Trade_Invest.pdf.

Goel, Vindu. 2014. Facebook Tinkers with Users' Emotions in News Feed Experiment, Stirring Outcry. *The New York Times*, June 29, Sec. Technology. https://www.nytimes.com/2014/06/30/technology/facebook-tin kers-with-users-emotions-in-news-feed-experiment-stirring-outcry.html.

Gomez, Christopher, and Heather Purdie. 2016. UAV-Based Photogrammetry and Geocomputing for Hazards and Disaster Risk Monitoring—A Review. *Geoenvironmental Disasters* 3 (1): 23. https://doi.org/10.1186/s40677-016-0060-y.

Gorelick, Noel, Matt Hancher, Mike Dixon, Simon Ilyushchenko, David Thau, and Rebecca Moore. 2017. Google Earth Engine: Planetary-Scale Geospatial Analysis for Everyone. *Remote Sensing of Environment, Big Remotely Sensed Data: Tools, Applications and Experiences* 202 (December): 18–27. https://doi.org/10.1016/j.rse.2017.06.031.

Hayes, Sean. 2015. Korea's Cyber Defamation Law: Basics of Libel and Slander in Korea. *The Korean Law Blog*. https://www.thekoreanlawblog.com/2015/08/korea-defamation-lawyers.html.

Head, Tom. 2019. David Mabuza: Acting President Stumped by EFF's Tech Question. *The South African*. https://www.thesouthafrican.com/technology/what-were-first-three-industrial-revolutions-david-mabuza-ndlozi-4ir/.

Hellman, Matilda, Tim M. Schoenmakers, Benjamin R. Nordstrom, and Ruth J. van Holst. 2013. Is There Such a Thing as Online Video Game Addiction? A Cross-Disciplinary Review. *Addiction Research & Theory* 21 (2): 102–112. https://doi.org/10.3109/16066359.2012.693222.

Hern, Alex. 2018. Cambridge Analytica: How Did It Turn Clicks into Votes? *The Guardian*, May 6, Sec. News. https://www.theguardian.com/news/2018/may/06/cambridge-analytica-how-turn-clicks-into-votes-christopher-wylie.

Hong, Sok Chul, and Jungmin Lee. 2015. People on the Verge of Death: Evidence from Impacts of Celebrity Suicides. *Applied Economics* 47 (7): 710–724. https://doi.org/10.1080/00036846.2014.980571.

Hughes, Siobhan. 2018. Mark Zuckerberg: Facebook Made Mistakes on 'Fake News,' Privacy. *Wall Street Journal*, April 9, Sec. Tech. https://www.wsj.com/articles/mark-zuckerberg-facebook-made-mistakes-on-fake-news-privacy-1523289089.

Hundley, Richard O. 1999. *Past Revolutions, Future Transformations: What Can the History of Revolutions in Military Affairs Tell Us about Transforming the U.S. Military?* Santa Monica, CA: RAND Corporation.

IARC Classifies Radiofrequency Electromagnetic Fields as Possibly Carcinogenic to Humans. 2011. Lyon, France: World Health Organization International Agency for Research on Cancer.

Ith, Tracy. 2017. Technology Helps the UN Advance the Protection of Human Rights in New Ways. *Microsoft*. https://news.microsoft.com/features/technology-helps-un-advance-protection-human-rights-new-ways/.

Jeon, Jong-Soo. 2014. A Study on the Effects of Internet Games Shutdown Policy in Korea. *Journal of Korea Game Society* 14 (6): 99–108. https://doi.org/10.7583/JKGS.2014.14.6.99.

Jin, Dal Yong, Florence Chee, and Seah Kim. 2013. Transformative Mobile Game Culture: A Sociocultural Analysis of Korean Mobile Gaming in the Era of Smartphones. *International Journal of Cultural Studies* 18 (4): 413–429. https://doi.org/10.1177/1367877913507473.

Kang, Jiyeon. 2016. *Igniting the Internet: Youth and Activism in Postauthoritarian South Korea*. Honolulu: University of Hawai'i Press.

Kang, Shin Chul. 2015. Greeting. *Korean Association of Game Industry*. http://www.gamek.or.kr/index-eng/.

Kelly, Richard. 2018. *Constructing Leadership 4.0: Swarm Leadership and the Fourth Industrial Revolution*. New York, NY: Palgrave Macmillan.

Kim, Kyunghee, and Kisook Kim. 2015. Internet Game Addiction, Parental Attachment, and Parenting of Adolescents in South Korea. *Journal of Child & Adolescent Substance Abuse* 24 (6): 366–371. https://doi.org/10.1080/1067828X.2013.872063.

Kim, Yong Cheol, and June Woo Kim. 2009. South Korean Democracy in the Digital Age: The Candlelight Protests and the Internet. *Korea Observer* 40 (1): 53–83.

Kirman, Ben, Shaun Lawson, Conor Linehan, Francesco Martino, Luciano Gamberini, and Andrea Gaggioli. 2010. Improving Social Game Engagement on Facebook Through Enhanced Socio-Contextual Information. In *Proceedings of the SIGCHI Conference on Human Factors in Computing Systems*, 1753–1756. CHI '10. Atlanta, Georgia, USA: Association for Computing Machinery. https://doi.org/10.1145/1753326.1753589.

Kosinski, Michal, David Stillwell, and Thore Graepel. 2013. Private Traits and Attributes are Predictable from Digital Records of Human Behavior. *Proceedings of the National Academy of Sciences* 110 (15): 5802–5805. https://doi.org/10.1073/pnas.1218772110.

Kramer, A.D.I., J.E. Guillory, and J.T. Hancock. 2014. Experimental Evidence of Massive-Scale Emotional Contagion Through Social Networks. *Proceedings of the National Academy of Sciences* 111 (24): 8788–8790. https://doi.org/10.1073/pnas.1320040111.

Lasi, Heiner, Peter Fettke, Hans-Georg Kemper, Thomas Feld, and Michael Hoffmann. 2014. Industry 4.0. *Business & Information Systems Engineering* 6 (4): 239–242. https://doi.org/10.1007/s12599-014-0334-4.

Lee, Claire. 2018. Inside 'Druking' Scandal: Between Freedom of Expression and Illegal Opinion Rigging. *The Korean Herald*. http://www.koreaherald.com/view.php?ud=20180417000859.

Lee, Changho, and Ocktae Kim. 2017. Predictors of Online Game Addiction Among Korean Adolescents. *Addiction Research & Theory* 25 (1): 58–66. https://doi.org/10.1080/16066359.2016.1198474.

Li, De-Kun, Hong Chen, Jeannette R. Ferber, Roxana Odouli, and Charles Quesenberry. 2017. Exposure to Magnetic Field Non-Ionizing Radiation and the Risk of Miscarriage: A Prospective Cohort Study. *Scientific Reports* 7 (1): 1–7. https://doi.org/10.1038/s41598-017-16623-8.

Lupton, Deborah. 1999. Introduction: Risk and Sociocultural Theory. In *Risk and Sociocultural Theory: New Directions and Perspectives*, edited by Deborah Lupton. Cambridge, UK: Cambridge University Press. http://public.ebookcentral.proquest.com/choice/publicfullrecord.aspx?p=4637452.

Lupton, Deborah. 2013. *Risk*. 2nd ed. London; New York: Routledge.

Marketforce, and TIBCO Software. 2017. *The Fourth Industrial Revolution in Insurance*. https://www.tibco.com/sites/tibco/files/resources/Algo-marketforce-Fourthindustrialrevolution-Brief.pdf.

Menon, Abhilash. 2019. Digital Twins: The Next Frontier in Operational Risk Management. *Oilfield Technology*. https://www.oilfieldtechnology.com/digital-oilfield/01112019/digital-twins-the-next-frontier-in-operational-risk-management/.

Moon, Chang-seok, and Seung-joo Park. 2019. Druking Sentenced Three Years and Six Months in Prison in His First Trial for 'Distorting Voters' Political Decision-Making Process. *News1*. http://news1.kr/articles/?3537260.

Moon, Yong-pil. 2018. Looking into the Flooding Piles of 'Portal Regulatory Bills.' *The PR News*. http://www.the-pr.co.kr/news/articleView.html?idxno=40153.

Neff, Gina, and Dawn Nafus. 2016. *Self-Tracking*. Cambridge, MA: The MIT Press.

Peper, Erik, and Richard Harvey. 2018. Digital Addiction: Increased Loneliness, Anxiety, and Depression. *NeuroRegulation* 5 (1): 3–8. https://doi.org/10.15540/nr.5.1.3.

Perrow, Charles. 1984. *Normal Accidents: Living with High-Risk Technologies*. New York: Basic Books.

Petrillo, Antonella, Fabio De Felice, Raffaele Cioffi, and Federico Zomparelli. 2018. Fourth Industrial Revolution: Current Practices, Challenges, and Opportunities. In *Digital Transformation in Smart Manufacturing*. Rijeka, Croatia: InTech. https://www.intechopen.com/books/digital-transformation-in-smart-manufacturing/fourth-industrial-revolution-current-practices-challenges-and-opportunities.

"Presidential Committee on the Fourth Industrial Revolution." 2019. Accessed 18 Nov. https://www.4th-ir.go.kr/home/en.

Schwab, Klaus. 2016. *The Fourth Industrial Revolution*. Geneva: The World Economic Forum.

Schwab, Klaus, and Nicholas Davis. 2018. *Shaping the Fourth Industrial Revolution*. New York, NY: Currency.

Sehgal, Vivek Kumar, Anubhav Patrick, Ashutosh Soni, and Lucky Rajput. 2015. Smart Human Security Framework Using Internet of Things, Cloud and Fog Computing. In *Intelligent Distributed Computing*, edited by Rajkumar

Buyya and Sabu M. Thampi, 251–263. Advances in Intelligent Systems and Computing. Switzerland: Springer International Publishing.

Shim, Seohyeon. 2020. Internet Companies Have Opposed to the 'Real-Time Search Law', Which Would Make Companies Like Naver Responsible for Future Druking Incidents. *JoongAng Daily*. https://news.joins.com/article/23672622.

Shin, Seonjin, and Joon Koh. 2017. Analysis of Mobile Broadband Service Penetration in South Korea. *Journal of Computer Information Systems* 57 (1): 31–38. https://doi.org/10.1080/08874417.2016.1181491.

Summerton, Jane, and Boel Berner. 2003. Constructing Risk and Safety in Technological Practice: An Introduction. In *Constructing Risk and Safety in Technological Practice (Routledge Advances in Sociology; 4)*, ed. Boel Berner, Jane Summerton, and Max Novick. London: Routledge.

Sung, Tae Kyung. 2018. Industry 4.0: A Korea Perspective. *Technological Forecasting and Social Change* 132 (July): 40–45. https://doi.org/10.1016/j.techfore.2017.11.005.

Tandoc Jr, C. Edson, Zheng Wei Lim, and Richard Ling. 2018. Defining 'Fake News.' *Digital Journalism* 6 (2): 137–153. https://doi.org/10.1080/21670811.2017.1360143.

Tapscott, Don, and Alex Tapscott. 2016. *Blockchain Revolution: How the Technology Behind Bitcoin Is Changing Money, Business, and the World*. New York: Portfolio/Penguin.

The Institute of Internal Auditors. 2019. *5G and the Fourth Industrial Revolution—Part I*. FLA: Lake Mary.

Varnali, Kaan. 2019. Online Behavioral Advertising: An Integrative Review. *Journal of Marketing Communications* 0 (0): 1–22. https://doi.org/10.1080/13527266.2019.1630664.

Wang, K. 2016. Intelligent Predictive Maintenance (IPM) System—Industry 4.0 Scenario. In *Advanced Manufacturing and Automation V*, edited by K. Wang, Y. Wang, J. O. Strandhagen, and T. Yu. Southhampton, Boston: WIT Press.

Wang, Shiyong, Jiafu Wan, Di Li, and Chunhua Zhang. 2016. Implementing Smart Factory of Industrie 4.0: An Outlook. *International Journal of Distributed Sensor Networks* 12 (1): 3159805. https://doi.org/10.1155/2016/3159805.

Wassom, Brian. 2015. *Augmented Reality Law, Privacy, and Ethics: Law, Society, and Emerging AR Technologies*. Waltham, MA: Syngress.

Wu, Tim. 2017. *The Attention Merchants: The Epic Scramble to Get Inside Our Heads*. New York, NY: Vintage Books.

Xu, Min, Jeanne M. David, and Suk Hi Kim. 2018. The Fourth Industrial Revolution: Opportunities and Challenges. *International Journal of Financial Research* 9 (2): 90. https://doi.org/10.5430/ijfr.v9n2p90.

Xue, Su, Meng Wu, John Kolen, Navid Aghdaie, and Kazi A. Zaman. 2017. Dynamic Difficulty Adjustment for Maximized Engagement in Digital Games. In *Proceedings of the 26th International Conference on World Wide Web Companion*, 465–471. WWW 17 Companion. Republic and Canton of Geneva, Switzerland: International World Wide Web Conferences Steering Committee. https://doi.org/10.1145/3041021.3054170.

Yuen, Steve, Gallayanee Yaoyuneyong, and Erik Johnson. 2011. Augmented Reality: An Overview and Five Directions for AR in Education. *Journal of Educational Technology Development and Exchange (JETDE)* 4 (1). https://doi.org/10.18785/jetde.0401.10.

Yun, Seongjin, Jun-Hong Park, and Won-Tae Kim. 2017. Data-Centric Middleware Based Digital Twin Platform for Dependable Cyber-Physical Systems. In *2017 Ninth International Conference on Ubiquitous and Future Networks (ICUFN)*, 922–926. https://doi.org/10.1109/icufn.2017.7993933.

CHAPTER 8

School Safety Management: International Framework and Japanese Practice

Aiko Sakurai

RISKS AND CRISIS MANAGEMENT AND SAFETY AT SCHOOL

According to the International Organization for Standardization (ISO), a risk is defined as the "effect of uncertainty on objectives." Risk is expressed in terms of "risk sources" that refer to elements that alone or in combination have the potential to give rise to risk (ISO 2009). Risk management involves coordinated activities that include risk assessment, risk treatment, risk acceptance, and risk communication to direct and control an organization regarding risk. Based on risk management, crisis management is a holistic management process that identifies potential impacts that threaten an organization and provides a framework for building resilience, with the capability for an effective response that

---

A. Sakurai (✉)
International Research Institute of Disaster Science, Tohoku University, Sendai, Japan

Toyo Eiwa University, Yokohama, Kanagawa Prefecture, Japan

© The Author(s), under exclusive license to Springer Nature Singapore Pte Ltd. 2021
Y. Jing et al. (eds.), *Risk Management in East Asia*,
https://doi.org/10.1007/978-981-33-4586-7_8

167

safeguards the interests of the organization's key stakeholders, reputation, brand, and value-creating activities, as well as effectively restoring operational capabilities.

In contrast, the term "safe" is the state of being protected from recognized hazards that are likely to cause harm. The ISO noted that "the state of being protected from all hazards" is a misunderstanding of the definition of "safe." It is important to be aware that some level of risk is inherent in products or systems (ISO 2014). As seen from these definitions, securing safety and managing risk are inextricably linked. Therefore, school risk and crisis management are called school safety management.

A school is a place for pupils and students to gather, learn from each other, build friendships, and build a foundation for character formation. Therefore, a school should be a safe and secure place for children. Children should develop their abilities at school through education to protect themselves as well as be protected from threats.

As post-modern society is called a risk society (Beck 1999), environments surrounding children have changed dramatically. Tragic incidents that take students' lives keep occurring. Children are exposed to diversified risk, including traffic incidents, injuries during athletic activities, natural disasters, bullying, infections, drugs, predators, and Internet and social networking service activities. Children are also surrounded by these risks at home, on the way to and from school, and in other situations.

Targets for school safety differ according to the school environment in the country. For example, in the United States, more attention is given to school safety against school violence and school shootings. In Japan, because the country is disaster-prone, school safety focuses on disaster safety among three focuses: disaster safety, traffic safety, and daily life safety. Of course, injuries in sports activities and death by incidents have been long concerned about school safety in Japan. According to statistics available for incidents involving children in Japan, the most common incidents that caused the deaths of children under school supervision in 2001–2008 were traffic incidents, followed by death from drowning (Ehara 2012). Although there is a trend of declining deaths by unexpected incidents and traffic incidents under school supervision in Japan before 2011, the number of deaths of children leaped when a large-scale earthquake, the 2011 Great East Japan earthquake, occurred.

Therefore, given the focus on school safety during natural disasters, this paper is composed of two parts: the evolution of the international framework and the development of Japanese practice. A case from the 2011

Great East Japan earthquake is examined to draw lessons learned from experiences to make schools safer. The chapter also provides suggestions for future collaboration to enhance school resilience through risk management at school to protect children under school supervision, and the need to exchange experiences and regional collaboration in Asia.

INTERNATIONAL FRAMEWORK FOR SCHOOL SAFETY

Comprehensive School Safety

Comprehensive school safety is a framework aiming to reduce the risks of all hazards to the education sector. Comprehensive school safety rests on three pillars: safe school facilities, school disaster management, and risk reduction education (Fig. 8.1, Tables 8.1 and 8.2; Global Alliance for Disaster Risk Reduction and Resilience in the Education Sector (GADRRRES 2017). The framework has been developed since

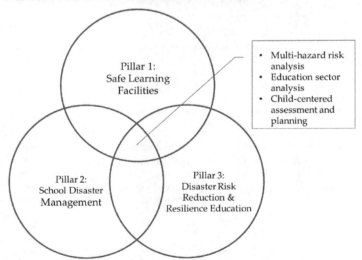

Fig. 8.1 Comprehensive school safety (*Source* Created by the author based on GADRRRES 2017)

170 A. SAKURAI

Table 8.1 Details of the three pillars of comprehensive school safety

Pillar 1: Safe Learning Facilities	Pillar 2: School Disaster Management	Pillar 3: Disaster Risk Reduction and Resilient Education
• Safe site selection • Building codes • Disaster-resilient and 'green' design • Performance standards • Builder training • Construction supervision • Quality control • Remodeling • Retrofitting • Water, sanitation and hygiene	• Assessment and planning • Physical, environmental and social protection • Response skills and provisions • Representative/participatory SDM linked to school-based management • Educational continuity planning • Standard operating procedures • Contingency planning	• Education for sustainable development • Child-centred learning • Formal curriculum Integrations and infusion • National consensus-based key messages • Teacher training and staff development • Extracurricular and community-based informal education • Conflict sensitive education for diversity acceptance, peace and social cohesion

Source Created by the author based on Global Alliance for Disaster Risk Reduction and Resilience in the Education Sector 2017

Table 8.2 Details of the overlap between pillars

Overwrapping between Pillar 1 & Pillar 2	Overwrapping between Pillar 1 & Pillar 3	Overwrapping between Pillar 2 & Pillar 3
• Building maintenance • Non-structural mitigation • Fire safety • Green school practices	• Structural safety education • Construction as educational opportunity • Community engagement in construction	• Household disaster plan • Family reunification plan • School drills • Learning without fear • School as zones of peace

Source Created by the author based on GADRRRES (2017)

2012 by GADRRRES, which includes United Nation agencies, such as UNESCO, UNICEF, UNDRR, the World Bank Group's Global Facility for Disaster Reduction and Recovery (GFDRR), and major international child-support Non-Governmental Organizations (NGOs), such as Save the Children, World Vision, Plan, and Child Fund. The framework includes emergency response agencies, such as the International Federation of the Red Cross and Red Crescent Societies, and the Inter-Agency Network for Education in Emergencies, in addition to regional Asian agencies, such as Asia Disaster Preparedness Center (ADPC), Asia Disaster Reduction and Response Network (ADRRN), and Southeast Asian Ministers of Education Organization (SEAMEO).

The Hyogo Framework for Action (HFA) 2005–2015, which was agreed at the second UN World Conference on Disaster Risk Reduction, set a Priority for Action 3 to use knowledge innovation and education to build a culture of safety and resilience at all levels (UNISDR 2005). Under the HFA, the international community supported integrating disaster knowledge and information in the existing curriculum to promote disaster education globally. However, earthquakes have caused many tragedies at schools. For example, six thousand eight hundred and ninety-eight schools were fully destroyed by the 2008 Sichuan earthquake that occurred at 14:28 on May 12, 2008, in China, with a moment magnitude of 7.9. More than eleven thousand students died during class hours due to the collapse of the school buildings. In 2010, UNISDR launched the global One Million Safe Schools and Hospitals Campaign to raise awareness of the urgency of making schools and hospitals safe from disasters, especially those located in disaster-prone regions. The 2008 Sichuan earthquake led the international community to emphasize a comprehensive approach to create safer schools by integrating safe learning facilities, school disaster management, and disaster risk reduction education as shown in the three pillars.

Comprehensive school safety is composed of three pillars by presenting key responsibilities and actions that can be taken through changes in education policy and practices aligned with disaster management at the national, regional, district, and local school site levels (Fig. 8.1). In the 2017 updates by GADRRRES, child-centered and evidence-based efforts are brought into focus to promote disaster risk reduction throughout the education sector and to assure universal access to quality education. This focus allows education sector partners to work more effectively and to link with similar efforts in other sectors. Comprehensive school safety is

172   A. SAKURAI

also aligned with the Sustainable Development Goals 2015–2030 and the Sendai Framework for Disaster Risk Reduction priorities for action and indicators for the education sector.

Comprehensive School Safety in Terms of Disaster Risk Reduction

In terms of school disaster safety, it is important to further understand the link between comprehensive school safety and the Sendai Framework for Disaster Risk Reduction 2015–2030 (the Sendai Framework, hereafter; UNISDR 2015). The Sendai Framework is an internationally agreed framework to be achieved by 2030 through partnerships among the stakeholders to reduce disaster risk at the global, regional, country, local, and citizen levels. In the Sendai Framework, education became embedded and recombined into an entire disaster cycle as one of the integrated and inclusive measures for preventing and reducing disaster-related risk (Sakurai and Sato 2016). The framework outlines seven global targets for measuring progress made by all countries on reducing disaster risk by the year 2030. Table 8.3 shows the relationship between the seven global targets in the framework and the application of the targets to the education sector. Comprehensive school safety is specifically mentioned as a means of promoting international cooperation in global target 6. Besides, the pillar and education sector investments and strategies are integrated into the seven targets. Reducing casualties at school and the disruption of educational services at school during and after a disaster is an internationally promoted goal under the Sendai Framework.

Other International Efforts to Promote Safe Schools

International Safe Schools (ISS) is part of the worldwide certifying movement led by the World Health Organization's (WHO's) Collaborating Centre for Development and Research on Community Safety Promotion to prevent injuries, incidents, and violence at school. Started in 2001, as of 2013, there were 130 ISS in 10 countries, including Sweden, Czech Republic, South Korea. Once a school is approved as an ISS, a safe school promotion mechanism is established and functions at the school. ISS status is reviewed every three years and does not imply that the school is a 100% safe school. The designated school creates a whole school and community-wide governing body on safety promotion, prepares for and implements a plan and programs for target groups

Table 8.3 Linking the Sendai Seven Targets to the education sector

The "Sendai Seven" Targets	Global Targets for the Education Sector
1. Substantially reduce global disaster mortality by 2030, aiming to lower average per 100,000 global mortality between 2020–2030 compared to 2005–2015	Minimize the number of deaths and injuries due to hazard impacts on schools
2. Substantially reduce the number of affected people globally by 2030, aiming to lower the average global figure per 100,000 between 2020–2030 compared to 2005–2015	Substantially reduce the number of school children affected by disaster impacts of all sizes
3. Reduce direct disaster economic loss in relation to global Gross Domestic Product (GDP) by 2030	Reduction education sector investment losses due to hazard impacts
4. Substantially reduce disaster damage to critical infrastructure and disruption of basic service, among them health and educational facilities, including developing their resilience by 2030	Minimize school days lost due to hazard impacts
5. Substantially increase the number of countries with national and local Disaster Risk Reduction strategies by 2020	Countries have education sector risk reduction strategies
6. Substantially enhance international co-operation to developing countries through adequate and sustainable support to complement their national actions for implementing this framework by 2030	Countries work together to achieve Comprehensive School Safety
7. Substantially increase the availability of and access to multi-hazard early warning systems and disaster risk information and assessments to people by 2030	Schools have access to, and use early warning systems

Source Created by the author based on GADRRRES (2017)

identified by a baseline survey, documents the data and progress, evaluates the program, and plans to achieve a safer environment at the school (International Safe Schools Certifying Centers 2014). A spin-off from the International Safe Schools initiative is the Safety Promotion School (SPS), which was customized based on the Japanese approach by the National Support Center for School Crisis by Osaka Kyouiku University (http://nmsc.osaka-kyoiku.ac.jp/). SPS has been promoted under the Five-Year Plan to Promote School Safety in Japan.

174   A. SAKURAI

Safe Schools Declaration and Guidelines for Protecting Schools and Universities from Military Use during Armed Conflict is an international initiative led by the Global Coalition to Protect Education from Attack (GCPEA) to promote and protect the right to education and to facilitate the continuation of education in situations of armed conflict. The Safe Declaration explained the situation in conflict areas:

> Worldwide, schools and universities have been bombed, shelled and burned, and children, students, teachers, and academics have been killed, maimed, abducted, or arbitrarily detained. Educational facilities have been used by parties to armed conflict as, inter alia, bases, barracks or detention centres. Such actions expose students and education personnel to harm, deny large numbers of children and students their right to education and so deprive communities of the foundations on which to build their future. In many countries, armed conflict continues to destroy not just school infrastructure, but the hopes and ambitions of a whole generation of children.

The Guidelines urge that parties to armed conflict not to use schools and universities for any purpose in support of their military effort and realize safe schools for all (Global Coalition to Protect Education from Attack 2014).

THE 2011 GREAT EAST JAPAN EARTHQUAKE AND THE EDUCATION SECTOR IN JAPAN

Damage and Impact of the 2011 Disaster on the Japanese Education Sector

The magnitude 9.0 Tohoku earthquake occurred at 14:46 on March 11, 2011. The epicenter was 130 kilometers southeast of the Ojika Peninsula of Ishinomaki City and had a depth of 24 kilometers. The earthquake resulted in the generation of a massive tsunami, which caused the Great East Japan earthquake and tsunami disaster, resulting in 15,884 deaths and 2633 missing persons (as of March 10, 2014, according to the National Police Agency of Japan).

The 2011 disaster caused substantial damage to the education sector. When the earthquake occurred at 14:46 on Friday, many children were still at school, having recently finished their classes and not yet left for home. Although Japanese citizens have experienced many earthquakes, this was the first time Japanese schools had to deal with such a disaster on such a large scale. As of September 14, 2012, the disaster had caused 659 deaths in the education sector. Of these deaths, 616 were children, including the 74 who died or went missing in the tragedy of Okawa Elementary School in Ishinomaki, Miyagi Prefecture. As of March 28, 2012, 241 children had been orphaned by the disaster, according to the Ministry of Welfare and Labour.

A total of 6284 schools were damaged by the earthquake and tsunami. Of these, 930 schools (15%) completely or partially collapsed and required rebuilding. Inspections revealed that the damage was mainly caused by the tsunami rather than earthquake tremors. Although the disaster damaged many facilities, no deaths were reportedly caused by the collapse of school buildings during the earthquake; all were attributed to the subsequent flooding. Before the 2011 disaster, 71 schools were located within tsunami inundation areas in the tsunami hazard maps prepared by the prefecture, and 53 of these schools (74.6%) were inundated by the tsunami. The tsunami affected an additional 69 schools in the area (Ministry of Education, Culture, Sports, Science and Technology [MEXT] 2014).

In Japan, public schools and community centers are designated evacuation shelters by municipal governments. Although education services were disrupted at schools that served as evacuation shelters after the 1995 Kobe earthquake, after the 2011 earthquake during the peak evacuation period, 622 schools were used as shelters in the Tohoku and Kanto regions of Japan because of the scale of the damage. According to the MEXT report, almost 30% of schools were used as evacuation shelters in the most heavily affected prefectures, Iwate, Miyagi, and Fukushima. The longest time for which a school was used as a shelter was until early November 2011. It took almost eight months for all the school shelters to be closed. Almost 30% of the schools that were used as shelters faced problems reopening for children's education. In addition to the school buildings, many playgrounds were used for temporary housing after the 2011 disaster because the amount of flat land was limited in the tsunami-affected coastal areas. Students lost space for physical exercise and extracurricular and sports club activities (MEXT 2012d).

In Japan, the school year starts in April and ends the following March. Since the disaster occurred in March, classes for the remainder of the 2010–2011 school year were suspended, and closing and graduation ceremonies were postponed at the schools affected by the disaster. The new

176   A. SAKURAI

school year was supposed to start in April 2011, but schools in the affected areas remained closed for at least a month, and in the longest case, for two months, including spring vacation. Even after the resumption of school services, many schools were forced to share classrooms with other schools, rent classrooms at other schools or other public facilities, or conduct classes in temporary classrooms. It took six years in the longest case to rebuild the damaged schools.

MEXT's Response to the 2011 Disaster Regarding School Disaster Safety

In response to the 2011 disaster, MEXT took immediate action to support the early resumption of education in disaster-affected areas, which entailed bearing the costs of building temporary classrooms and reconstructing damaged school facilities. Also, MEXT secured educational opportunities for affected students by distributing free textbooks, allowing affected students to go to schools in resettled or evacuated areas, providing economic assistance to affected students, reassigning teachers to schools in tsunami-affected areas, and dispatching school counselors to care for children's psychological needs.

Following the six-month emergency period, MEXT took a series of actions to review the comprehensive safety of Japanese schools based on the 2011 disaster experiences. Regarding school learning facilities, in July 2011 MEXT issued an emergency proposal by advisors for improving school facilities based on the damage caused by the 2011 Great East Japan earthquake disaster (MEXT 2011a). It also published the report *A Concept on a Disaster-Resilient School Facility: Strengthening Tsunami Countermeasures and Disaster Prevention Function as an Evacuation Shelter* (MEXT 2017). To review the existing disaster education and disaster management policies, MEXT asked the Advisors' Council on Disaster Prevention Education and Management in July 2011 to analyze schools' experiences during the 2011 disaster, and the council produced two reports within a year of the 2011 disaster (MEXT 2011b, 2012a). These reports identified issues related to Japanese Disaster Risk Reduction (DRR) in the education sector and made recommendations for enhancing it. In addition, a survey on school responses to the 2011 disaster was conducted and a report issued in May 2012. The report stated that the schools' tsunami disaster preparedness had not been adequate. Forty percent of schools that were predicted to be inundated in the tsunami hazard maps did not conduct tsunami evacuation drills before the 2011 disaster (MEXT 2012d).

The lessons learned from the 2011 disaster in terms of school disaster management emphasized localizing school disaster manuals for the context of each school. Considering that schools are located in different geographic areas, the disaster manuals and drills should be tailored to the local characteristics of the schools' surroundings. To localize disaster management efforts at school, schools are encouraged to collaborate with parents, disaster-related divisions of municipal governments, and the local community. Also, MEXT has recommended that each school disaster manual should include response procedures for post-disaster crisis management, such as shelter management and preparation efforts (including conducting evacuation drills and sharing information with parents on procedures for releasing children from schools to their parents).

Based on lessons from the 2011 disaster, MEXT published the *Handbook for Schools for Preparing a School Disaster Preparedness and Response Manual* (for earthquake and tsunami disasters; MEXT 2012c). The handbook aims to urge all schools to review their disaster manuals and to reconsider their practicality within the school's local context. The handbook also encourages schools to establish a plan-do-check-action (PDCA) cycle for disaster management when there are changes in school personnel or the local environment.

SCHOOL SAFETY IN JAPAN

School Health and Safety Act

In Japan, the School Health and Safety Act, which was enacted in 2009 as a substantial revision of the School Health Act of 1958, describes the division of responsibilities among educational administration for school safety. In particular, the School Health and Safety Act greatly expanded the content of school safety from the previous School Health Act, which led to the change in the name of the law. One of the reasons for the revision was to respond to challenges to school safety that included the increasing number of traffic accidents during commuting from/to school, series of large earthquakes, and a school massacre at Ikeda Elementary School in Osaka, where eight pupils were killed and fifteen were wounded in a stabbing spree by a man who ran amok inside the school in 2001.

It specifies the obligation of the national government, local authorities, and schools regarding school health and school safety (Takayama 2010). 1 of the Act specifies that national and local governments should collaborate to implement school safety efforts at the school level and provide financial support and other necessary assistance based on the latest knowledge and information on DRR. The Act also stipulates that the national government should formulate a school safety plan that promotes school safety efforts and that the local government should follow the national government's guidelines. Article 3 specifies school safety issues and articulates a school's roles and responsibilities, including preparing a school safety plan, ensuring a safe school environment, creating a crisis management manual, and promoting collaboration between the school and the community.

This clear definition of roles and responsibilities among authorities in educational governance helps mainstream school safety within the education sector. In the vertical structure of Japanese educational governance from MEXT down to prefectural boards of education, municipal boards of education and schools, each level promotes school safety. Mainstreaming school safety in this structure supports schools that have the main responsibility for securing children's safety (Fig. 8.2).

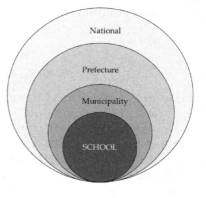

Level	Roles and Responsibilities
National	• Financial support • Development of school safety promotion plan
Prefecture	• Financial support • Support implementation of national plan by municipalities and schools
Municipality	• Establishment of a school • Prevent any risky events related to pupils and students • Improving facilities, equipment, and operational management organization at school
School	• Development of school safety plan and crisis response manual • Promoting collaboration with parents, community organizations, and local residents

Fig. 8.2 Roles and responsibilities for school safety in the educational structure (*Source* Created by the author based on MEXT 2019)

Institutional Structures for School Safety

Under the Order for the Organization of MEXT, school safety is located in the gender equality, cohesive society learning, and safety division under the Education Policy Bureau. In the last five years, the location of the division dealing with school safety has been changed three times. School safety is a newly recognized field in school education policies. Previously, the division was under the Primary and Secondary Education Bureau with school health education. However, with the restructuring of MEXT, the division was moved under the General Policy Education Bureau. Also, the Department of Facilities Planning and Administration under the minister's secretariat is responsible for school facility safety. The promotion of school safety in Japan occurs within these legislative and institutional frameworks.

In Japan, school safety is composed of three areas: disaster safety, traffic safety, and daily life safety (Fig. 8.3). Life safety covers daily incidents

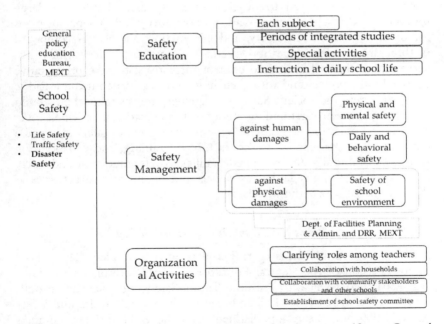

Fig. 8.3 School safety system in the Japanese education sector (*Source* Created by the author based on MEXT 2019)

and cases, including protecting students from predators, kidnapping, and assault. Traffic safety covers various traffic hazard countermeasures. Disaster safety deals with preparedness for and responses to all types of natural disasters, including earthquakes, tsunamis, volcanic activity, climate-related disasters, and nuclear incidents. Food poisoning at school meals, school sanitation, narcotic abuse, crimes related to illegal and harmful Web sites, and violence among students are covered in the school meal, school health, and student guidance areas.

Three Areas of School Safety

School safety aims at nurturing the competencies and capacities of students to respect their lives and others', behave safely, and contribute to the safety of others and society, in addition to building secure environments for students. School safety is composed of three activities: safety education, safety management, and organizational activities (Fig. 8.3). Each school is required to develop its safety plan. Under the large umbrella of the school safety plan, schools also develop separate plans for disaster safety, traffic safety, and life safety. Each plan is composed of three areas. Safety education teaches students to predict various risks surrounding themselves and to control these risks, to take preventative actions by themselves and with their judgment, and to contribute to the safety of others and society. Safety management means that schools build a safe environment surrounding students. Organizational activities cover an entire school effort with the development of a school safety plan and a crisis management manual, in-school teacher training, and collaboration with the community and students' families. Safety education and safety management can be regarded as wheels and organizational activities as the axle that supports the wheels.

Plans for Promotion of School Safety

MEXT is responsible for preparing a plan on school safety. The School Safety Division of the Central Education Council formulated the Five-Year (2012–2016) Plan to Promote School Safety and then the Second-term Five-Year (2017–2021) Plan based on the School Health and Safety Act of 2009 and the lessons learned from the 2011 disaster. Findings from the series of reports prepared by MEXT after the 2011 disaster were incorporated into the Five-Year (2012–2016) Plan to Promote School Safety (MEXT 2012b).

The Plan aims to promote comprehensive and effective school safety measures empirically based on an idea of "safety promotion," which tries to prevent injuries and incidents through collaboration beyond departments and to evaluate interventions scientifically with the goal of zero deaths due to incidents and disasters at a school. The Plan set 43 indicators under 12 targets to monitor the progress of the efforts, in terms of (i) enhancing disaster education, (ii) improving school safety plans, (iii) enhancing school facilities and equipment, (iv) preventing incidents through a PDCA cycle, and (v) collaborating with households, communities, and related agencies in each school district.

MEXT reviewed the achievements of the First-term Five-Year Plan and concluded that adequate student safety could not be achieved according to the development stages of the children and the geographic, and socioeconomic conditions of each school. Thus, the Second-term Five-Year Plan, which began in April 2017, emphasizes filling in the gaps among regions, schools, and teachers, and making more of an effort to promote school safety at all schools in Japan. The Plan also carried over the same goal of zero deaths due to incidents and disasters at a school (MEXT 2017).

At the end of the First-term Five-Year Plan, it was found that 19 among 43 indicators, including the development of a school safety plan (96.5%), development of a school crisis management manual (97.2%), regular mandated review of the school safety plan (96.5%), and review of a crisis management manual (92.9%), were achieved at more than 90% of all schools. All schools at all levels throughout Japan were encouraged to improve. However, issues were identified in terms of collaboration with households, communities, and related agencies. Further efforts should be made beyond the school to promote collaboration with the community (MEXT 2017) (Table 8.4).

Table 8.4 Status of school collaboration with households and communities in 2015 (N = 48,497 Schools)

Indicators	Status (2015) %
Percentage of schools that organized a meeting to request collaboration and exchange information among households, communities, and relevant agencies	87.3
Percentage of schools that established a collaborative mechanism to prepare school evacuation shelters among the municipal DRR section and the local residents	63.5
Percentage of schools that establish an advisory mechanism for school safety plans and evacuation drills led by experts	33.1

Source MEXT (2017)

LESSONS LEARNED FROM THE OKAWA ELEMENTARY SCHOOL INCIDENT

Okawa Elementary School Incident

Okawa Elementary School (hereafter as OES) was a public elementary school in Ishinomaki City in Miyagi Prefecture. The prefecture population was more than 160,000 before the 2011 disaster. In the city, 2978 deaths and 669 missing persons were recorded for the 2011 disaster (as of October 2011), the highest rate of casualties among the disaster-affected municipalities, and 22% of the overall death toll. The highest recorded tsunami by the earthquake in the city was more than 8.6 meters high, which washed away 15,941 houses.

The damage to the whole education sector in Ishinomaki City was also substantial. Among school-aged children from kindergarten to high school in Ishinomaki City, 166 children were killed, and 16 went missing. All 71 educational facilities in the city were damaged. At OES, 74 of 108 pupils and 10 teachers were lost under school supervision along with numerous local persons by the 2011 tsunami that came upstream along the Kitakami River. Okawa Elementary School was located on the riverside but 4.5 kilometers inland northeast from the mouth of the river. The two-story school building was inundated up to the roof and destroyed.

On March 11, the principal was off-duty, so the vice principal was the decision-maker in charge of evacuating the students. The students, along with teachers and individuals from the local community, remained on the

Fig. 8.4 A photo of the remaining building of OES (taken by the author in July 2019)

Fig. 8.5 A photo of the Kitakami River Bridge (left) and OES (right) (taken by the author in July 2019)

school grounds for more than 40 minutes. Then, they were fleeing to an area near a bridge over the Kitakami River, about 6 meters higher than the school grounds, when they were struck by the tsunami around 15:37 (Figs. 8.4 and 8.5).

Twenty-Four Recommendations in the Investigation Report by the OES Incident Investigation Committee

A third-party investigation board completed their final report in March 2014 with 24 recommendations for actions-related agencies, residents, educational personnel, and DRR experts should take to avoid a repeat of the tragedy at other schools (Okawa Elementary School Incident Investigation Board 2014).

The report described multiple issues related to the teachers' actions and decision making on the day of the disaster, school administrators' and local authorities' insufficient steps taken, and education provided before and after the disaster (Okawa Elementary School Incident Investigation Board 2014). Based on analyses conducted by 10 investigating committee members, comprising 108 interviews of 196 persons involved (including survivors), 24 recommendations were put forth as proposals for future disaster preparedness.

The OES incident was so catastrophic that the recommendations should strongly influence DRR policymaking and practices. Although the report received much criticism because it could not find causes of the children's loss, the 24 recommendations cover a wide range of school risk and crisis management aspects. Moreover, although the so-called successes or failures of school evacuations are distinct from each other, a thorough examination of school evacuations at the 2011 disaster suggested that many so-called successes were uncomfortably close to being failures (Seo 2014). For example, in one case, a school's roof was only a few meters above the inundation line, and the entire structure could easily have been flooded in a slightly more severe tsunami. These examinations emphasized the need to establish systemic DRR programs for teachers who could be called upon to make crucial life-and-death decisions during future disasters (Oda 2017).

Ishinomaki City and its Board of Education established a Committee on School Disaster Prevention Promotion and have been enhancing school safety at schools to realize the 24 recommendations. Since it is worthwhile sharing what could be done to make the school safety efforts more practical and substantial, in terms of comprehensive school safety, based on the lessons learned from the OES incident, a summary of the 24 recommendations is shown in Table 8.5.

Court Decisions in the Okawa Elementary School Case

Following the release of the final report by the investigation board, 23 of the victims' families sued the Miyagi Prefecture and Ishinomaki City governments in civil court to pursue answers to the question: "What happened at OES on March 11?"

Table 8.5 Summary of recommendations by the investigation committee of OES incident

Recommendations for prevention countermeasures to avoid further incidents

Education for teachers and staff on disaster prevention and crisis management
1. Mandate pre-service teacher training on DRR (For MEXT and each teacher training universities)
2. Implement substantial in-service training to raise schools' awareness of DRR. Share training experiences among teachers and staff at school (for MEXT and prefectural and municipal boards of education and schools)
3. Develop crew resource management (CRM) training or its equivalent non-technical skill training (for MEXT and prefectural and municipal boards of education and schools)

Improvement of school disaster response manual
4. Choose appropriate evacuation locations, routes, and measures according to potential natural hazards based on the understanding of the local disaster risk and environment at each school. Municipal boards of education should support these school efforts by providing necessary professional knowledge through their collaborative networks
5. Municipal boards of education should guide to improve the school disaster response manual through regular supervision

Importance of information gathering and securing measures for communication at school
6. Municipal governments should take countermeasures to communicate evacuation information promptly and without fail to schools, designated evacuation locations, and shelters
7. Each school should clarify measures to disseminate information proactively, to acknowledge disaster risk around the school immediately, and establish a communication mechanism with firefighters and neighborhood associations
8. Each school should facilitate collaboration with parents and community organizations for school disaster prevention and crisis management. Municipal governments and BOEs should support the collaboration by setting occasions for meetings
9. Municipal governments should establish an evacuation shelter management mechanism at the school evacuation shelter to avoid heavy dependence on the school and to realize resident-driven management. Municipal BOEs should cooperate with municipal governments

Collaboration with the community and parents
10. Each school should be involved in the decision of whether the school is appropriate as a shelter for residents according to each natural hazard. Municipal BOEs should provide support to schools to prepare a disaster response manual based on the assumption that schools are used as community evacuation shelters, and examine how schools could be used as a shelter and a school to provide education services at the same time

(continued)

Table 8.5 (continued)

Recommendations for prevention countermeasures to avoid further incidents

---

Disaster evacuation drills and disaster education

11. Each school should predict possible natural disasters as much as possible and conduct evacuation drills. BOEs should provide appropriate guidance and support
12. Each school should conduct the regular practice of the procedures for releasing children to their parents
13. Each school should conduct disaster education seamlessly with evacuation drills by understanding the local environment of the school neighborhood

Location of school and designs and layout

14. MEXT should stipulate standards for school locations in terms of student safety and DRR. When building a school, the geographic condition of the school site should be considered, especially near the coast and rivers. When it is difficult to build a school on higher ground, evacuation routes to higher ground should be created
15. School facilities should be designed to consider the local disaster risk and environment, as well as possible natural disasters

Proper understanding of hazard maps

16. Municipalities should review and examine the development process of current and future hazard maps based on the local geographic features and geomorphology. Residents should check hazard maps in their area and attempt to understand local disaster risk by making their maps. Each school should compare the hazard maps and the school district's local hazards, and prepare an evacuation map
17. Experts should help residents understand disaster risk correctly through active dissemination and communication of information

Disaster response in the municipal disaster risk reduction division

18. Municipalities should distinguish clearly the difference between emergency evacuation locations and evacuation shelters, and designate evacuation locations according to the type of hazard, equip these locations with communication measures, and share information with the public
19. Municipalities should take countermeasures to ensure correct communication with schools and residents during a disaster

Recommendations for appropriate response postvention

Incident response headquarters

20. Municipalities should prepare a plan to establish a countermeasure headquarters to gather information on damage, support for school management, requests from those affected, and the bereaved once schools are affected by a disaster

Support to victims and the bereaved

21. MEXT should set guidelines for supporting victims and the bereaved
22. Each school and municipal BOE should examine, plan, and implement training to conduct hearings from students during the investigation regarding the human casualties of an incident/disaster at school

Investigation and verification of the incident

23. MEXT should prepare for guidelines for incident investigation and verification
24. Any person who is involved in the incident investigation should judge with discretion on how much information to disseminate to the public

Source Created by the author with translation based on the 2014 Okawa Elementary School Incident Investigation Board report

In October 2016, the Sendai District Court ruled that the Ishinomaki City and Miyagi prefectural governments were negligent and that the school could have expected the arrival of the tsunami when city vehicles urging evacuation passed at around 15:30. The court also acknowledged that the school failed to choose a nearby mountain for evacuation where pupils could have been saved and ordered the city and the prefecture to pay a total of roughly JPY 1.4 billion to the relatives of the victims in compensation. Both the plaintiffs and defendants appealed the case to the high court.

In April 2018, the Sendai High Court ordered the Ishinomaki City and Miyagi Prefecture governments to pay about JPY 2.3 billion to the families. The court decision stated that the deaths of the elementary school children could have been prevented if the prefecture and city governments had updated their disaster contingency plans. The judgment stated that the school had obligations to set a third evacuation area for the tsunami, as well as clarify evacuation areas and evacuation routes in the school's risk management manual and that the school had failed to do so due to negligence (The Mainichi Newspaper, April 27, 2018). The Supreme Court rejected the appeal by the city and prefectural governments and upheld the high court's ruling on October 10, 2019.

Table 8.6 shows a summary of the arguments and court decisions. The Sendai District Court decision was mainly about the tsunami evacuation behavior on March 11, 2011, but the Sendai High Court decision pointed out that the school could have foreseen the tsunami arrival risk and could have prepared for the third evacuative location in their disaster response manual based on articles 26 and 29 in the School Health and Safety Act of 2009. Although the school was not located in a tsunami inundation area on the City's tsunami hazard map, the court concluded that the map did not exclude tsunami arrival risk at the school by considering other available information, such as the school's location. The high court decision also pointed out that the school principal is requested to accumulate more disaster risk information than residents to secure student safety based on the School Health and Safety Act.

Following the finalization of the high court decision, in December 2019 MEXT issued a notification letter to all boards of education and others in charge of kindergartens, nurseries, elementary, junior high, high, and vocational schools, and universities to improve school safety management against natural disasters, and to promote practical disaster education (MEXT 2019). The letter requested educational authorities urge all

8 SCHOOL SAFETY MANAGEMENT: INTERNATIONAL ... 189

Table 8.6 Allegations and judgment in the OES incident case

Points of contention	23 families of victims (Plaintiff)	City and Prefecture Governments (Defendant)	Sendai District Court Judgment (October 2016)	Sendai High Court Judgment (April 2018)
Foresee ability	The school could foresee the risk of tsunami arrival	It was not possible to foresee the risk	The school was warned 7 minutes before the tsunami arrived	The school could have foreseen the tsunami arrival risk based on the information on April 30, 2010
Organizational negligence	The City Board of Education (CBE) failed to instruct the school to improve its disaster risk manual	The CBE provided adequate guidance to schools	The school did not have an obligation to improve the manual	The school failed to improve its manual, and the CBE failed to guide the school
Avoidable consequences	If the school had decided in advance where to evacuate, all the victims could have survived	It was not possible to evacuate all the students with knowledge and information about the timing	Teachers have some negligence because they did not evacuate students	If the evacuation place had been decided in advance, the consequences could have been avoided

Source Created by the author with translation based on the Sendai High Court's (2016) decision

schools to review, check, and improve their school safety management and disaster education to prepare for future natural disasters, focusing on school safety plans, school disaster response manuals, and collaboration mechanisms among the school, households, the community, and related agencies.

DISCUSSION

This chapter articulated school risk and crisis management vis-à-vis school safety against natural disasters articulated from international and Japanese perspectives. Two important approaches to school disaster risk and crisis management were identified. The first is a comprehensive approach to ensure school safety in a natural disaster, while the second is a DRR approach to minimize the impact of a natural disaster at school. These approaches are integrated into the Sendai Framework for Disaster Risk Reduction and became one of the global targets for DRR. More concretely, minimizing deaths and injuries of children at school is the most important goal of school disaster risk and crisis management. To achieve this goal, comprehensive efforts are urgently requested at schools to secure the safety of the school learning facilities, school disaster management, and disaster risk reduction education under educational policies, and plans aligned to national, sub-national, and local disaster management plans.

In Japan, school safety has been promoted since the 1995 Hanshin Awaji earthquake disaster and has been evolved based on lessons learned from experiences since then (Sakurai and Sato 2016). Legal and institutional school safety plans are implemented within the Japanese educational structure, and national plans for promoting school safety have been implemented since 2012. Many reference materials, handbooks, and sub-reading materials have been prepared by MEXT and prefectural boards of education, and they are freely available on the web as "School Safety X MEXT" (https://anzenkyouiku.mext.go.jp/).

Although disaster and safety plans were in place, the 2011 disaster challenged their effectiveness for protecting children's lives at schools. The OES incident and the high court ruling recommended all schools prepare for effective and practical school disaster safety based on the school district's risk assessment with the support of the municipal board of education. This, effectiveness and practicality of school disaster safety is the second important points, identified from the Japanese experiences, to approach school safety.

The ruling that each school should foresee its own local disaster risk was challenging, because the possible types of natural disasters, degree of the disaster, and its impact on the school vary according to the geographic, socioeconomic conditions of the school and its school district. Nonetheless, the ruling recommends all schools should be prepared with an effective contingency plan.

This recommendation was based on the fact that a school is a public facility that provides education for students organizationally and as planned. Parents send their children to the school to implement their duty to receive compulsory education as a citizen of Ishinomaki City. Thus, the school should secure the safety of children based on trust from their parents. If not, the school is negligent.

As an example, in assessing the local disaster risk at each school, contour maps and geomorphological maps are started to be utilized at school to increase understanding of local hazard maps by school children and teachers. The Reconstruction and Disaster Risk Reduction Mapping Program is an educational program implemented at elementary and junior high schools in the City since 2012 (Sakurai et al. 2019). In the program, students compare the latest contour map and the previous contour map to identify different patterns of land use, understand geographic features of their school district, and figure out safe and dangerous locations by comparing these maps and hazard maps of their school district in the classroom. After in-class learning, students go out into the school district to confirm what they understand from the maps and to interview local community residents to understand previous disaster experiences and the efforts to recover from the disaster. Based on this information, reconstruction and disaster risk reduction maps are produced as children's outputs of the Reconstruction and Disaster Risk Reduction Mapping Program. In addition, an in-service training program for teachers was initiated in 2019 (Sakurai et al. 2019). The training was organized to improve teachers' map reading skills, help them identify the school district's local disaster risk, and revise their school disaster manual based on the local disaster risk. A key approach is the provision of a package of maps that contain local disaster risk information for each school district.

CONCLUSIONS

This chapter mainly discussed school disaster risk and crisis management in the case of Japan. Not only in Japan, but school safety efforts have also been promoted in China and South Korea in the East Asian region. In China, the School Safety Law was proposed at the 12th National Committee of the Chinese People's Political Consultative Conference (CPCC) in 2017, and the Department of Basic Education of the Ministry of Education of China is in charge of school safety. In South Korea, the School Safety Law was enacted in 2018, and the School Safety Division, Educational Safety Information Bureau of the Ministry of Education of South Korea is in charge. Bilateral collaboration on school safety has also been promoted. For example, the Japanese Agency for International Cooperation (JICA) supported a technical cooperation project for promotion and capacity development of disaster mitigation education in 2015–2018. Among university researchers, collaborative research has accumulated as Japan and China are disaster-prone countries, especially after the 2008 Sichuan earthquake and recovery. Exchanges of experiences have occurred between South Korea and Japan, especially after the Sewol incident, in terms of providing mental healthcare for surviving students and communication with bereaved families.

Also, the governments of China, South Korea, and Japan support the Association of Southeast Asian Nations (ASEAN) to promote regional collaboration on DRR. ASEAN has ASEAN Committee on Disaster Management (ADCM) as a regional body that promotes and monitors implementation of the Sendai Framework. Disasters are inevitable daily phenomena in ASEAN, and the region is on the verge of losing USD 8.35 trillion, which is three times ASEAN's nominal gross domestic product (GDP) in 2018 (AHA Centre 2019). ASEAN is improving regional collaboration based on the ASEAN Vision on Disaster Management 2025 and the ASEAN Socio-Cultural Community Blueprint 2025. In 2011, ASEAN established the ASEAN Coordinating Centre for Humanitarian Assistance on Disaster Management (AHA Centre), a coordinating center for humanitarian assistance on disaster management to promote regional collaboration and realize "One ASEAN One Response." Regarding school safety, there is a mechanism called the ASEAN Safe School Initiative based on the ASEAN Common Framework for Comprehensive School Safety. However, much space remains to promote further collaboration not only within the East Asia region but also in the South East Asia region.

In a risk society, schools face diversified risk. Therefore, regardless of the types of risk, it is important to keep exchanging experiences and lessons learned on school safety to protect children's lives at school. Experiences of a school regardless of whether it is a success or failure should be shared with other schools in the country, the regions, and the world for promoting the realization of a safer school.

REFERENCES

The ASEAN Coordinating Centre for Humanitarian Assistance on Disaster Management (AHA Centre). 2019. *ASEAN Risk Monitor and Disaster Management Review*. Jakarta: AHA Centre.

Beck, Ulrich. 1999. *World Risk Society*. Cambridge: Polity Press.

Ehara, Etsuko. 2012. Jido seito no jiko saigai ni yoru shibou hasseiritsu no hachinennkan no hikaku [Comparison of Students' Fatality Incidence Rate by Incidents and Disasters]. Hyogo: Hyogo University of Teacher Education. http://52.197.196.111/dspace/bitstream/10132/6017/1/YV3 1501001.pdf. Accessed 20 Feb 2020.

Global Alliance for Disaster Risk Reduction and Resilience in the Education Sector (GADRRRES). 2017. *Comprehensive School Safety*. Geneve: UNISDR and GADRRRES. https://www.undrr.org/publication/comprehensive-school-safety. Accessed 20 Feb 2020.

Global Coalition to Protect Education from Attack (GCPEA). 2014. *Safe Schools Declaration and Guidelines on Military Use: Global Coalition to Protect Education from Attack*. New York: GCPEA. http://www.protectingeducation.org/safe-schools-declaration-guidelines. Accessed 20 Feb 2020.

International Organization for Standardization (ISO). 2009. *ISO/DIS 22300(en) Security and resilience—Terminology*. Geneve: ISO. https://www.iso.org/iso-31000-risk-management.html. Accessed 20 Feb 2020.

International Organization for Standardization (ISO). 2014. *ISO/IEC GUIDE 51:2014 Safety Aspects—Guidelines for Their Inclusion in Standards*. Geneve: ISO. https://www.iso.org/standard/53940.html. Accessed 20 Feb 2020.

International Safe Schools (ISS) Certifying Centers. 2014. *International Safe Schools*. Tucson: ISS. https://internationalsafeschool.com/. Accessed 20 Feb 2020.

Investigation Committee of Okawa Elementary School Incident. 2014. *Okawa shogakko jiko kensho hokokusho* [Investigation Report of Okawa Elementary School Incident]. Ishinomaki, Miyagi: Ishinomaki City. https://www.city.ishinomaki.lg.jp/cont/20101800/8425/20140303164845.html. Accessed 20 Feb 2020.

Ministry of Education, Culture, Sports, Science and Technology (MEXT). 2011a. *Higashinihon daishinsai wo uketa bosai kyoiku bosai kanri nado ni kansuru yushikishakaigi chukan torimatome* [Mid-Term Report from Council on Disaster Prevention Education and Management in the Wake of the Great East Japan Earthquake]. Tokyo: MEXT. https://www.mext.go.jp/b_menu/shingi/chousa/sports/012/toushin/__icsFiles/afieldfile/2011/10/05/131 1688_01_1.pdf. Accessed 20 Feb 2020.

Ministry of Education, Culture, Sports, Science, and Technology (MEXT). 2011b. *Higashinihon daishinsai niokeru gakko shisetsu no tsunami higai jokyo ni tsuite* [Situation Report on Damage to School Facilities by Tsunami of the Great East Japan Earthquake Disaster]. Tokyo: MEXT. Accessed 20 Feb 2020. https://www.mext.go.jp/b_menu/shingi/chousa/shisetu/013/007/shiryo/__icsFiles/afieldfile/2013/07/29/1335813_02.pdf. Accessed 20 Feb 2020.

Ministry of Education, Culture, Sports, Science and Technology (MEXT). 2012a. *Higashinihon daishinsai wo uketa bosai kyoiku bosai kanri nado ni kansuru yushikishakaigi saishu hokoku* [Final Report from Council on Disaster Prevention Education and Management in the Wake of the Great East Japan Earthquake]. Tokyo: MEXT. https://www.mext.go.jp/b_menu/shingi/cho usa/sports/012/toushin/__icsFiles/afieldfile/2012/07/31/1324017_01. pdf. Accessed 20 Feb 2020.

Ministry of Education, Culture, Sports, Science and Technology (MEXT). 2012b. *Gakko anzen no suishin ni kansuru keikaku* [Five-Year (2012–2106) Plan to Promote School Safety]. Tokyo: MEXT. https://www.mext.go.jp/a_menu/kenko/anzen/__icsFiles/afieldfile/2012/05/01/1320286_2.pdf. Accessed 20 Feb 2020.

Ministry of Education, Culture, Sports, Science and Technology(MEXT). 2012c. *Gakko no kiki kanri manyuaru sakusei no tebiki* [Handbook for Schools on Preparing a Crisis Management Manual: Earthquake and Tsunami Version]. Tokyo: MEXT. https://www.mext.go.jp/a_menu/kenko/anzen/1323513. htm. Accessed 20 Feb 2020.

Ministry of Education, Culture, Sports, Science and Technology (MEXT). 2012d. *Higashinihon daishinsai ni okeru gakko tou no taiou ni kansuru chosa kenkyu hokoku* [Research Study on Schools' Response to the 2011 Great East Japan Earthquake Disaster]. Tokyo: MEXT. https://www.mext.go.jp/a_menu/kenko/anzen/1323511.htm. Accessed 20 Feb 2020.

Ministry of Education, Culture, Sports, Science, and Technology (MEXT). 2014. *Gakko niokeru anzen kyoiku no jyujistsu ni tuite shingi no matome* [Summary of Discussion on Enhancing Safety Education at School]. Tokyo: MEXT. https://www.mext.go.jp/component/b_menu/shingi/toushin/__ics Files/afieldfile/2014/11/19/1353563_02_3_1.pdf. Accessed 20 Feb 2020.

Ministry of Education, Culture, Sports, Science, and Technology (MEXT). 2017. *Dai niji gakko anzen no suishin ni kansuru keikaku* [Five-Year (2017–2021) Plan to Promote School Safety]. Tokyo: MEXT. https://www.mext.go.jp/a_menu/kenko/anzen/__icsFiles/afieldfile/2017/06/13/138 3652_03.pdf. Accessed 20 Feb 2020.

Ministry of Education, Culture, Sports, Science, and Technology (MEXT). 2019. *Shizen saigai ni taisuru gakko bosasi taisei no kyoka oyobi jissenteki na bosai kyoiku no suishin ni tsuite, irai* [Request to Strengthen School Safety Structure Against Natural Disasters, and to Promote Practical Disaster Education, Ministerial Notification Letter]. Tokyo: MEXT. https://www.mext.go.jp/a_menu/kenko/anzen/1422067_00001.htm. Accessed 20 Feb 2020.

Oda, Takashi. 2017. Schools, Teachers, and Training in Risk Reduction After the 2011 Tohoku Disaster. Chap. 5 in *Disaster Resilience of Education Systems*, edited by Koichi Shiwaku, Aiko Sakurai, and Rajib Shaw, 53–71. Tokyo: Springer.

Sakurai, Aiko, and Takeshi Sato. 2016. Promoting Education for Disaster Resilience and the Sendai Framework for Disaster Risk Reduction. *Journal of Disaster Research* 11 (3): 402–412.

Sakurai, Aiko, Sanae Kitaura, Takeshi Sato, and Yoshiyuki Murayama. 2019. Chiiki ni nezashita saigai hukko bosai kyoiku puroguramu no kaihatsu, Ishinomaki shiritsu gakko deno hukko bosai mappu dukuri gonen kan no jissen wo humaete [Development of a Community-Based Disaster Recovery and Disaster Prevention Program-Based on the Five-Year Implementation at Public Schools in Ishinomaki City, Miyagi Prefecture]. *The Japanese Journal of Safety Education* 18 (1): 23–36.

Sakurai, Aiko, Takashi Oda, Yoshiyuki Murayama, and Takeshi Sato. 2019. Linking Geomorphological Features and Disaster Risk in a School District: The Development of an in-Service Teacher Training Programme. Abstract for the 12th Aceh International Workshop on Sustainable Tsunami Disaster Recovery Sharing Tohoku-Aceh Experience, Knowledge, and Culture. Sendai, November 8.

Sendai High Court. 2016. *Hanketsu Heisei 28 nen (ne) dai 381 go kokkabaisho tou seikyuu kouso jiken* [Decision No. 381 on Initial Appeal to a High Court].

Seo, K. 2014. Tsunami saigai to gakko-Higashi Nihon Daishinsai no hinan kodo kara manada koto [Tsunami and Schools: What We Learned from Evacuation Behaviors During the 3.11 Tsunami]. *Bulletin of Support Center for Revival in Education* 1: 1–14. Miyagi University of Education. http://fukkou.miy akyo-u.ac.jp/report/pdf/no2/01.seo.pdf. Accessed 20 Feb 2020.

Takayama, Ken. 2010. Recent Tasks of School Health Administration in Japan. *Journal of the Japan Medical Association (JMAJ)* 53 (3): 144–147. https:// www.med.or.jp/english/journal/pdf/2010_03/144_147.pdf. Accessed 20 Feb 2020.

UNISDR. 2005. *Hyogo Framework for Action 2005–2015*. Geneva: UNISDR.

UNISDR. 2015. *Sendai Framework for Disaster Risk Reduction 2015–2030*. Geneva: UNISDR.

PART IV

International Cooperation in Risk Management

CHAPTER 9

Aid Policies in Disaster Risk Reduction: Japan and the Development Assistance to Disaster-Prone Developing Countries

Hazuki Matsuda and Keiichi Ogawa

INTRODUCTION

As a country vulnerable to natural catastrophes, Japan has built several disaster prevention and preparedness mechanisms based on its experiences. The lessons learned, as well as innovative technologies, have been transferred to disaster-prone developing nations through development assistance channels to help them cope with crisis uncertainties and mitigate both human and economic losses. This chapter discusses how the disaster risk reduction (DRR) framework has evolved in the context of aid, thereby identifying policy and practice changes in addressing natural calamities. By reviewing the DRR instrument from the Yokohama

---

H. Matsuda (✉) · K. Ogawa
Graduate School of International Cooperation Studies, Kobe
University, Hyogo Prefecture, Japan
e-mail: matsuda.hazuki@people.kobe-u.ac.jp

K. Ogawa
e-mail: ogawa35@kobe-u.ac.jp

© The Author(s), under exclusive license to Springer Nature
Singapore Pte Ltd. 2021
Y. Jing et al. (eds.), *Risk Management in East Asia*,
https://doi.org/10.1007/978-981-33-4586-7_9

Strategy, the Hyogo Framework for Action 2005–2015 (HFA), and the Sendai Framework for Disaster Risk Reduction 2015–2030, this chapter explores implications for Japan's DRR cooperation policies. Although the first technical cooperation was recorded in the 1960s with the deployment of experts to Iran for post-disaster reconstruction, aid policies at the time were centered on restoring damaged infrastructure. Since the 1990s, a more socially oriented, humanitarian approach has been adopted. The first part of this chapter covers the conceptual framework of DRR to assess the Yokohama Strategy, as well as the HFA and Sendai Framework, underscoring that Japan played an influencing role in determining some of its policies. Subsequently, the chapter outlines the historical evolution of Japan's development cooperation from the DRR perspective, examining some cases of DRR programs implemented in disaster-prone developing nations. It concludes that Japan's development cooperation policies transformed along with changes in the international environment, and these shifts also affected, to some extent, the national DRR framework, adjusting to new global circumstances. Although joint efforts that integrate local stakeholders in devising strategies are crucial, the incorporation of traditional or indigenous methods to complement modern technology can also lessen risks in disaster-prone aid recipient states.

Conceptual Framework of Disaster Risk Reduction

The term DRR evolved gradually to adapt to new international policies and practices in addressing natural disaster issues. In 2004, the United Nations International Strategy for Disaster Reduction (UNISDR) defined the first DRR concept in the context of sustainable development (UNISDR 2004, 17). Later, after the HFA was adopted, the notion was revised under the "2009 UNISDR Terminology on Disaster Risk Reduction" to standardize the understanding of the term (UNISDR 2009) at the global level. Finally, in 2016, the "Open-ended intergovernmental expert working group on indicators and terminology relating to disaster risk reduction," established by the UN General Assembly (UNGA), presented a new version of the idea to implement the Sendai Framework, which the UNGA accepted in 2017.

Today, DRR is defined as a political framework "aimed at preventing new and reducing existing disaster risk and managing residual risk, all of which contribute to strengthening resilience and, therefore, to the achievement of sustainable development" (A/171/644) (UNGA 2016,

16). This concept entails prevention, mitigation, and preparedness as it seeks to avoid or alleviate the impacts of eventual hazards and ensure countries to be prepared to respond to disaster situations and recover from adverse events. The UNGA explains that the DRR is an objective of disaster risk management, and it has its unique strategies and plans (UNGA 2016, 16) based on several measures (e.g., preventive awareness) to attain sustainable development.

Disaster management can be categorized into three components. The first is composed of prevention, mitigation, and preparedness and constitutes a fundamental stage in minimizing disaster risks. Response and recovery, as the second and third components, involve attending to people's needs in emergencies and assisting in repairing damage in devastated areas (see Fig. 9.1). This chapter focuses on the first aspect due to its crucial role in diminishing the impacts of potential losses, which include social, economic, and environmental assets. Based on experience and knowledge, donors such as Japan can contribute significantly

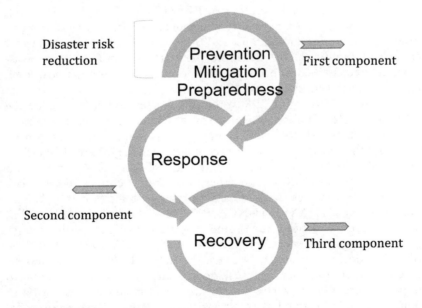

Fig. 9.1 Components of disaster management (*Source* Created by the authors based on UNDRR 2020; UNGA 2016)

in this phase, transferring technology to and increasing capacity building in disaster-prone developing countries.

DRR and International Cooperation: Historical Overview

The UN's involvement in DRR systems has a long history, and its policies and priorities have evolved gradually, changing specific international assistance patterns. The UN Office for Disaster Risk Reduction (UNDRR) traced a series of historical stages of DRR that outline how assistance started from a merely technical approach and became applicable on a global scale, integrating the goals of sustainable development (UNDRR 2020). The first measure adopted to tackle disasters took place in the 1960s with the Buyin-Zara earthquake in northwestern Iran. The UN called for technical aid and cooperation from the international community in the field of seismological research and earthquake engineering to design adequate earthquake-resistant structures and other warning systems and relief actions (see UN Resolution A/RES/1753(XVII)) (UNGA 1962, 28). Japan was one of the nations that deployed its technical team to investigate damages to buildings and other concerned structures in that country (Omote et al. 1962). From the 1960s onward, technical assistance for reconstruction plans began to occur at the international level, aiming to cope with devastation in developing states.

From the 1970s to the 1980s, the UN created and strengthened the UN Disaster Relief Office (UNDRO) in the context of "assistance in cases of natural disasters" to work on prevention, mitigation, preparedness, response, and reconstruction. Further, it encouraged global collaboration, inviting development agencies, the International Bank for Reconstruction and Development (IBRD), and other international entities to formulate and improve measures, such as early warning systems (see UN Resolution A/RES/2717(XXV)) (UNGA 1970, 83–84), in light of the need for global organizations to assume a greater role in assisting countries suffering from a catastrophic situation (UNGA 1971, 409). The Bhola cyclone, which struck then East Pakistan in 1970, provided lessons to enhance coordination between donors and aid recipient nations to respond more efficiently. Despite the emergency circumstances, owing to domestic political turmoil, the East Pakistani government refused to coordinate with international and national organs within its borders (Saban

2014, 21), leading to delayed responses, thus affecting local vulnerable people (Hossain 2018).

Post-1990, the natural disaster reduction principle entered into the international policy agenda due to the emergence of ongoing calamities, such as hurricanes and typhoons, in many developing nations. To address increasing natural disaster issues, the International Decade for Natural Disaster Reduction (IDNDR) was established, and the international community was called upon to implement it under the UN Resolution A/RES/45/185 (UNGA 1990, 113), with the aim to act jointly. The proposal of IDNDR, made by Japan (Bosai Hakusho 1996), was pivotal and led to further political resolutions (Nishikawa and Hosokawa 2015, 116–117) in the context of the UN. In subsequent years, disaster reduction strategies and plans of action were produced, including the Yokohama Strategy and the Plan of Action for a Safer World, the HFA, and the Sendai Framework, in line with new catastrophic events and the need to reinforce international commitments on sustainable development. This chapter analyses the three abovementioned DRR mechanisms against the background of international cooperation to link them to Japan's aid policies in development.

THE YOKOHAMA STRATEGY AND THE PLAN OF ACTION FOR A SAFER WORLD

In 1994, Japan hosted the World Conference on Natural Disaster Reduction, a global summit in which member countries of the UN, non-governmental organizations (NGOs), international organizations, epistemic groups, and the private sectors gathered to deliberate the mid-term accomplishment and failures of the IDNDR, as well as to define the principles, strategies, and the plan of action for DRR activities.

The IDNDR's mid-term report described limitations, rather than achievements, and, from the perspective of aid, included some of the points given below (IDNDR 1994, 10):

- Awareness of the potential benefits of disaster reduction is still limited to specialized circles and has not yet been successfully communicated to all sectors of society, in particular policymakers and the general public. This is due to a lack of attention for the issue, insufficient commitment and resources for promotional activities at all levels;

- At the same time, however, activities during the first years of the decade in training, technical applications and research at local, national, and international levels and in regional cooperation, have had positive results in some regions in reducing disaster losses;
- Equally, the creation of the organizational framework called for by the General Assembly, which includes National Decade Committees and Focal Points and, at the international level, the Special High-Level Council, the Scientific and Technical Committee and the Decade Secretariat, has laid the basis for intensified preventive and preparedness efforts in the second half of the Decade;
- These new efforts in the field of disaster reduction have not systematically been part of multilateral and bilateral development policies.

The international community recognized some failures of the IDNDR, and the Yokohama Framework defined a series of principles affirming the importance of disaster prevention and preparedness mechanism. It included principles that integrate a cooperative approach from domestic to international scale. Grounded in the standpoint of aid, the following tenets are highlighted (IDNDR 1994, 8):

- Disaster prevention and preparedness should be considered integral aspects of development policy and planning at national, regional, bilateral, multilateral, and international levels.
- The international community accepts the need to share the necessary technology to prevent, reduce, and mitigate disaster; this should be made freely available and promptly as an integral part of technical cooperation.
- Each country bears the primary responsibility for protecting its people, infrastructure, and other national assets from the impact of natural disasters. The international community should demonstrate strong political determination required to mobilize adequate and make efficient use of existing resources, including financial, scientific and technological means, in the field of natural disaster reduction, bearing in mind the needs of the developing countries, particularly the least developed countries.

Based on the above assumptions, a series of "Strategies for the year 2000 and beyond" was created, such as the reinforcement of traditional techniques along with modern scientific and technical know-how; the application of preventive steps at communal level; the promotion of community-based programs on disaster reduction; the development of a culture of prevention; the adoption of a self-reliance policy; and the allocation of resources for capacity building (IDNDR 1994, 9, 12), the last two patterns being standards practiced and incorporated into the Japanese culture.

In line with the defined principles and strategies, a plan of action was also established. In the context of aid policies, some actions were suggested, such as providing extra-budgetary resources to implement the IDNDR; integrating natural disaster prevention, mitigation, and preparedness into development assistance programs through bilateral and multilateral channels; ensuring cooperation for scientific research and technology in the area of natural disaster reduction; and enhancing capacity building in developing countries (IDNDR 1994, 16, 17). Within the global culture of prevention, after the strong earthquake that hit Turkey in 1999, the Japan International Cooperation Agency (JICA) not only responded to emergency needs, but also provided technical assistance for earthquake disaster mitigation and encouraged disaster prevention education in local schools.

A year after the abovementioned conference, in 1995, a catastrophic urban earthquake with a magnitude of 7.3 struck Japan. Known as the Great Hanshin-Awaji Earthquake, it destroyed the city of Kobe, demolished buildings and houses, and generated thousands of casualties. The primary lessons learned were that reporting system for damages and casualties from the municipal sector to prefectural and central governments was weak (Nishikawa and Hosokawa 2015, 120); there was a slow emergency response (Toyoda 2012, 241); and there were limits regarding making predictions and alleviating natural disasters (Toyoda 2016, 318). However, in the following years, urban planning, and infrastructure development (e.g., the construction of earthquake-resistant homes, buildings, and communication systems) improved. Scientific research has advanced in the abovementioned fields, thereby improving domestic public awareness.

The HFA (2005–2015)

With the conclusion of the IDNDR, the UNISDR was established as a successor to the first; its agency opened branches in Geneva and Kobe. In 2005, in order to review the Yokohama Strategy, the second world conference on DRR, known as HFA, was held in Hyogo Prefecture under the auspices of Japan. New challenges were identified, and a call for action was made in the following areas (UNISDR 2005, 2):

- Governance: organizational, legal, and policy frameworks;
- Risk identification, assessment, monitoring, and early warning;
- Knowledge management and education;
- Reducing underlying risk factors; and
- Preparedness for effective response and recovery.

The review of the Yokohama Strategy led to the adoption of five priorities for action on DRR, as follows (UNISDR 2005, 6):

- Ensure that disaster risk reduction is a national and a local priority with a strong institutional basis for implementation;
- Identify, assess and monitor disaster risks and enhance early warning;
- Use knowledge, innovation, and education to build a culture of safety and resilience at all levels;
- Reduce the underlying risk factors; and
- Strengthen disaster preparedness for effective response at all levels.

From the angle of international cooperation, states as well as regional and global bodies were encouraged to support the Framework of Action, mobilizing the resources needed to execute the action plan, including the provision of financial and technical aid, as well as technology transfer in disaster-prone developing countries through multilateral and bilateral channels. The HFA also suggests to "mainstream disaster risk reductions measures appropriately into multilateral and bilateral development assistance programmes including those related to poverty reduction, natural resource management, urban development and adaptation to climate change" (UNISDR 2005, 18–19). Some of them relate to the Millennium Development Goals (MDGs) adopted in 2000 (such as eradicating poverty, ensuring environmental sustainability, and creating a global partnership for development).

At the conference, the Japanese government announced the "Initiative for Disaster Reduction through ODA," which became the underlying policy for DRR in the context of international cooperation. It stated Japan's intention to proactively advance the self-help effort principle, which aimed to build disaster-resilient societies through several DRR programs in developing countries (MOFA 2005). After the HFA was formed, the International Recovery Platform (IRP) was established to provide and disseminate information on post-disaster recovery to the global community.

In line with the HFA, disaster management organizations and systems were set up in many nations (Priority 1), and disaster response systems (Priority 5) were strengthened (Cabinet Office 2015, 3). Moreover, educational materials on tsunamis were devised in developing countries to raise awareness (Priority 3). Early warning systems (Priority 2) were advocated for through the Asian Disaster Reduction Center (ADRC), founded by Asian states. Technology was actively transferred to developing countries such as Indonesia and the Philippines. In Indonesia, after the Great Indian Ocean Earthquake and Tsunami, Japan assisted in opening the National Disaster Management Agency (NDMA) and form the National Disaster Management Plan (NDMP). The NDMA provided technical assistance on disaster management at the local community level so that a more bottom-up approach could be instituted. In the Philippines—a country that suffers frequent typhoon damages—Japan has been working in the sphere of flood management over the Pasig/Marikina River, which crosses the Philippines' metropolitan region, helping to control the flow of the water (Cabinet Office 2014, 48–49). However, despite the progress, some challenges have been recognized such as the need to tackle global risks, including those related to urbanization, globalization, and meteorological disasters (Cabinet Office 2015, 3).

The Sendai Framework (2015–2030)

Prior to the third world conference in Sendai, Japan suffered another historical natural catastrophe in March 2011. The 9.0 magnitude earthquake struck the northeastern part of the country, and the subsequent tsunami took more than 18,000 lives, destroying buildings and houses throughout the region. Despite the severe human and material damage, it is believed that Japan's disaster prevention culture and advanced technology lessened the impact. Nonetheless, at the third UN World

Conference on DRR hosted by Japan in March 2015, lessons learned were presented and improvements were suggested to reduce future disaster risks.

At the conference, the Sendai Framework was created as a successor instrument to the HFA. The Sendai Framework encourages the international community to improve policies and practices surrounding DRR to prevent new disaster risks, underscoring the need to take action on delicate issues such as poverty, climate change, and unplanned and rapid urbanizations. The Sendai Framework calls for strengthening international and regional cooperation to help developing countries through bilateral and multilateral channels, as requested at previous world conferences, as a way to ensure the implementation of capacity building and provide financial and technical assistance, including the transfer of technology (UNISDR 2015, 9–10).

Following the HFA's implementation, four priorities for action were renewed in the Sendai Framework as follows (UNISDR 2015, 14):

- Understanding disaster risk, entailing prevention, mitigation, and preparedness, using among others "traditional, indigenous and local knowledge and practices, as appropriate, to complement scientific knowledge in disaster risk assessment";
- Strengthening disaster risk governance to manage disaster risk, through collaboration and partnership with relevant stakeholders;
- Investing in disaster risk reduction for resilience, through the allocation of resources into structural and non-structural measures; and
- Enhancing disaster preparedness for effective response and to "Build Back Better" in recovery, rehabilitation, and reconstruction.

In the context of international cooperation, several pertinent concerns were listed to implement the priority actions established in the Sendai Framework, such as the need to aid developing countries in their efforts to mitigate disaster risks and to boost technology transfer due to the disparity on their technological innovation and research capacity. It included considerations to offer support through partnerships to vulnerable nations with high disaster risk levels, and with limitations to respond to—and recover from—calamities, including small island and African states; to strengthen the North-South cooperation, South-South, and Triangular cooperation; and to offer assistance with capacity building (UNISDR 2015, 24–25).

From the authors' perspective, in reviewing the DRR instruments from the Yokohama Strategy to the HFA and Sendai Framework, two points have been identified regarding development efforts. While the first instrument outlined general strategies to promote a global culture of prevention, the second determined a framework for DRR, establishing a series of clear priorities (e.g., the use of knowledge and education to foster a culture of disaster prevention and resilience), through which technical aid has been provided. The third instrument, the Sendai Framework, is an improved version and provides a comprehensive DRR configuration that defines the action priorities by considering the special needs of small island and African states. It underscores the vital role of North-South, South-South, and Triangular cooperation, as well as partnerships with all relevant stakeholders.

On the other hand, alluding to the three abovementioned DRR tools, and given the critical observations about the community involvement in DRR (Tozier de la Poterie and Baudoin 2015), local knowledge and traditional techniques need to be incorporated into aid programs as concrete disaster prevention practices, when applicable, and merged with modern scientific technology. Various indigenous case studies have been identified as good practices based on the experiences of Asian countries (UNISDR 2008), and can be used as references to integrate them into DRR aid programs (depending on the local circumstances and applicability). This will encourage a more bottom-up approach, thereby contributing to the international goals and objectives of DRR.

In aid programs for which donor countries use their resources to conduct projects, it is crucial to involve local communities because traditional knowledge and practices can offer unique insights to improve the design of prevention measures. Toyoda presents a particular case in which failures were found in DRR projects implemented in Indonesia (Toyoda 2016, 323). Aid programs conducted without considering local circumstances and needs might fail. Hence, more thorough DRR practices need to be articulated in aid programs in order to attain sustainable development in developing nations.

Donor Countries' Commitment to DRR

Donor countries and multilateral organizations have different development policy approaches to DRR programs. However, a common agreement was made at the three world conferences (from the Yokohama Strategy to the HFA and Sendai Framework) to work on DRR in the context of aid, listing a series of priority actions. Although a wide range of commitments have been made in DRR frameworks, indices show that from 1991 to 2010, low priority was given to DRR compared to aid for emergency response, as well as reconstruction and rehabilitation. During this time, $3 trillion was spent on development aid; of this, the international community invested $106.7 billion in disasters, out of which, $13.5 billion was allocated to DRR measures or prevention and preparedness, $69.9 billion on emergency response, and $23.3 billion to reconstruction and rehabilitation. The $13.5 billion only represented 12.7% of the total aid designated for disasters during the two decades of that period (Kellet and Caravani 2013, 5–6). Hence, development assistance for DRR only accounted for a small fraction of overall international aid. Moreover, disaster-prone developing states and the least developing countries that are highly vulnerable to natural catastrophes (e.g., Kenya, Somalia, and Djibouti) received a disproportionate quantity of DRR aid compared to other nations (e.g., China, India, Turkey) despite the high mortality risk of the latter group (Watson et al. 2015, 4).

Notwithstanding the general low number of DRR investments provided by the international community, Japan has been the largest direct donor to DRR comprising 64% ($3.7 billion) of the total funding between 1991 and 2010. The most significant funding was for flood prevention and control projects, with Asian countries being the primary beneficiaries (Indonesia, the Philippines, China, Brazil, and Sri Lanka, in order of the amount received, from 1991 to 2010) (Kellet and Caravani 2013, 39–40). This share shows that Japan is advanced worldwide in terms of disaster prevention and preparedness and is aware of the importance of tackling this essential phase of DRR in developing and emerging countries.

JAPAN'S DEVELOPMENT COOPERATION FRAMEWORK AND THE EVOLUTION OF DRR POLICIES

Foreign aid policies in Japan are embedded in its Official Development Assistance (ODA) Charter (now called the Development Cooperation Charter). The first charter was enacted in 1992 and revised twice in 2003 and 2015, based on adjustments made due to international environment changes. Prior to the establishment of the ODA Charter, agencies engaged in Japan's ODA administration, such as JICA (then the Overseas Technical Cooperation Agency [OTCA]), was mandated to provide assistance in order to contribute to the economic development of aid recipient nations. This is because the general principle of the Ministry of Foreign Affairs consisted of giving aid under the premise that help provided to countries in need would contribute to world peace and stability, and therefore to Japan's own peace and prosperity (Gaiko Seisho 1986). In this context, technical cooperation was granted to aid recipient states recovering from natural disasters, as explained earlier, with the purpose of boosting their economic growth.

Against the background of catastrophes and humanitarian cooperation, emergency responses were launched with the creation of Japan Medical Team in 1979, and the Japan Medical Team for Disaster Relief (JMTDR) in 1982, the predecessor of the current Japan Disaster Relief (JDR). The JDR Law was enacted in 1987; since then, wide-ranging assistance, through the deployment of the JDR team, has been provided in disaster situations in developing countries, starting with the flood that occurred in Venezuela that same year (JICA 2017a, 6). Therefore, since the 1980s, Japan's cooperation in disaster emergency and recovery has increased, raising awareness of the importance of preventing calamities. As explained previously, Japan helped to draft the proposal of the International Framework of Action of the IDNDR, adopted by the UNGA in 1987, showing its commitments to reducing disaster risks.

1992 Japan's ODA Charter and DRR

In 1989, Japan became the world's largest donor in terms of bilateral aid; this situation continued for ten consecutive years (MOFA 2012, 51). Although Japan became a top contributor, criticism emerged both internationally and domestically regarding the forms in which it allocated funding. Globally, peer DAC members stressed that Japan's ODA was primarily directed toward economic infrastructure instead of social infrastructure. The focus on hardware assistance implied that Japan's inclination toward modernization was tied to expanding industrialization and trade (Fujisaki et al. 1996–1997) in aid recipient countries. On the other hand, domestically, aid scholars, NGOs, and mass media maintained their skepticism as to whether the aid contributed to the stability and welfare of impoverished peoples in developing states or whether it was merely a façade to support Japan's own economic and political interests. Critics underscored the need to clarify Japan's ODA philosophy, to define its foreign aid policy, to demonstrate transparency and effectiveness (Murai 1989, 4–5; Murai and Kaida 1987, 2; Tsurumi 1989, 38; Sasanuma 1991, 119; Fujisaki et al. 1996–1997), and to foster assistance programs in accordance with the new post-Cold War era.

The seeming response to these criticisms is that the Japanese government adopted its ODA Charter for the first time in history—the Cabinet ratified it in 1992. The ODA Charter, now a legal policy tool of Japan's foreign assistance, aims to strengthen aid not only in the realm of economic growth, but also in the areas of social welfare, environmental conservation, peacekeeping, and self-help efforts (MOFA 1992). Although the charter does not explicitly mention DRR, within its basic philosophy, Japan reaffirms its position to help maintain global peace and stability and to ensure international prosperity (MOFA 1992); this highlights the understanding that disaster prevention and preparedness reinforce that principle. During the 1990s, various initiatives were carried out in the field of DRR. The Yokohama Strategy was formed, and funding for DRR increased greatly, accounting for over 80% in 1998, as reported by the Global Facility for Disaster Reduction and Recovery (GFDRR) (Kellet and Caravani 2013, 30–40), despite the serious damage caused by the Great Hanshin-Awaji Earthquake of 1995.

2003 Revised Japan's ODA Charter and DRR

In 2000, the international community created the MDGs, which aimed (among other goals) to eradicate extreme poverty and ensure environmental sustainability. After its adoption, in 2003, the original 1992 ODA Charter was revised. Although the essential features of the old charter were maintained, the 2003 Charter adopted a new cooperation strategy to confront emerging global threats (e.g., environmental and humanitarian problems, the latter including poverty and natural disasters), as well as to forge joint aid efforts with governments, international organizations, and stakeholders (MOFA 2003). The more recent charter included "human security" as a basic policy of Japan's ODA, together with encouraging self-help effort principle, guaranteeing equity, transferring technologies, and building partnerships with a several entities (MOFA 2003). The "human security" paradigm was introduced in 1994 to shift the notion of security from a territorial concept to a more people-centered one. Japan was one of the countries that took a leading role in disseminating this idea at the international level. Within the human security paradigm, early prevention is considered a tool to ensure human security (UNDP 1994, 22–23, 29), since environmental problems (such as earthquakes and floods) constitute a threat to human beings.

In 2005, the "Initiative for Disaster Reduction through ODA" was established and announced as part of the HFA. Human security became a fundamental policy of this initiative and stressed the importance of promoting disaster reduction from the human security perspective, thereby deepening the community's capacity to protect people from disasters (MOFA 2015a). After the 1990s, JICA gradually shifted its assistance from implementing projects grounded in structured-measures or hard infrastructure (such as the construction of river banks) to more non-structure, or soft measure (including warning systems and evacuation planning). This involves more communities and local governments in disaster assistance programs to prepare them for eventual calamities and combines both steps using a bottom-up approach (JICA 2011).

2015 Japan's Development Cooperation Charter and DRR

In 2015, Japan's ODA Charter was modified for the second time. The term "ODA" was changed to "development cooperation" to expand the scope of international cooperation activities to other affiliated agencies, such as Other Official Flows (MOFA 2015b). With this revision, the Japanese government intended to not only buttress collaboration and coordination with stakeholders (such as NGOS, emerging countries, and private organs), but also to cope with internal budgetary constraints and gain public support on economic cooperation projects (MOFA 2011, 18–20). While the reduction of disaster risk was embedded in the human security principle within the 2003 ODA Charter, the revised Development Cooperation Charter explicitly includes the DRR approach in its priority policies. For example, the policy of "building a sustainable and resilient international community through efforts to address global challenges" states that Japan will address disaster issues by mainstreaming DRR in development. The human security principle continues to be a key pillar of Japan's development cooperation schemes. In terms of the charter's mechanisms, it stipulates that the government is responsible for formulating development cooperation strategies, and that the government will improve its collaboration with JICA (which is responsible for carrying out the government's policies) (MOFA 2015b). JICA considers the charter's first priority policy (eradicating poverty for purposes of growth) to include DRR as a vital tool to boost resilience and to break the cycle of poverty among vulnerable people (JICA 2018a).

In the same year that the new Development Cooperation paradigm was adopted, the UNGA endorsed the Sustainable Development Goals (SDGs) as part of a post-2015 agenda; the Sendai Framework was also approved for implementation. According to JICA, the SDGs reflect the human security notion, a chief pillar of the 2015 Development Cooperation policies. In the context of DRR, the following SDGs were integrated into all of JICA's assistance programs: Goal #1 (No Poverty), Goal #2 (Zero Hunger), Goal #9 (Industry, Innovation and Infrastructure), Goal #11 (Sustainable Cities and Communities), and Goal #13 (Climate Action). These goals are related to DRR because prevention, mitigation, and preparedness can contribute to lessen the impacts of natural disasters, hence addressing the aforementioned objectives (JICA 2018a; UNISDR 2015). Even though JICA implements DRR programs in line with the four priority actions outlined in the Sendai Framework, some countries have denounced their own lack of financial resources, claiming that this dearth hinders them from performing DRR actions (JICA 2018b). Still, the limited financial resources of developed and developing states should be used effectively in "the pre-disaster stage" (Toyoda 2016, 320) to alleviate the effects of disasters and socioeconomic losses.

In this section, we have discussed the historical evolution of Japan's foreign aid policies in the context of DRR. We argue that Japan's ODA Charter was ratified and reviewed twice in parallel with changes in the international arena, and that in concordance with this shift, disaster prevention, mitigation, preparedness, and the DRR framework have been revamped (see Fig. 9.2). The human security principle has played a key role in Japan's aid policies. According to this idea, development cooperation began to promote more people-centered assistance programs, involving local communities and governments in disaster risk programs.

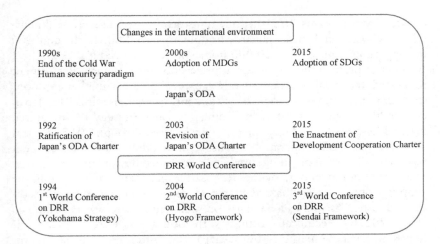

Fig. 9.2 Japan's ODA and the evolution of DRR framework (*Source* Created by the Authors)

Meanwhile, prior to the 1990s, aid programs focused more on economic growth.

Cooperation on Disaster Risk Reduction: Case of Brazil

Based on its experience with natural disasters, Japan has developed technology and know-how to alleviate associated hazards. Besides its Early Earthquake Detection System and Risk Maps for Disaster Prevention, recently, the National Research Institute for Earth Science and Disaster Resilience started using the Monitoring of Waves on Land and Seafloor (MOWLAS) system, an observation network for natural catastrophes (including earthquakes, tsunamis, and volcanoes) throughout Japan (JICA 2018c).

These kinds of technology are gradually being transferred to disaster-prone developing nations. In Brazil, urban zones are vulnerable to landslides, floods, and debris flows. Due to population density, many houses are built near unstable hillsides, and, owing to the weak construction systems, areas such as Nova Friburgo in Rio de Janeiro have been affected by rainstorms. In 2011, one rainstorm caused a severe sediment-related disaster in Rio de Janeiro, leading to over 800 deaths and 400 missing people; more than 20,000 homes were destroyed (JICA 2018b). In order to prepare the region for future events, the Brazilian government requested technical assistance from Japan, aiming to implement non-structural measures based on risk assessment. In response, in 2013, Japan created the "Project for Strengthening National Strategy of Integrated Natural Disaster Risk Management," which lasted through 2017. For this initiative, technical cooperation was based on building water and sediment risk mapping, urban planning, prediction and warning systems, prevention and rehabilitation, and guidelines for disaster management. Regarding the project's outcomes, a "hazard map and risk mapping manual for sediment disaster" as well as a database on sediment disasters were produced (JICA 2017b). Technical meetings with local actors were held without imposing Japanese methods, but rather taking into account local circumstances (JICA 2018b). This can be considered a good practice that leads to the transfer of technology in line with local needs. The appropriate transfer of technology and knowledge congruent to the local environment is crucial in the project implementation process. Otherwise, adverse effects may follow, such as the failed aid program conducted in Aceh to recover from the great Indian Ocean Tsunami (Toyoda 2016, 323).

Trilateral Cooperation Among Japan, Korea, and China in DRR

In terms of trilateral cooperation, Japan, China, and Korea continue to build joint programs to bolster their relationships, particularly in the realm of DRR, aiming to lessen casualties in vulnerable states. In 2008, the first Japan-China-South Korea Summit was held in Japan; the high representatives of the three countries announced their trilateral collaboration in disaster management. As a result, since 2009, the Trilateral Ministerial Meeting on Disaster Management has been held on a rotating basis in each member country (Cabinet Office 2019). At the sixth meeting held in South Korea in 2019, the Trilateral Joint Statement on Disaster Management Cooperation was signed by the heads of government agencies for disaster management. In this joint declaration which was meant to boost the three nations' disaster prevention capacity, it was decided that each country would share prevention policies based on information related to disaster prevention and reduction, to learn about each state's advanced disaster management system, and to arrange exchanges with experts on calamities and safety (TCS 2019). Even though each country has its own development cooperation policies, as leading donor nations, their exchange of knowledge and information on DRR can help them incorporate new risk reduction technologies and reinforce domestic efforts to tackle natural catastrophes in disaster-prone developing states.

DISCUSSION AND CONCLUSION

Japan has experienced severe natural disasters over the years. From the lessons learned, knowledge and technology in relation to disaster preparedness have been developed and transferred to vulnerable developing nations in order to minimize physical damage and human casualties. Since long ago, the government of Japan has been aware of the importance of reducing natural disaster risks. Hence, internationally and as a donor country, Japan has played a key role in investing in DRR programs, becoming the world's single biggest direct donor in the context of DRR. The proposal to implement the IDNDR (which was adopted in 1990), the World Conference on Disaster Risk Reduction hosted by Japan (which led to the establishment of the Yokohama Strategy in 1994), and the HFA and Sendai Framework all show Japan's efforts to tackle disaster risks on a global level.

Aid policies in DRR seem to have evolved to adapt to changes in the international environment. In the 1990s, the Cold War ended, and globalization began to speed up. In the same decade, Japan ratified its first ODA, the IDNDR came into force, and the Yokohama Strategy for Action on DRR was adopted by the international community. Furthermore, in 1994, the human security paradigm emerged, constituting a central pillar of Japan's ODA policies. Later, the MDGs were adopted in 2000, and the ODA Charter was revised in 2003 for the first time, integrating the human security concept to become a guiding principle in order to implement DRR-related development programs. In this setting, the HFA and the "Initiative for Disaster Reduction through ODA" were established, and funds were allocated for implementation. Finally, in 2015, the Development Cooperation Charter was formed as a new version of Japan's ODA Charter, underscoring the importance of working in partnership with stakeholders in aid programs. That same year, the SDGs and the Sendai Framework were produced, becoming a foundation for collaboration to cope with eventual natural disasters in the international community. The building of aid policies and DRR approaches demonstrates that DRR policies have shifted in accordance with emerging global issues. In the context of Japan's aid programs, assistance has been transformed and improved upon based on lessons learned, and new technology has been created for transfer to disaster-prone developing countries.

Although adaptation to international changes is pivotal, DRR programs should be congruent with local circumstances and needs. Climate conditions and types of natural disasters, as well as local perceptions of disasters, can differ according to each nation and region; hence, appropriate disaster risk planning needs to take the local situation into account. Furthermore, collaboration and partnerships with local governments are imperative in implementing DRR programs. However, involving local people in designing prevention measures is also essential because traditional and indigenous techniques can complement modern technologies to prevent disasters, when applicable.

References

Bosai Hakusho. 1996. *Heisei 8 Nenban Bosai Hakusho.* http://www.bousai.go.jp/kaigirep/hakusho/h8hakusho.html. Accessed 15 Mar 2020.

Cabinet Office (Government of Japan). 2014. *Disaster Management in Japan.* Tokyo: Cabinet Office.

Cabinet Office (Government of Japan). 2015. *White Paper: Disaster Management in Japan 2015 Summary.* Tokyo: Cabinet Office.

Cabinet Office (Government of Japan). 2019. *Dai Rokkai Nicchiukan Bosai Tanto Kakuryokyu Kaigo ni okeru kyodoseimei ni Tsuite.* http://www.bousai.go.jp/kokusai/bilateral/pdf/dai6kai_nityubousai.pdf. Accessed 22 Mar 2020.

Fujisaki, T., F. Briscoe, J. Maxwell, M. Kishi, and T. Suzuki. 1996–1997. Japan as Top Donor: The Challenge of Implementing Software Aid Policy. *Pacific Affairs* 69 (4): 519–539.

Gaiko Seisho. 1986. *Waga Gaiko no Kinkyou. Part 1, Chapter 3, Section 3.* https://www.mofa.go.jp/mofaj/gaiko/bluebook/1986/s61-contents.htm. Accessed 20 Mar 2020.

Hossain, N. 2018. The 1970 Bhola Cyclone, Nationalist Politics, and the Subsistence Crisis Contract in Bangladesh. *Disasters* 42 (1): 187–203.

IDNDR (International Decade for Natural Disaster Reduction). 1994. *Yokohama Strategy and Plan of Action for a Safer World: Guidelines for Natural Disaster Prevention, Preparedness and Mitigation.* Geneva: IDNDR.

JICA (Japan International Cooperation Agency). 2011. *JICA's Assessment of Its Contribution to the Hyogo Framework for Action*. Tokyo: JICA.

JICA (Japan International Cooperation Agency). 2017a. *Disaster Relief and JICA: Striving to Make a Difference*. Tokyo: JICA.

JICA (Japan International Cooperation Agency). 2017b. *Brazil Koku Togoshizensaigai Risk Kanrikokka Senryaku Kyoka Project Shuryo Hyoka Chosa Hokokusho*. Tokyo: JICA.

JICA (Japan International Cooperation Agency). 2018a. *JICA Bosai Bunya Position Paper*. https://www.jica.go.jp/activities/issues/disaster/ku57pq00002c y5n0-att/position_paper_disaster.pdf. Accessed Mar 21 2020.

JICA (Japan International Cooperation Agency). 2018b. *JICA's World, Disaster Risk Reduction, Building a Foundation for Our Future (10) 1*. Tokyo: JICA.

JICA (Japan International Cooperation Agency). 2018c. *Highlighting Japan, Technologies for Disaster Mitigation (118) 2018*. Tokyo: JICA.

Kellet, J., and A. Caravani. 2013. *Financing Disaster Risk Reduction, A 20 Year Story of International Aid*. London and Washington, DC: ODI and GSDRR.

MOFA (Ministry of Foreign Affairs). 1992. *Seifu Kaihatsu Enjo Taiko (Kyu ODA Taiko)*. https://www.mofa.go.jp/mofaj/gaiko/oda/seisaku/taikou/sei_1_1. html. Accessed 30 Mar 2020.

MOFA (Ministry of Foreign Affairs). 2003. *Japan's Official Development Assistance Charter*. https://www.mofa.go.jp/policy/oda/reform/revision0308. pdf. Accessed 30 Mar 2020.

MOFA (Ministry of Foreign Affairs). 2005. *Japan's Official Development Assistance, White Paper 2005*. Tokyo: MOFA.

MOFA, Ministry of Foreign Affairs of Japan. 2011. *Japan's Official Development Assistance, White Paper 2010*. Tokyo: Ministry of Foreign Affairs.

MOFA (Ministry of Foreign Affairs). 2012. *Japan's Official Development Assistance, White Paper 2011*. Tokyo: MOFA.

MOFA (Ministry of Foreign Affairs). 2015a. *Bosai Kyoryoku Initiative*. https:// www.mofa.go.jp/mofaj/gaiko/kankyo/kikan/wcdr_initiative.html. Accessed 21 Mar 2020.

MOFA (Ministry of Foreign Affairs). 2015b. *Cabinet Decision on the Development Cooperation Charter*. https://www.mofa.go.jp/files/000067701.pdf. Accessed 30 Mar 2020.

Murai, Y. 1989. *Musekinin Enjo ODA Taikoku Nippon*. Tokyo: JICC.

Murai, Y., and M. Kaida. 1987. *Dareno Tame no Enjo?*. Tokyo: Iwanami Shoten.

Nishikawa, S., and Y. Hosokawa. 2015. Institutionalizing and sharing the culture of prevention: The Japanese Experience. In *Disaster Risk Reduction for Economic Growth and Livelihood*, ed. I. Davis, K. Yanagisawa, and K. Georgieva. Oxon: Routledge.

Omote, S., K. Nakagawa, H. Kobayashi, S. Kawabata, and E. Nakaoka. 1962. A Report on the Buyin Earthquake (Iran) of Sept. 1, 1962. *Indian Institute of Technology Kanpur* 3: 27–44.

Saban, L.L. 2014. *Disaster Emergency Management: The Emergence of Professional Help Services for Victims of Natural Disasters*. New York: State University of New York.

Sasanuma, M. 1991. *ODA Enjo Hihan wo Kangaeru*. Tokyo: Kogyo Jiji Tsushinsha.

TCS (Trilateral Cooperation Secretariat). 2019. *Trilateral Joint Statement on Disaster Management Cooperation*. https://tcs-asia.org/en/cooperation/overview.php?topics=6. Accessed 22 Mar 2020.

Tozier de la Poterie, A., and M.A. Baudoin. 2015. From Yokohama to Sendai: Approaches to Participation in International Disaster Risk Reduction Frameworks. *International Journal of Disaster Risk Science* 6: 128–139.

Toyoda, T. 2012. Disaster Management and Policy. In *Economic and Policy Lessons from Japan to Developing Countries*, ed. T. Toyoda, J. Nishikawa, and H. Kan Sato. New York: Palgrave Macmillan.

Toyoda, T. 2016. The Framework of International Cooperation for Disaster Management and Japan's Contribution. In *Asian Law in Disasters: Towards a Human-Centered Recovery*, ed. Y. Kaneko, K. Matsuoka, and T. Toyoda. New York: Routledge.

Tsurumi, K. 1989. *ODA Enjo no Genjitsu*. Tokyo: Iwanami Shoten.

UNDP (United Nations Development Programme). 1994. *Human Development Report 1994*. New York: UNDP.

UNGA (United Nations General Assembly). 1962. *Resolutions Adopted on the Reports of the Third Committee, General Assembly Seventeenth Session*. https://undocs.org/en/A/RES/1753(XVII). Accessed 31 Mar 2020.

UNGA (United Nations General Assembly). 1970. *Resolutions Adopted on the Reports of the Third Committee, General Assembly Twenty-fifth Session*. https://research.un.org/en/docs/ga/quick/regular/25. Accessed 31 Mar 2020.

UNGA (United Nations General Assembly). 1971. *Agenda Item 59, Assistance in Cases of Natural Disaster: Report of the Secretary-General. Consideration of Draft Resolution, Twenty-sixth Session*. https://digitallibrary.un.org/record/806908. Accessed 31 Mar 2020.

UNGA (United Nations General Assembly). 1990. *Resolutions Adopted on the Reports of the Second Committee, General Assembly Forty-fifth Session. International Decade for Natural Disaster Reduction*. https://undocs.org/en/A/RES/45/185. Accessed 31 Mar 2020.

UNGA (United Nations General Assembly). 2016. *Seventy-first Session, Agenda Item 19 (c), Sustainable Development: Disaster Risk Reduction. Report of the Open-ended Intergovernmental Expert Working Group on Indicators and*

Terminology Relating to Disaster Risk Reduction. UNGA. https://www.pre ventionweb.net/files/50683_oiewgreportenglish.pdf. Accessed 31 Mar 2020.

UNDRR (United Nations Disaster Risk Reduction). 2020. *Milestones in the History of Disaster Risk Reduction.* https://www.undrr.org/about-undrr/his tory. Accessed 24 Mar 2020.

UNISDR (United Nations International Strategy for Disaster Reduction). 2004. *Living with Risk: A Global Review of Disaster Reduction Initiatives.* Geneva: UNISDR.

UNISDR (United Nations International Strategy for Disaster Reduction). 2005. *Hyogo Framework for Action 2005–2015: Building the Resilience of Nations and Communities to Disasters.* Geneva: UNISDR.

UNISDR (United Nations International Strategy for Disaster Reduction). 2008. *Indigenous Knowledge for Disaster Risk Reduction: Good Practices and Lessons Learned from Experiences in the Asia-Pacific Region.* Bangkok: UNISDR.

UNISDR (United Nations International Strategy for Disaster Reduction). 2009. *2009 UNISDR Terminology on Disaster Risk Reduction.* Geneva: UNISDR.

UNISDR (United Nations International Strategy for Disaster Reduction). 2015. *Sendai Framework for Disaster Risk Reduction 2015–2030.* Geneva: UNISDR.

Watson, C., A. Caravani, T. Mitchell, J. Kellet, and K. Peters. 2015. *Finance for Reducing Disaster Risk: 10 Things to Know.* London: ODI.

CHAPTER 10

Transboundary Fine Dust and "PM 2.5 Diplomacy" in Northeast Asia: Cooperation and Future Challenges

Muhui Zhang

INTRODUCTION: RISING "PM 2.5 DIPLOMACY" IN NORTHEAST ASIA

The countries of Northeast Asia face serious environmental threats that necessitate effective regional cooperation. In recent years, air pollution has become the most critical public health issue in this region. According to the World Health Organization (WHO), particulate matter (PM)—generally known as "fine dust" and including PM 10 and PM 2.5—is among the most important components of air pollutants. PM10 is most visible in the context of dust transport, but it is of less concern for causing health problems. In contrast, PM 2.5 can easily penetrate human skin and the respiratory system, can enter the lungs much more easily and deeply, and can cause many diseases. The worsening of PM 2.5 pollution began

---

M. Zhang (✉)
Graduate School of International Studies, Pusan National
University, Busan, South Korea
e-mail: muhui_zhang@pusan.ac.kr

© The Author(s), under exclusive license to Springer Nature
Singapore Pte Ltd. 2021
Y. Jing et al. (eds.), *Risk Management in East Asia*,
https://doi.org/10.1007/978-981-33-4586-7_10

223

in the northern part of China in 2012 and brought about severe haze weather in major Chinese cities. In January 2013, Beijing recorded an extremely high PM 2.5 record (as high as 993 $\mu g/m^3$)—nearly 40 times higher than the 24-hour mean concentration of 25 $\mu g/m^3$ recommended by the WHO. A research report indicated that in 2015, air pollution killed approximately 4000 people and caused 17% of all deaths in China (Rohde and Muller 2015). In the meantime, China is not the only country that has been suffering from the PM 2.5 pollution. South Korea has also been also confronted with the haze weather in recent years.

Unlike other categories of wastes and pollutants that are locally based, air pollution can be highly transnational. However, the source and diffusion paths of air pollution are harder to track than those of other types of waste and pollution. Among China, Japan, and South Korea, scientists have issued varying versions of research reports regarding the responsibilities of air pollution. In 2017, the Seoul Metropolitan Government, citing a study conducted by the Seoul Institute, stated that the portion of Seoul's fine dust pollution that originate from China and other foreign countries had increased to 55%, compared to 49% in 2011 (The Korean Times 2017). Despite experiencing significantly less pollution than South Korea, the western part of Japan has also been affected by transboundary air pollutants (Matsuoka 2017). Japanese researchers have highlighted that China's contribution of PM 2.5 amounts to 61% in the Kyushu region, 59% in the Chugoku region, and 59% in the Shikoku region (Kanaya 2013). On the other hand, China's scientists claim that China's contribution to the air pollution in neighboring countries is rather limited, and the majority of PM 2.5 pollutants comes from indigenous sources (Wang and Zhang 2015). To note, a new research report was released in 2019 and claimed that China's contributions to major cities in South Korea were 32.1%, and to major cities in Japan 24.6% (Secretariat of Working Group for LTP Secretariat 2019). This report thus suggests an in-between perspective that the PM 2.5 pollution is a mixed result of local emission and transboundary pollution. The report came from the Long-range Transboundary Pollution (LTP) program—a joint study project organized by the three governments. For these reasons, the research outcome appears to have better neutrality and scientific reliance.

Resolving long-range transboundary air pollution requires transnational cooperation between neighboring countries. At present, China and South Korea are the two most affected countries in Northeast Asia, and the two countries are trapped in disputes over the pollution sources. This study investigates environmental policy interactions in Northeast Asia and endeavors to address two key research questions. First, what is the performance of existing multilateral frameworks? Second, what obstacles have impeded the advancement of regional air cooperation? This paper also seeks to outline the main limitations of the current regional institutions.

The main argument of this article is twofold. First, the issues of air pollution issue have been listed as the top priority among all other environmental issues in this region. The deterioration of air quality has drawn substantial attention from policymakers. The rapid spread of environmental cooperation has made it a pivotal area for trilateral cooperation between China, Japan, and South Korea (Zhang 2018; Cui 2013 ; Yoshimatsu 2010). On bilateral and multilateral occasions, scientific joint research and policy exchanges are dynamic, and a variety of cooperative actions have occurred. Second, ongoing cooperative projects have remained noncommitted and nonbinding, which means that a great variety of obstacles and ongoing disputes remain unresolved. This article contends that the transboundary fine dust issue appears to be more of a "political" issue than merely an "environmental" issue. It can be highly subject to changes in domestic politics and the diplomatic climate. In a broader sense, the politicization of the transboundary fine dust issue also implies that there is a hybrid regional "air governance" that mixes environmental concerns with diplomatic interests.

This chapter comprises the four following parts. The first part links environmental issues with the scholarly debates of international politics and explores an analytical framework in understanding "air governance" in Northeast Asia. The second part summarizes the existing multilateral mechanism in Northeast Asia and examines the specific cooperative outcomes in recent years. The third part addresses the governmental positions of China and provides explanations to its perspectives. Finally, the chapter explores ongoing challenges and obstacles. Arguably, "air governance" has emerged in Northeast Asia, but it definitely remains in its initial stages of development. There does not seem to be much cause for optimism, however, given that the issue of PM 2.5 appears to be becoming increasingly politicized. In this regard, "air governance" mirrors the complexity of geopolitics in Northeast Asia, a region that has been struggling for decades in rule-making and with rivalry for leadership.

"Air Governance" and the Politicization of Transboundary Fine Dusts

In recent decades, environmental pollution has largely transformed from localized issues, such as waste disposal or unclean water supplies, to risks with global dimensions, which call for dynamic transnational cooperation. Environmental protection appears to no longer comprise purely technical issues that can be dealt with by the local or central governments of one single nation. Similar to governance on global trade, environmental issues have become hybrid bargains among varying countries and among diversified domestic interest groups. The past decades have witnessed a huge growth in the number of multilateral negotiations and wider diplomatic initiatives over environmental conflicts (Benedick 1998, 4–5) In this regard, the issue of climate change marks a perfect case of the politicization of environmental conflicts. The evolution of global climate change governance from the 1993 UN Framework Convention on Climate Change to the 1997 Kyoto Protocol on Climate Change, and then to the ongoing Conference of the Parties (COP), shows the deepening division among participating nations. Climate change has become a political battlefield among the varying camps of developed countries and emerging economies.

Likewise, transboundary air pollution in Northeast Asia is closely tied to political maneuvers. The problem of PM 2.5 pollution bears political connotations in two aspects. First, "air diplomacy" can be perceived as an extension of domestic politics. In South Korea, there has been rising demand for regulatory policies on air quality, and public opinion has converged to put pressure on the government's environmental policy. In a recent public survey, an overwhelming majority of respondents choose "air pollution" as the most pressing environmental threat (72.7%). The number was substantially higher than other kinds of environmental concerns such as waste management (36.3%), radioactive waste (26.8%), and climate change (25.6%) (Choi et al. 2020). In China's case, heavy fine dust pollution has emplaced severe social distrust against the government and has lowered public support of the current regime (Alkon and Wong 2018). It is critical to note that the amelioration of domestic conditions serves as the primary driving force for the Chinese government's participation in transnational cooperation on air pollution.

Second, PM 2.5 pollution also acts as a diplomatic issue, as many of the bilateral and multilateral agreements have been conducted via political-diplomatic channels. In addition to the environmental ministries and technical experts, the involvement of foreign ministries or even political leaders are vital. Meanwhile, the outbreak of air pollution has damaged China's international image. A public opinion poll in 2013 indicates that more than 90% of the South Korean people expect the government to pressure the Chinese government through diplomatic channels, and if not working well, eventually to file an international lawsuit against China (Asian Citizen's Center for Environment and Health 2013). China's foreign policymakers are certainly aware of these voices of dissatisfaction from its neighboring countries and have realized the necessity of taking cooperation actions.

This study also analyzes the concept of "air governance" in Northeast Asia. It features a highly intergovernmental approach and refers to the fact that each national government predominates the process and approaches of how cooperation can be facilitated (Elliott 2017; Yoshimatsu 2010). Many previous studies have highlighted the roles of well-developed transnational epistemic communities in tacking environmental problems. Haas (1992, 3) defined an "epistemic community" as "a network of professionals with recognized expertise and competence in a particular domain and an authoritative claim to policy-relevant knowledge within that domain or issue-area." Solid epistemic community-building needs a combined set of multiple actors among state governments, nongovernmental organizations (NGOs), and international organizations. For a successful environmental regime, NGOs and international organizations can create networks of experts, and thus provide authoritative advice to national governments (Kim 2007, 453; Lee 2013; Yarime and Li 2017). Such nongovernmental and supranational arrangements can reduce uncertainty for policymakers, while the emergence of legally binding transnational instruments could also help to regulate government behaviors. However, the power of epistemic communities in Northeast Asia remains limited. Instead, the construction of "air diplomacy" in Northeast Asia is politics-oriented and has been carried out via diplomatic channels. The reaching of agreements demands consensus among the highest-level officials, or even the convergence of top political will. The advancement of cooperative actions has been attained through the convening of summit-level or minister-level meetings. In this regard, the rule-making of "air governance" in Northeast Asia remains largely undeveloped, given that countries in this region favor nonbinding norms and volunteer-based codes of conduct, and do not welcome legalized instruments.

EMERGING MULTILATERAL FRAMEWORKS AND JOINT ACTIONS

Regional cooperation on transboundary fine dust coexists in three different channels: the Tripartite Environmental Ministers Meeting (TEMM), the Northeast Asian Sub-regional Programme for Environmental Cooperation (NEASPEC), and Long-range Transboundary Pollution (LTP). These three parallel frameworks share similarities in their scientific aspects and have all developed research arms. In all cases, the main focus of air pollution has shifted from sulfate and sandstorms in previous years, to fine dust in recent years. On the other hand, the three mechanisms have different organizational structures and operate in different approaches.

Tripartite Environmental Ministers Meeting (TEMM)

TEMM is the only minister-level environmental mechanism in Northeast Asia with three participants: China, Japan, and South Korea. TEMM was initiated in 1999 and is considered to be the most well-developed mechanism among all other areas of trilateral cooperation (China–ASEAN Center 2018), and it was even launched prior to the first trilateral summit meeting. TEMM has an intergovernmental nature and has been managed by the environmental ministries from the three countries. TEMM covers a great variety of sub-fields, including e-waste, water pollution, sandstorms, maritime pollution, and air pollution. In recent years, the three countries have recognized the deterioration of air quality as being the most urgent environmental problem. At the 17th TEMM in 2015, the three countries updated a five-year Tripartite Action Plan on Environmental Cooperation (2015–2019), and the new action plan was further reconfirmed via a Joint Statement at the 6th trilateral summit in the same year (JMOFA 2015). The new action plan highlighted "air quality improvement" as the top priority among nine pivot areas, and confirmed the "compelling need of tackling air pollution caused by fine particulate matters (PM 2.5), ozone (O3), and volatile organic compounds (OVC) in a prompt and effective manner" (JMOE 2015).

Against this backdrop, the three countries initiated a Trilateral Policy Dialogue on Air Pollution (TPDAP) under the TEMM in 2014, with a special focus on the issue of fine dust. TPDAP began as a loose policy-based dialogue. Following the 3rd meeting in 2016, the dialogue started to cover technical fields by establishing two working groups. The first group works on scientific joint research on emission controls and standards (such as fuels standards and non-road sources including vessels and construction equipment). The second targets at the monitoring and prediction of air pollutants. The three countries have been working toward a real-time data share system, so that Japan and South Korea can mobilize the data from China in order to develop an effective forecasting system on fine dust weather in the future (JMOE 2019; Chu 2018; Shim 2017).

Long-Range Transboundary Pollution (LTP)

LTP is another environmental regional mechanism among China, Japan, and South Korea that specifically deals with air pollution. LTP has a longer history than the TEMM and is run primarily by experts. It was initiated by the South Korean government in 1995, and the National Institute of Environmental Research (NIER) of South Korea acts as an interim secretariat for the LTP and manages regular communication and administrative issues (Kim 2007 and 2014). To date, South Korea has displayed leadership in bringing the national environment research institutes of China and Japan into the joint research program, and South Korea is also the main financial supporter for LTP activities. The LTP project has two expert groups, focused on monitoring and modeling. The monitoring group studies the state of air quality in each of the three countries. The modeling group examines the source–receptor (S-R) relationship to identify the cross-border transmission of air pollutants. Each country has set up two monitoring sites and has produced data for comparison and analysis.[1] Since 2000, four out of the five stages of these joint research studies have been concluded, with the 4th stage (2013–2017) specifically focusing on the S-R relation of PM 2.5 concentration over China, Japan, and South Korea. At present, experts are working on the action plan for the 5th stage (2018–2022), which will enable researchers to co-operate with Pandora, a network of remote monitoring equipment that covers a larger spatial area (Secretariat of Working Group for LTP Secretariat 2015).

Unlike the TEMM, LTP is run primarily by experts. LTP produces summary report for each of its 5-year-long research phase. In 2019, LTP issued the summary report to the 4th stage of joint research on transnational PM 2.5 (2013–2017), suggesting that China's contributions to major cities in South Korea were 32.1%, and to major cities in Japan 24.6% (Secretariat of Working Group for LTP Secretariat 2019). As the study was conducted by the three countries in a joint way, it can be considered as a scientific consensus on transboundary PM 2.5 pollution at present.

Northeast Asian Sub-Regional Programme for Environmental Cooperation (NEASPEC)

The NEASPEC represents another example of environmental cooperation in Northeast Asia. Proposed by South Korea, the NEASPEC was initiated in 1993. It is the only regional environmental entity that incorporates all six countries in this region (China, Japan, South Korea, Mongolia, North Korea, and Russia). The local Incheon office of the United Nations Economic and Social Commission for Asia and the Pacific (UNESCAP) has been acting as a permanent secretariat since 2010. The senior official's meeting (SOM) serves as the main governing body, which takes charge of providing policy guidance and project coordination. For this, the governance structure of the NEASPEC reflects a semi-intergovernmental approach. The SOM meeting has been convened annually on a rotating basis, with decisions being made by consensus. The NEASPEC differs from LTP and the TEMM, and has the status of an international organization. The NEASPEC has two main funding sources. One comes from the Asian Development Bank (ADB), which pays for most of the organizational costs. The other source of funding is voluntary contributions from participating countries through the establishment of a "Core Fund." However, NEASPEC is severely limited by its budget, as its funds appear to be insufficient and lacks predictability (Pak 2012, 10; Kim 2014, 153).

In 2017, NEASPEC launched a "Northeast Asia Clean Air Partnership (NEACAP)" project that primarily focused on particulate matter (PM 2.5 and PM 10). The program has been developed based on two tracks: science-based cooperation and policy-oriented collaboration. To compare, NEASPEC lies between the policy-based TPDAP and the research-based LTP. With the support of a standing organization, NEASPEC appears to have developed clearer policy goals and corresponding working agendas than LTP and TEMM. NEACAP proposed cooperative plans in three directions: first, to build emission inventories as common information basis; second, to strengthen the compatibility among various national databases and create an open platform for scientific communication;[2] and third, to promote and encourage the use of integrated assessment modelling (IAM) among member states (NEASPEC Secretariat 2018 and 2019b).[3] The IAM approach has been widely applied and practiced by the Convention on Long-range Transboundary Air Pollution (CLRTAP) in Europe. It helps to link scientific results with real environmental policies and presents various scenarios of cost-effective emission reductions. In East Asia, the modeling and monitoring standards vary by country. The use of different calculation models or scenarios creates problems of incompatible scientific research outcomes and data monitoring.

To summarize, three parallel multilateral frameworks are currently involved in transboundary air pollution in Northeast Asia. Nonetheless, these three mechanisms have different organizational structures and operate in different approaches. Table 10.1 shows their functions in a comparative manner. The TEMM (including TPDAP) primarily targets policy exchanges; LTP, on the other hand, represents a purely technical approach. The NEASPEC presents an integrated approach and seeks to establish a region-wide network of scientific research and policy dialogues. There has been visible and steady progress in transnational cooperation on

Table 10.1 Multilateral frameworks on transnational fine dust

Body	Initiated in	Member States	Area of Focus	Participating Agency	Level
TEMM	1999	China, Japan, South Korea	policy-oriented (all environmental issues)	Ministry of Environment	minister-level
(TPDAP)	2014		mainly policy exchanges		director-level
LTP	1995	China, Japan, South Korea	scientific joint research	experts	experts
NEASPEC	1993	China, Japan, two Koreas, Russia, Mongolia	mixed (policy exchanges and scientific research)	Ministry of Foreign Affairs	experts and working-level

Source Compiled by the author

the subject of air pollution, as various action plans and working agendas have materialized in recent years. Notably, cross-border cooperation over PM 2.5 pollution has displayed substantial institutional solidarity. TEMM, LTP, and NEASPEC mechanisms are convened on an annual basis, and these institutions have never been interrupted or canceled, even during periods of diplomatic tensions in the region (Park 2019, 93–94). In this sense, nascent "air governance" in Northeast Asia has been developing in recent years.

Explain China's "Air Diplomacy": Why Co-Operate, and Why not?

The people of China have lived under the shadow of haze weather in recent years. "Haze" refers to low atmospheric visibility and is mainly caused by the increased loading of fine fraction particles—mostly PM 2.5 (Aunan et al. 2018, 283). People in China normally refer to the haze as "smog," or "*wumai*" in Chinese. The main pollution source of PM 2.5 comes from the energy sectors and heavy industries, as China remains heavily dependent on coal-fired energy. During the Beijing Asia-Pacific Economic Cooperation (APEC) Summit in 2014, the second World War 70th-anniversary military parade in 2015, and the Hangzhou G20 Summit in 2018, the temporary massive shutdown of power plants and polluting industries was substantially effective in reducing PM 2.5 emissions, for which people hailed the resulting blue skies, and calling them "APEC blue" and "G20 blue."

At the beginning of the 2010s, the Chinese government was cautious on the opening of environmental data. However, since approximately 2015, China has started its environmental "open-up." The central government changed to being increasingly transparent regarding the release and sharing of data. Importantly, China's "PM 2.5 diplomacy" is highly associated with the change of domestic air quality. China showed rising willingness to engage in cross-border cooperation, on the condition that its domestic air condition improved. Hence, China began to embrace more confidence regarding transnational cooperation on PM 2.5 cooperation. In this regard, domestic politics became a decisive variable in China's environmental diplomacy.

In 2013, the Chinese government became determined to tackle smog and environmental pollution. The PM 2.5 crisis also brought about reforms in the Chinese Communist Party (CCP)'s cadre appointment system. The CCP gradually abandoned the past standards of its rating system for local officials. The new standards lowered the scores for economic development and gross domestic product (GDP) growth, while adding points for local officials' performance regarding environmental protection. The Chinese government's highly centralized governance structure enables it to adopt an approach of "authoritarian environmentalism" (Ahlers and Shen 2018). This theory concedes that authoritarian governments can react in a faster way, and allow for more rigorous responses to environmental problems (Gilley 2012, 288). The Xi Jinping administration officially declared war against haze weather and highlighted the reduction of PM 2.5 emissions as a political task for party officials. In the following years, the State Council of China issued the "Air Pollution Prevention and Control Action Plan (2013–2017)" and committed to reducing PM 2.5 concentrations by approximately 2015 in major industrialized regions. The Action Plan covered ten specific tasks, and was characterized by the Chinese media as "iron fisted." This PM 2.5 policy set included various compulsory measures, combining environmental regulations with technological, industrial, economic, and legal reforms (Jin et al. 2016).

Indeed, the government-led massive mobilization of political and social resources has been taking effect in recent years. China has adopted more rigorous environmental standards and has shut down a substantial number of polluting industries. Scientific research has given evidence for China's improving air quality (see Fig. 10.1), as the annual PM 2.5 concentration has shown a steadily decreasing trend (Aunan et al. 2018; Brombal 2017; Zheng et al. 2018). The years 2015 and 2016 represented a turning point for China's air quality, or at least represented a halt in its continuing deterioration. In 2018, the average PM 2.5 concentrations in 74 major Chinese cities (implementing the Ambient Air Quality Standard) fell by 42%; in three key regions (Beijing–Tianjin–Hebei region, the Yangtze River Delta, and the Pearl River Delta), the average PM 2.5 concentration dropped by 48%, 39%, and 32%, respectively, from 2013 (JMOE 2019). Consequently, China also released a "Three-year Action Plan for Winning the Blue-Sky War" in 2018 in order to achieve continuous improvement of air quality by 2020. For cities where PM 2.5 standards were not met in the previous cycle, the urban concentration of PM 2.5 was targeted to be reduced by at least 18%, and the aim was set to reduce highly polluted days by at least 25%. The annual number of days with fairly good air

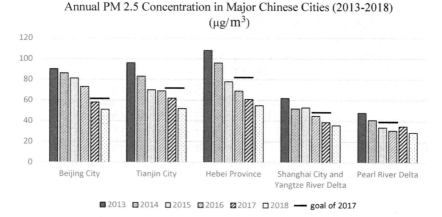

Fig. 10.1 Annual PM 2.5 concentration in Major Chinese Cities (2013–2018) (*Source* Clear Air Asia (2019), compiled by the author)

quality was expected to increase by 80%, compared with 2015 (NEASPEC Secretariat 2019c).

Against this backdrop, China began to show an "open-up" stance with the international community. The improvement of domestic air quality was synchronized with China's increasing communication and engagement with its neighboring countries. This indicates that the mitigation of domestic pollution has led to increased confidence in the government regarding international negotiations. As analyzed in the previous section, it was after 2015 that China started to respond to South Korea's request for closer coordination. In particular, China's agreement on PM 2.5 real-time data exchange with South Korea can be considered as a big step forward. China's increasing commitments to LTP also present one of the strongest pieces of evidence. Despite the fact that LTP produces annual reports, the Chinese government did not agree to publicize these report until 2017. Since the TEMM 20 in 2018, China has shown increasing openness and consented to do so.[4]

At present, the Chinese government stresses the necessity of international cooperation for resolving transboundary air pollutions and clearly opposes to approaches of mobilizing the environmental issue for political purposes. On March 6, 2019, the spokesperson of China's foreign ministry said, "I am not sure whether we have sufficient evidence that

South Korea's fine dust is coming from China...we should follow the science on this issue." In particular, Chinese scholars of environmental science and international studies have widely pointed out that the key for joint actions lies in the areas of city-to-city local cooperation and transfer of technologies (Wang and Zhang 2015; Ren and Li 2019). The Chinese government also eagerly welcomes advanced technologies regarding environmental protection and green economy from developed countries.

In the meantime, the basic position of China's environmental diplomacy is to oppose any intervention in China's domestic affairs by the maneuvering of environmental issues (Won 2002). This also explains China's low engagement and uncooperative stances within the framework of the Acid Deposition Monitoring Network in East Asia (EANET),[5] as China is concerned by Japan's continuous attempts to legally institutionalize it (Shapiro 2018; Wang and Zhang 2015). Japanese and Korean scholars tend to identify clear responsibilities and duties among different countries and argue to bring in the Polluter Pays Principle (PPP) as an international environmental norm, which places the burden of handling pollution squarely on the polluting country (Lee 2019; Park 2019, 89). However, China favors a scientifically based approach and sees this politicized approach as unhelpful in the resolving of common environmental challenges (Dong 2017). As such, some Chinese scholars illustrate the case of sulfide emission and pollution, and point out the "historical responsibilities" of Japan and South Korea during their years of high-speed development. As such, China, as a later developer, firmly sides with other developing countries and claims for its equal "emission rights" in this regard (Liu and Wang 2017). China also refuses to take responsibilities that do not match with its status as a developing country.

Can "Air Diplomacy" Move Forward? Identifying Issues of Rule-Making and Governance

Environmental cooperation in Northeast Asia has its own style. Yoshimatsu (2010) called it "regulatory governance," referring to the predominating roles of national governments and the complicated net of intergovernmental meetings and dialogues. This section illustrates three aspects of the ongoing shortcomings. In addition to an interest-based perspective to understanding the varying pursuits from each country, we also highlight a normative approach, in the sense that a commonly acknowledged set of rules for cooperation remain as yet under-developed. Conflicting codes of conduct and stagnancy of rule-making exist at the scientific level, and this also extends to political–diplomatic and institutional levels.

Scientific Data and Standards

Environmental monitoring data is essential to informing decision-making processes relevant to the management of transboundary air pollutants. The real-time exchange of accurate PM 2.5 data is the very foundation for transnational cooperation. However, regional multilateral frameworks such as TEMM, LTP, and NEASPEC have not established any data-sharing system. The China-South Korea bilateral data exchange has been initiated, yet a closer examination on the exchange mechanism also reveals its shortcomings. The real-time data exchange between China and South Korea is limited to PM 2.5 concentrations and emissions, for which environmental researchers in South Korea complain that the current data exchange remains at a superficial stage. South Korean experts argue that annual overall emissions are not always the ideal criteria for measuring the severity of PM 2.5 pollution. Instead, they argue that the count of "severe pollution days" (PM 2.5 > 75 $\mu g/m^3$) is far more critical than that of yearly based PM 2.5 concentrations, and should be used as a key index for monitoring air quality. Also, for the purposes of scientific research and accurate weather forecasting, comprehensive PM 2.5 data exchange regarding the composition and routes for transmission are also necessary.[6] However, this information has not yet been widely shared between the two countries. For this reason, in-depth data exchange and joint research still play as the "first step" toward China–South Korea cooperation on fine dust reduction (Lee 2019).

In addition, the use of different environmental standards points to another scientific barrier for understanding the sources of transboundary air pollution, and for designing effective PM 2.5 reduction measures. However, China, Japan, and South Korea have each adopted their own national emission inventories, based on preferred industries or compositions of air pollutants that vary from country to country.[7] This brings about the problems of comparability and compatibility among these differing information inventories and standards, as well as the accuracy and reliability of each country's data. At present, the NEASPEC is actively engaged in this scientific and technical process. It has selected the interaction and integration among diversified emission inventories as a working priority for its expert group meetings (NEASPEC Secretariat 2019a). In spite of ongoing efforts, significant challenges for building a scientific-based epistemic community in Northeast Asia still remain, let alone the subsequent policy-based steps.

Overlapping Cooperative Institutions and the Issue of Leadership

Relatedly, the different interests and pursuits of varying countries have also caused overlap, or even competition, among environmental institutions. Foremost, it appears that bilateral cooperative frameworks still largely precede multilateral and regional ones at the current stage, as there have been more tangible cooperative outcomes from bilateral approaches between China and South Korea. On the surface, the TEMM has demonstrated remarkable efforts regarding environmental institution-building among China, Japan, and South Korea by means of incorporating and integrating three pairs of bilateral cooperation into a single trilateral framework. In reality, however, this trilateral umbrella remains more "symbolic" than "substantive." Normally, the agenda of TEMM is that bilaterally based environmental minister meetings will be held on the side-line of TEMM. TEMM, as a three-party dialogue, features a pattern of consensus making and settles on "lowest common denominator" agreements that may be insufficient to reach common actions. However, core issues and difficult negotiations are more likely to be addressed in bilateral occasions. This explains why the sharing of real-time monitoring data between China and South Korea—one of the most convincing outcomes for "PM 2.5 diplomacy" in Northeast Asia—is bilateral, rather than multilateral. This also seemingly implies a complex nexus between bilateralism and multilateralism in Northeast Asia. In the near future, multilateral approaches may work well in providing cooperative agendas and venues, whereas currently they remain unable to replace the roles of bilateral approaches (Zhang 2018).

Further, the current situation of "PM 2.5 diplomacy" leads to issues such as program overlap and conflicts of interest among the different players. The existing regional environmental frameworks (LTP, TEMM, NEASPEC, and EANET) do not seem to have a clear division of tasks. All mechanisms have been advancing in both technical and policy branches, with similar functions. In this sense, the ambiguity of regional environmental governance in Northeast Asia resembles the "spaghetti-bowl effect" of regional trade governance, leading to the multiplication of the transaction costs, and a decline in cooperation efficiency. Meanwhile, Northeast Asian countries have significant differences in their national interests and approaches to environmental cooperation. This means that they treat environmental issues as an arena of rivalry for regional leadership. Japan, for example, has displayed leadership in EANET, which focuses on acid rain. It has a strong preference for a broader pan-East Asia cooperative framework. However, South Korea and China have revealed passive stances toward EANET (Park 2019, 100). Unlike Japan, South Korea is keener on Northeast Asia-based sub-regional cooperation. South Korea does not welcome Japan's exertion of regional leadership and has aspired to act as a leader through the NEASPEC and LTP programs (Jung 2016; Shim 2017, 20). Likewise, China is also reluctant to engage in Japan's display of leadership and remains hesitant regarding a full-scale sharing of environmental data within EANET. These stances help to understand why TEMM still acts as the best multilateral performing platform to address transnational environmental challenges. Furthermore, its high minister-level architecture enables strong political commitments. It is also important that TEMM is running on a strictly equal basis. TEMM, together with its affiliated sub-mechanisms, is convened on a rotating basis among China, Japan, and South Korea, with equal shares regarding financial contributions. Without an explicit leadership, the institutional design of TEMM guarantees that its member states' are as comfortable as possible.

Bureaucratization and the Absence of Legalized Arrangements

In Northeast Asia, state bureaucracies have long been the predominant actors in the formulation of environmental policies and the legislation of environmental laws. The strength of state bureaucracies starkly contrasts with the weaknesses of scientific communities and international institutions. For instance, despite the LTP providing policy reports on each of its five-year-long research phases, these research results have not been fully reflected in the policy-making process (Shim 2017). In addition, the environmental ministries do not have the authority to draft "air diplomacy" in this region. Instead, the foreign ministries have had considerable impacts in addressing transboundary air pollution, and in many circumstances appear to be the main agencies in charge of environmental cooperation. The operations of the NEASPEC provide a telling example in this regard. The NEASPEC was initially proposed and supported by South Korea's Ministry of Foreign Affairs. Even today, China's participation in the NEASPEC is strictly controlled by the foreign ministry. The power of foreign ministries thus represents further evidence that the issue of transboundary fine dust bears political–diplomatic consequences, for which any major decision making requires the delegation of mandates from top political leaders. However, the leading roles of foreign ministries in transboundary air cooperation is not always a good signal, considering that foreign relations experts may lack specific knowledge and technical expertise (Lee 2013; Jung 2016). Furthermore, the working style of foreign ministries has complicated the bureaucratic process and has increased the administrative workload (Park 2019, 92–93). These problems may include hierarchical reporting processes, excessive emphasis on protocols, and intra-ministry buck-passing, all of which can slow down the process of multilateral coordination.

Meanwhile, "air governance" in this region remains largely underdeveloped, as cooperative actions remain overwhelmingly limited to preliminary and "soft" approaches, such as exchanging of data and holding joint seminars. LTP and TEMM do not yet have an organizational base. The NEASPEC, despite having a permanent small secretariat, is also confronted with limited financial budgets and capacity building. More importantly, a long-term plan for legally binding agreements and enforcement mechanisms is not forthcoming (Kim 2007; Komori 2010; Yoon 2007; Nam 2002). In this sense, the European experience is instructive. In the 1970s, the United Nations Economic Commission for Europe adopted the CLRTAP, through which a series of multilateral binding agreements were established (Lee 2013; Drifte 2005; Yarime and Li 2017). In 2012, the Convention was revised and updated to include fine dust and PM 2.5 problems. It also adopted new goals for emissions for each participating member state by 2020. The European model points to differentiated responsibilities regarding emission reductions among its members, so that each member state shoulders international responsibilities when formulating their domestic environmental policies. In the meantime, it also enables certain punishment mechanisms in case any member state fails to achieve its goal of emission reductions (Dong 2017; Xue and Zhang 2013). Clearly, it would appear that the European model does not fit the context of Northeast Asia at this moment.

Conclusion

Transboundary cooperation on air quality in Northeast Asia has gone through many changes over the past decades. In the past, the air pollution issue was mainly embodied by non-PM pollutants such as acid rain and yellow dust. In recent years, air quality has remained poor, and the haze weather caused by fine dust has posed a new environmental challenge. PM 2.5 pollution is far more harmful to people's health than other pollutants, and environmental scientists have more difficulties in identifying its transmission routes.

This chapter examines how Northeast Asian countries have responded to the atmospheric crisis, and sheds light on the current conditions of multilateral environmental cooperation. There are both encouraging and discouraging prospects. Studies into international relations (IR) tend to examine the three facets of "governance": actors, processes, and outcomes. In this regard, this chapter has seen spreading transnational networks, the start of data-sharing systems, and scientific joint research in recent years. In this regard, this chapter contends that preliminary "air governance" has taken shape in Northeast Asia. Environmental regionalism has stood the test of geopolitical uncertainties in this region and has demonstrated its vibrant institutional solidarity, given that existing environmental frameworks have not been suspended due to conflicts such as THAAD deployment, historical territorial disputes, or rising nationalist sentiments.

Yet, the future vision of regional cooperation on transboundary air pollution in Northeast Asia remains unclear. This study finds that the problem of air quality is never a purely environmental issue, but rather a political challenge with mixed concerns of domestic politics and diplomatic interests. China's environmental "open-up" is vital, and China's "air diplomacy" is largely a side product of its domestic environmental politics. China has been showing increasing openness and cooperative stances, while China declines the criticism from neighboring countries that sees China as the source of pollution.

To conclude, "air diplomacy" in this region still has a long way to go in the future. The current achievements regarding PM 2.5 reduction are a credit to each country's individual domestic efforts, but they have much less to do with the convergence of transnational efforts. Many factors are still hindering the advancement of bilateral, trilateral, and regional cooperation on PM 2.5 mitigation. This study highlights the key word of "rule-making" in Northeast Asia and points out the chaos, if not a total absence, of shared norms at scientific, diplomatic, and institutional levels. International institutions can hardly bypass national governments, and their roles are limited. Park (2019, 62–63 and 99–100) formulated a five-stage Regional Environmental Development Model that extends from the "total absence of environmentalism and rigid state sovereignty" to "multidimensional global and inter-regional spillovers." He argued that the environmental regionalism in Northeast Asia stops at the second stage—"asymmetry in environmentalism." Northeast Asian countries are still engaged in ceaseless blame games and are unable to work out an environmental community with clear duties and responsibilities. Indeed, the underdeveloped "air diplomacy" in this region is not a unique case. It mirrors the fragility of regional governance in Northeast Asia, which is reflected in the bilateralism–multilateralism nexus, "organizational gaps," and continuous rivalry for leadership. These impediments can explain the geopolitical paradox in Northeast Asia and also explain the regional environmental diplomacy.

NOTES

1. The monitoring sites of each country are: Dalian and Xiamen in China, Oki and Rishiri in Japan, and Kangwha and Kosan in South Korea (NEASPEC secretariat 2012).
2. Against this backdrop, NEASPEC convened a science and policy committee and launched the first meeting in July 2019 (NEASPEC secretariat 2019a).
3. IAM is an integrated set of scenario analysis, air quality assessment, and cost-efficient abatement measures to be delivered to policymakers. The use of IAM is widely considered as a cornerstone of interactive processes between science and policy by analyzing emission trends and their impacts on health and environment.
4. Interview with Professor Kim Cheol-hee, Pusan National University, South Korean representative for NEASPEC, January 15, 2020, Busan, South Korea.
5. EANET was established in 2001 as an intergovernmental initiative to create a common understanding on the state of acid deposition problems in East Asia. At present, it has 13 member states in both Northeast Asia and Southeast Asia. Japan plays the role of leadership within EANET. In comparison with the LTP, the EANET puts focus on acid rain and other long-term transitional air pollutants.

6. Interview with Dr. Cho, Kyeong Doo, director-general of Incheon Climate and Environmental Research Center, The Incheon Institute, January 16, 2020, Incheon, South Korea.
7. These emission inventories include: China—Chinese Research Academy of Environmental Sciences (CRAES) and Multi-resolution Emission Inventory (MEIC); Japan—Asia Center for Air Pollution Research (ACAP); South Korea—Clean Air Policy Support System (CAPSS).

REFERENCES

Ahlers, Anna L., and Yongdong Shen. 2018. Breathe Easy? *Local Nuances of Authoritarian Environmentalism in China's Battle Against Air Pollution, the China Quarterly* 234: 299–319.

Alkon, Meir, and Erik H. Wong. 2018. Pollution Lowers Support for China's Regime: Quasi-experimental Evidence from Beijing. *The Journal of Politics* 80 (1): 327–331.

Asian Citizen's Center for Environment and Health. 2013. Report of National Survey of Environmental Policy about Chinese Smog and Domestic Fine Dust, 173, December 23, http://eco-health.org/bbs/board.php?bo_table=sub02_02&wr_id=172. (assessed April 3, 2020).

Aunan, Kristin, Mette H. Hansen, and Shuxiao Wang. 2018. Introduction: Air Pollution in China. *The China Quarterly* 234: 279–298.

Benedick, Richard E. 1998. *Diplomacy for the Environment: The New Generation of Environmental Danger, conference report on environmental diplomacy (November 18)*, 3–13. American Institute for Contemporary German Studies: The Johns Hopkins University.

Brombal, Daniele. 2017. Accuracy of Environmental Monitoring in China: Exploring the Influence of Institutional. *Political and Ideological Factors, Sustainability* 9 (3): 324.

Center, China-ASEAN. 2018. *Report on China-Japan-Korea Tripartite Environmental Cooperation and its Outlook.* Beijing: China-ASEAN Environmental Cooperation Center.

Choi, Hyeonjung, James J. Kim, and Chungku Kang. 2020. South Korean Perception on Climate Change, the ASAN Institute for Policy Studies Issue Brief (February 18).

Chu, Jiang Min. 2018. Resilience Evaluation of the TEMM Cooperation: DSS and Air Pollution, Institute of Developing Economies—Japan External Trade Organization (IDE-JETRO) research project, www.ide.go.jp/English/Research/Project/2018/2017220009.html?media=pc. (assessed March 3, 2020).

Clear Air Asia. 2019. *Daqi zhongguo 2019: zhongguo daqi wuran fangzhi Jincheng [Air China 2019: China's Air Pollution Prevention].* Beijing: Clear Air Asia.

Cui, Shunji. 2013. Beyond History: Non-traditional Security Cooperation and the Construction of Northeast Asian International Society. *Journal of Contemporary China* 22 (83): 868–886.

Dong, Liang. 2017. Wuhai zeren, huanjing waijiao yu zhongrihan hezuo [Smog, Environmental Diplomacy, and China-Japan-ROK Cooperation". *Dangdai Hanguo [Contemporary Korea]* 2: 1–14.

Drifte, Reinhard. 2005. Transboundary Pollution as an Issue in Northeast Asian Regional Politics, Asia Research Center working paper 12, London School of Economics and Political Science.

Elliott, Lorraine. 2017. Environmental Regionalism: Moving in from the Policy Margins. *The Pacific Review* 30 (6): 952–965.

Gilley, Bruce. 2012. Authoritarian Environmentalism and China's Response to Climate Change. *Environmental Politics* 21 (2): 287–307.

Haas, Peter M. 1992. *Knowledge*. Power and International Policy Coordination, South Carolina: University of South Carolina Press.

Japanese Ministry of Environment (JMOE). 2015. Joint Communiqué of the 17th Tripartite Environment Ministers Meeting among China, Japan and Korea. http://www.env.go.jp/earth/coop/temm/archive/pdf/commun ique_E17.pdf (March 3, 2020).

Japanese Ministry of Environment (JMOE). 2019. Tripartite Policy Dialogue on Air Pollution - Air Quality Policy Report: The Cooperation Progress and Outcome, https://www.env.go.jp/press/files/jp/112834.pdf (March 3, 2020).

Japanese Ministry of Foreign Affairs (JMOFA). 2015. Joint Statement on Environmental Cooperation, https://www.mofa.go.jp/files/000129792.pdf (March 3, 2020).

Jin, Yana, Henrik Andersson, and Shiqiu Zhang. 2016. Air Pollution Control Policies in China: A Retrospective and Prospects. *International Journal of Environmental Research and Public Health* 13 (12): 1219.

Jung, Woosuk. 2016. Environmental Challenges and Cooperation in Northeast Asia", *Focus Asia*, 16 (March).

Kanaya, Yugo. 2013. Nihon no PM2.5 wa doko kara kuruka? Ekkyo osen no kiyo wo saguru [where does Japan's PM 2.5 come from? An Exploration on the contribution of transboundary pollution], presentation at the seminar "Challenge for Transboundary Air Pollution" (November 1), Asia Center for Air Pollution Research, https://www.acap.asia/research-promotion/research-promotion-2/ (assessed February 9, 2020).

Kim, Inkyoung. 2007. Environmental Cooperation of Northeast Asia: Transboundary Air Pollution. *International Relations of the Asia-Pacific* 7 (3): 439–462.

Kim, Inkyoung. 2014. Messages from a Middle Power: Participation by the Republic of Korea in Regional Environmental Cooperation on Transboundary

Air Pollution Issues. *International Environmental Agreements: Politics, Law and Economics* 14 (2): 147–162.

Komori, Yasumasa. 2010. Evaluating Regional Environmental Governance in Northeast Asia. *Asian Affairs: an American Review* 37 (1): 1–25.

Lee, Jae-hyup. 2013. Transboundary Pollution in Northeast Asia: An International Environmental Law Perspective. *University of Hawaii Law Review* 35: 769–785.

Lee, Tae Dong. 2019. The First Step towards ROK-China Cooperation on Fine Dust Reduction: Achieve Consensus and Conduct Joint Research, the East Asian Institute Briefing, April 23.

Liu, Qiaoling, and Qi Wang. 2017. Zhongrihan kuajie daqi wuranzhong de zhongguo zeren shibie yanjiu [The Research on Identification of China's Responsibility in China-Japan-ROK Trans-boundary Air Pollution Issue]. *Dongbeiya Xuekan [Northeast Asia Forum]* 6: 77–91.

Matsuoka, Shunji. 2017. Japan's Long-range Transboundary PM2.5 Problem, the News Letter 77, summer 2017, International Institute for Asian Studies.

Nam, Sangmin. 2002. Ecological Interdependence and Environmental Governance in Northeast Asia: Politics versus Cooperation. In *International Environmental Cooperation: Politics and Diplomacy in Pacific Asia*, ed. Paul Harris, 167–202. Colorado: University Press of Colorado.

NEASPEC Secretariat. 2012. Review of the Main Activities on Transboundary Air Pollution in Northeast Asia, NEASPEC working paper (November 2012).

NEASPEC Secretariat. 2018. Review of Programme Planning and Implementation: Transboundary Air Pollution in North-East Asia, report at the 22nd Senior Officials Meeting (SOM) of NEASPEC (October 22–23).

NEASPEC Secretariat. 2019a. Conclusion of the First Meeting of NEACAP Science and Policy Committee and Technical Centers, report at the 1st meeting of Northeast Asia Clean Air Project Science and Policy Committee (July 5).

NEASPEC Secretariat. 2019b. Discussion Paper on the Workplan of the North-East Asia Clean Air Partnership, report at the 1st meeting of Northeast Asia Clean Air Project Science and Policy Committee (July 5).

NEASPEC Secretariat. 2019c. Review of Programme Planning and Implementation: Transboundary Air Pollution, report at the 23rd Senior Officials Meeting (SOM) of NEASPEC (October 9–10).

Park, Jeongwon Bourdais. 2019. *Regional Environmental Politics in Northeast Asia: Conflict and Cooperation.* London and New York: Routledge.

Pak, Sum Low. 2012. North & East Asian Sub-regional Programme for Environmental Cooperation: Challenges and Opportunities, working paper at the 17th Senior Officials Meeting of NEASCAP (December 20–21).

Ren, Xiaofei, and Shunlong Li. 2019. Dongbeiya quyu huanjing hezuo moshi tanxi [A study of regional environmental cooperative pattern in Northeast Asia]. *Dongyue Luncong* 40 (7): 120–26.

Rohde, Robert A. and Richard A. Muller. 2015. *Air Pollution in China: Mapping of Concentrations and Sources*, Berkeley Earth, http://berkel eyearth.org/wp-content/uploads/2015/08/China-Air-Quality-Paper-July-2015.pdf. (assessed February 9, 2020).

Secretariat of Working Group for LTP Secretariat. 2015. Annual Report, the 15th Year's Joint Research on Long-range Transboundary Air Pollutants in Northeast Asia.

Secretariat of Working Group for LTP Secretariat. 2019. Summary Report of the 4th stage (2013–2017) LTP Project, Joint Research Project for Long–range Transboundary Air Pollutants in Northeast Asia.

Shapiro, Matthew A. 2018. China-based Air Pollution and Epistemic Community Building in the Northeast Asian Region. In *Crossing Borders: Governing Environmental Disasters in a Global Urban Age in Asia and the Pacific*, ed. Michelle A. Miller, Michael Douglass, and Matthias Garschagen, 243–260. Singapore: Springer.

Shim, Changsub. 2017. Policy Measures for Mitigating Fine Particle Pollution in Korea and Suggestions for Expediting International Dialogue in East Asia, Japan International Cooperation Agency Research Institute working paper, 150 (November).

The Korean Times. 2017. Half of Fine Dust Smothering Seoul Comes from China, Other Countries: Report, http://www.koreatimes.co.kr/www/nat ion/2017/04/371_228411.html. (assessed February 9, 2020).

Wang, Zhifang, and Haibing Zhang. 2015. The Environmental Cooperative Strategy on Air Pollution for China in Northeast Asia under the New Normal [xinchangtaixia zhongguo zai dongbeiya daqi wuran huanjing hezuozhong de celue xuanze]. *Northeast Asia Forum [Dongbeiya Luntan]* 3: 94–103.

Won, Dong-wook. 2002. China, Japan and Korea's Environmental Diplomacy and Northeast Asian Environmental Cooperation [zhongrihan sanguo duiwai huanjing zhengce yu dongbeiya huanjing hezuo]. *Shijie Jingji Yu Zhengzhi Luntan [Forum of World Economics & Politics]* 3: 70–73.

Xue, Xiaopeng, and Haibin Zhang. 2013. Dongbeiya diqu huanjing zhili de moshi xuanze – ouzhou moshi haishi dongbeiya moshi? [Choices for Environmental Governance in Northeast Asia: The European Model or the Northeast Asian Model?]. *Guoji Zhengzhi Yanjiu [the Journal of International Studies]* 3: 52–68.

Yarime, Masaru and Aitong Li. 2017. International Cooperation for Tackling Air Pollution in East Asia: Overcoming Fragmentation of the Epistemic Communities, article presented at International Studies Association Hong Kong 2017 Conference (June 15).

Yoon, Esook. 2007. Cooperation for Transboundary Pollution in Northeast Asia: Non-binding Agreements and Regional Countries' Policy Interests. *Pacific Focus* 22 (2): 77–112.

Yoshimatsu, Hidetaka. 2010. Understanding Regulatory Governance in Northeast Asia: Environmental and Technological Cooperation among China. *Japan and Korea, Asian Journal of Political Science* 18 (3): 227–247.

Zhang, Muhui. 2018. Proceeding in Hardship: The Trilateralism-Bilateralism Nexus and the Institutional Evolution of China–Japan–South Korea Trilateralism. *The Pacific Review* 31 (1): 57–75.

Zheng, Bo, Dan Tong, Meng Li, Fei Liu, Chaopeng Hong, Guannan Geng, Haiyan Li, Xin Li, Liqun Peng, Ji Qi, Liu Yan, Yuxuan Zhang, Hongyan Zhao, Yixuan Zheng, Kebin He, and Qiang Zhang. 2018. Trends in China's Anthropogenic Emissions Since 2010 as the Consequence of Clean Air Actions. *Atmospheric Chemistry and Physics* 18: 14095–111.

INDEX

A

Accountability system, 31
Aceh, 47, 48, 216
Acid Deposition Monitoring Network in East Asia (EANET), 235, 237, 238, 241
Act on Support for Reconstructing Livelihoods of Disaster Victims, 43, 53, 56
Act on the Prevention of Contagious Animal Diseases, 64
Advocacy research, 95, 99, 100
Air governance, 11, 225, 227, 232, 239, 240
Air pollution, 158, 223–229, 232, 240
  in regional, 10
  in transboundary, 11, 224, 226, 231, 234, 236, 238, 240
Air quality, 225, 226, 228, 229, 232–234, 236, 240, 241
Algorithm, 153, 154
ASEAN Committee on Disaster Management (ADCM), 192

Association of Southeast Asian Nations (ASEAN), 192
Automation, 141, 143, 146, 149, 150, 155
Autonomy, 10, 50, 112, 127, 142–144, 146, 148, 150, 152, 154, 158

B

Basic Act, 40, 42–45, 55–57
Beck, Ulrich, 2, 99, 149, 150, 152, 168
Bottom-up risk assessment, 32
Build Back Better (BBB), 9, 38, 46–53, 56, 57, 208
Build resilient communities, 121
Bureaucratization, 238
Business model, 141, 142, 145, 154, 157, 158

C

Captivation, 152, 154, 159

© The Editor(s) (if applicable) and The Author(s), under exclusive license to Springer Nature Singapore Pte Ltd. 2021
Y. Jing et al. (eds.), *Risk Management in East Asia*,
https://doi.org/10.1007/978-981-33-4586-7

248 INDEX

Center for Research on the Epidemiology of Disasters (CRED), 62, 63

Central Disaster and Safety Countermeasure Headquarters (CDSCHQ), 6, 65, 69

Central Disaster Broadcasting Consultative Committee, 68

Central Emergency Rescue Control Group (CERCG), 69

Central Private-Public Cooperative Committee, 68

Central Safety Management Committee, 68, 69

China, 2, 4, 5, 7, 8, 10, 11, 15, 18, 20, 22–27, 29, 31, 32, 141, 171, 191, 192, 210, 216, 224–230, 232–242

Chinese Communist Party (CCP), 232

Citizen participation, 9, 10, 94, 95, 104, 106, 108, 114, 115, 123, 124

Citizens, 1, 7, 9, 32, 43, 56, 69, 94–97, 99–102, 104–109, 111, 113–115, 124, 128–130, 151, 152, 174

"Citizens' Disaster Prevention and Preparedness Manual", 130

Citizens' panels, 107–109

Civil society, 43, 99, 106, 107, 110, 121, 123

Climate change, 9, 72, 76, 79, 80, 83, 88, 115, 126, 146, 208, 226

Clinton, William, 47

Collaborative governance, 120, 122–125, 131

Collaborative Governance Regime (CGR), 122, 131

Collaborative network management, 121

Collaborative risk governance, 121, 126, 128, 132, 134, 135

Collective Action for Mobility Program of University Students in Asia (CAMPUS Asia), 8

Community(ies), 3, 8, 24, 38, 43, 46–51, 57, 63, 66, 68, 87, 119–121, 124, 127, 129–135, 150, 172, 174, 175, 177, 178, 180–182, 189, 191, 202–205, 207–210, 212–214, 217, 227, 234, 238, 241

Comprehensive emergency management, 21
all-hazard management, 21
all-phase management, 24
all-stakeholder management, 25

Comprehensive school safety, 169, 171, 172, 184, 192

Confucian norms, 4

Connectivity, 141, 145, 146, 148, 150

Consensus conference, 95, 104, 108, 109

Construction, 16, 39, 44, 53, 65, 83, 102, 105, 110–114, 122, 127, 205, 213, 215, 227, 229

Convention on Long-range Transboundary Air Pollution (CLRTAP), 231, 239

Coordination, 7, 17, 19–21, 25, 28–30, 69, 88, 112, 122, 131, 134, 202, 213, 230, 234, 239

Covid-19 pandemic, 1, 2, 5, 16, 20, 24, 26, 93, 94

Creative reconstruction, 47, 48, 52

Crisis Management Center under the National Security Council, 65

D

Data collection, 82, 145–147, 155, 158

Datafication, 10, 142, 145, 147, 148, 150, 154, 158
Datafication cycle, 144, 146–148, 150, 156, 158
Deliberative polling, 95, 104, 107–110, 112–114
Digital addiction(s), 10, 142, 155–158
Digitalization, 141, 145, 147
Digital twins, 148
Disaster Countermeasures Basic Act. *See* Basic Act
Disaster education, 27, 130, 171, 176, 181, 188, 189
Disaster Law, 45, 55
Disaster management, 6–9, 38–41, 43, 45, 46, 48, 49, 51, 52, 55–58, 65, 70, 71, 87, 120, 122, 124, 126, 132, 134, 171, 176, 177, 190, 192, 201, 207, 216, 217
Disaster mitigation, 8, 24, 28, 127, 192, 205
Disaster preparedness, 47, 130, 176, 184, 206, 217
Disaster Prevention and Protection Act, 126
Disaster Prevention and Protection Project (DPPP), 121, 127–135
Disaster Relief Act, 41, 51, 56, 57
Disaster resilience, 126
Disaster response manual, 188, 189
Disaster risk, 6, 38, 46, 48–50, 58, 63, 64, 78, 87, 88, 120, 127, 169–171, 189, 200, 201, 208, 211, 213, 214, 217, 218
Disaster risk management, 7, 9, 37, 46, 47, 61–65, 68–70, 72, 74, 79–81, 87, 88, 201
Disaster Risk Reduction (DRR), 6, 9, 10, 46, 63, 64, 127, 176, 191, 199, 200, 206, 208
Disaster risk reduction education, 171, 190

Disasters and Safety Act 2013, 64
Distinctive characteristics, 28
Distributed expertise, 95, 98
Distributed participation, 95, 100, 103
Domestic politics, 11, 225, 226, 232, 240
Droughts, 62, 73
Druking, 152–155

E

East Asia, 2, 4, 8, 10, 11, 141, 158, 192, 231, 238
Economic losses, 62, 63, 73, 74, 76, 88, 119, 199, 214
Economy(ies), 3, 49–51, 53, 57, 83, 141, 146, 157, 226, 235
Education, early resumption of, 176
Emergency communication, 26, 27
Emergency Events Database (EM-DAT), 62
Emergency management system, 4, 5
Emergency plan, 18, 21, 23, 24, 28, 29
Emergency preparedness, 28
Emergency rescue, 65, 66, 69
Emergency Response Law of the People's Republic of China, 20
Engagement, 127, 155–157, 234, 235
Environment, 10, 48–50, 53, 57, 64, 80, 122, 123, 126, 129, 130, 150, 168, 173, 177, 180, 200, 211, 216, 217
Environmental monitoring, 236
Environmental regionalism, 240, 241
Environmental risk management, 9
Environmental standards, 233, 236
Epistemic community, 227, 237
Evacuation behavior, 188
Evacuation centers, 46, 51
Evacuation drills, 46, 177
Expertise

250 INDEX

unitary expertise, 95, 96, 104, 114
Experts, 7, 47, 79, 93, 95–102,
104–112, 114, 146, 149, 151,
184, 200, 217, 227, 229, 230,
236, 239
Extreme temperatures, 62

F
Facebook, 145, 150, 151, 154
Failure of initiative, 28
Fake news, 10, 142, 152–155,
157–159
Fishkin, James S., 107, 108, 110, 111,
113
Flashflood, 74, 79, 80, 82, 87, 88
Flood Control Centers, 82, 86
Flood insurance, 62, 86, 88
Flood risk management, 61, 80–82,
86
Floods, 9, 39, 40, 42, 43, 50, 61, 62,
73, 133, 213, 215
Flood warning system, 86, 88
Focus groups, 104–106
Four River Basins, 82
Fourth Industrial Revolution (4IR), 4,
10, 141–152, 155–158
Fudan University, 8
Fukushima, 44, 53, 175
Future directions, 17

G
Game addiction, 155, 156
Global One Million Safe Schools and
Hospitals Campaign, 171
Goto, Shinpei, 40, 51, 52
Governance mechanism, 126, 129
2011 Great East Japan earthquake,
2, 5, 10, 43–45, 50, 52, 53, 57,
168, 169, 176

Great Hanshin-Awaji earthquake, 5,
38, 42, 43, 45, 47, 48, 52, 53,
56, 205
Great Kanto earthquake, 39, 51

H
Hazard map, 175, 177, 188, 191, 216
Hazards, 2, 4, 6, 24, 57, 64, 65, 142,
147, 149, 150, 152, 155, 157,
158, 168, 169, 201, 215
Haze weather, 224, 232, 233, 240
Historical evolution, 10, 17, 200, 214
Historical responsibility, 235
Human casualty, 6, 76, 217
Human decision-making, 6, 150, 155
Human rights, 147, 148, 157
Hyogo Framework for Action (HFA),
6, 10, 38, 46, 47, 171, 200, 203,
206–210, 213, 217

I
Indian Ocean tsunami, 47
Industrial accidents, 15, 16, 18, 21,
147, 150
Industry 4.0. *See* Fourth Industrial
Revolution (4IR)
Infectious Disease Control and
Prevention Act, 64
Institutional framework, 19, 61, 63,
79, 81, 179
Instrumental and value rationality,
94–99, 101–103, 114, 115
Integrated Assessment Modelling
(IAM), 231, 241
Interactions between government and
society, 26
Interaction with society, 17
Internal legitimacy, 124
International cooperation, 4, 10, 37,
46, 172, 203, 206–208, 213, 234
International Relations (IR), 240

INDEX   251

Internet addiction, 152, 155, 156
Internet of Things (IoT), 144, 148, 149

J
Japan, 2, 4–8, 10, 37–52, 55, 57, 58, 114, 119, 142, 168, 173, 175, 177, 179, 181, 190–192, 200–203, 207, 208, 210–212, 214–217, 224, 225, 228–230, 236–238
Joint research, 8, 225, 229, 230, 236, 240

K
Kaihara, Toshitami, 48
Kobe, 5, 7, 37, 38, 42, 43, 48, 52, 119, 205, 206
Kobe University, 8
Korea University, 8

L
Land-use planning, 46, 50
Laws, disaster-related, 40, 41
Leadership, 5, 10, 18, 127, 132, 146, 225, 229, 237, 238, 241
Legalized arrangements, 238
Legislation, 20, 40, 43, 44, 106, 238
Limited social participation, 28
Livelihood reconstruction, 44
Livelihood(s), 49, 51, 56, 57, 64, 120
Local disaster risk, 190, 191
Local knowledge, 101, 103, 208, 209
Long-range Transboundary Pollution (LTP), 224, 228–232, 234, 236–239, 241

M
Machizdukuri, 52

Mental integrity, 142, 152, 154
Ministry of Culture, Sports and Tourism, 156, 157
Ministry of Education, Culture, Sports, Science and Technology (MEXT), 175–181, 188, 190
Ministry of Emergency Management (MEM), 5, 19, 21, 23, 27
Ministry of Environment, 66, 78, 81–83, 85–87
Ministry of Foreign Affairs (MOFA), 69, 207, 211–214, 239
Ministry of Gender Equality and Family, 155, 157
Ministry of Land, Infrastructure and Transport, 81, 82
Ministry of the Interior and Safety, 6, 62, 65, 66, 69, 71, 74, 75, 81, 82
Modern state governance system, 5
Moon Jaein, 110, 114, 151
Multilateral frameworks, 225, 228, 231, 236
Multi-level governance, 131
Multi-purpose dam, 83, 84, 88
Municipality, 40, 41, 44, 52, 55–57, 182
Mutual trust, 124
Mutual understanding, 124, 125

N
Nankai Trough earthquake, 57
National Emergency Management Office (NEMO), 19, 22, 23
National Emergency Management System (NEMS), 9, 16–19, 21, 25, 28, 31
 challenges, 17
 future-oriented, 32
 modern, 17
National Fire Agency, 127, 128, 131

252 INDEX

Natural disasters, 2, 3, 5–7, 9, 15–18, 21, 38, 40, 50, 61, 62, 64, 74, 81, 87, 127, 129–131, 168, 180, 188–190, 202, 204, 205, 211, 212, 214, 215, 217, 218
Naver, 153
Negative externality, 10
Neighborhood Watch team, 130
Neopositivism, 96–100, 102, 104, 115
Network-based risk governance, 10
Network strategy, 125
  activating, 125
  framing, 126
  mobilizing, 126
  synthesizing, 126
Non-structural methods, 62
Northeast Asia, 223
Northeast Asia Clean Air Partnership (NEACAP), 230, 231
Northeast Asian Sub-regional Programme for Environmental Cooperation (NEASPEC), 228, 230, 231, 236–239
Nuclear disaster, 53, 110

O
Okawa Elementary School (OES), 175, 182, 184, 185, 189, 190
One Plan and Three subsystems, 18, 31
Online games, 156, 157
Ordinary knowledge, 101, 102
Over-response, 28

P
Participatory research, 95, 102–104
Participatory Survey, 95, 109, 114
Particulate Matter (PM), 223, 228, 230

PM 2.5, 223–230, 232–234, 236, 239, 240
PM 2.5 concentrations, 233, 234, 236
PM 2.5 diplomacy, 232, 237
PM 10, 223, 230
Personal data, 150, 154, 155
Physical assets, 42, 50
Physical-Digital-Physical Loop (PDP), 141, 145
Physical facility, 49, 50, 52, 56
Physical stock, 42, 57
Politicization, 99, 225, 226
Politicized approach, 235
Polling, 104, 110
Polluter Pays Principle (PPP), 235
Post-2015 Framework for Disaster Risk Reduction, 120
Postmodern technological hazards, 142, 150, 158
Post-positivism, 100–104
Predictive maintenance, 146–148
Preparedness, 2–6, 18, 24, 26, 32, 46, 64, 78–80, 86, 88, 120, 199, 201, 202, 204, 208, 210, 212, 214
Prevention policy, 80, 216
Public facility, 41, 43, 48, 176, 190
Public governance, 1, 4, 120
Public inquiry, 104, 106
Public physical facilities, 44

R
Rational planning, 97, 98
Real-time data, 148, 229
Real-time data exchange, 234, 236
Recent trends, 17
Reconstruction, 3, 8, 9, 24, 25, 38–40, 43, 44, 46, 48–53, 55–57, 86, 191, 200, 202, 208, 210
Reconstruction Agency, 52

INDEX 253

Recovery, 3, 8, 24, 26, 41, 43, 44, 46, 48, 50–53, 55–57, 70, 78–80, 86, 120, 124, 127, 192, 201, 206, 208, 211

Reluctant partner, 123

Resilience, 1, 2, 10, 46, 48–50, 57, 120, 130, 167, 169, 171, 200, 206, 208, 209, 214

Restoration, 49, 52, 56

Risk awareness, 3, 10, 129, 131

Risk management, 1–4, 6–9, 11, 61, 63, 93, 94, 97, 100–104, 129, 134, 142, 147, 167, 169, 188

Risk Management Experts in East Asia, 8

Risk management in school systems, 10

Risk society, 3, 146, 149, 150, 168, 192

Rule-making, 225, 227, 235, 236, 241

S

Safe school(s), 169, 172, 174, 178

Safety Policy Coordination Committee, 68

School disaster management, 169, 171, 177, 190

School Health and Safety Act, 177, 180, 188

School learning facilities, 171, 176, 190

School safety plan, 178, 180, 181, 189, 190

Scientific research, 10, 127, 205, 231, 233, 236

Sendai, 37, 38, 207

Sendai Framework for Disaster Risk Reduction 2015–2030 (SFDRR), 6, 8–10, 37, 38, 46, 47, 49–51, 57, 172, 190, 192, 200, 203, 208, 209, 214, 217

Severe Acute Respiratory Syndrome (SARS) crisis, 16

Severe pollution days, 236

Shared commitment, 123, 124

Shared-risk, 129

Shin-Gori Nuclear Reactors, 95, 109, 110, 114

Shutdown Law, 152, 156, 157

Sichuan, 120

2008 Sichuan earthquake, 2, 4, 171, 192. *See also* Wenchuan earthquake

South Korea, 2, 4, 6–10, 61–63, 65, 68–72, 74, 76, 78, 81, 82, 86–88, 109, 114, 141, 142, 151–153, 155, 158, 172, 191, 192, 216, 224–226, 228–230, 234–239

Storms, 40, 62, 74, 88

Structural measures, 62, 65

Sustainable Development Goals (SDGs), 172, 214

T

Tainan, 121

Taipei City Fire Department, 130, 131, 133

Taiwan, 121, 126, 129, 130, 134

Technical expertise, 93, 98, 101, 115, 239

Temporary housing, 42, 51, 57, 175

Tokyo Metropolitan earthquake, 57

Too little learning, 31

Too much accountability, 31

Top-down approach, 32

Torrential rainfall, 74, 79, 80, 87, 88

Transboundary fine dust, 225, 228, 239

Translational leaders, 132

Transnational cooperation, 224, 226, 231, 232, 236

254   INDEX

Trilateral cooperation, 7, 216, 225, 228

Trilateral Ministerial Meeting on Disaster Management, 7, 216

Tripartite Environmental Ministers Meeting (TEMM), 228–232, 236–239

Typhoon, 5, 9, 40, 42, 43, 62, 64, 71, 74, 76, 79, 80, 82, 83, 87, 88, 129, 130, 203, 207

Maemi, 62, 76–79

Rusa, 62, 63, 76–79

Typical coordination problems, 29

U

UN International Strategy for Disaster Reduction (UNISDR), 38, 48, 49, 63, 64, 171, 172, 200, 206, 208, 209, 214

Unitary participation, 95, 99, 100

United Nations (UN), 27, 37, 47, 119

UN Office for Disaster Risk Reduction (UNDRR), 37, 38, 46, 49, 171, 202

UN World Conference on Disaster Risk Reduction, 37, 57

V

Victims, 17, 39, 41–43, 50, 53, 56–58, 157, 188

Village Chiefs, 129, 132

Vulnerability, 48, 49, 62, 64, 73, 82, 120

W

Water-related disasters, 9, 61–63, 72–74, 80, 81, 87

Weber, Max, 94, 96, 101, 115

Wenchuan earthquake, 25–27

Wicked problems, 3, 98, 101–103

Wildfires, 62

Willingness to participate, 111, 124, 130, 133–135

World Bank, 47, 48

World Conference on Disaster Reduction (WCDR), 119, 120

World Conference on Disaster Risk Reduction (WCDRR), 37, 120, 217

X

Xi Jinping administration, 233

Y

Yokohama Strategy, 6, 10, 200, 203, 206, 209, 210, 212, 217

Z

Zoning of flood-prone areas, 86, 88

CPSIA information can be obtained
at www.ICGtesting.com
Printed in the USA
LVHW081911060321
680776LV00005B/55